ROBERT FROST

ROBERT FROST

THE WORK OF KNOWING

Richard Poirier

New York   OXFORD UNIVERSITY PRESS   1977

Copyright © 1977 by Oxford University Press, Inc.
Printed in the United States of America

Library of Congress Cataloging in Publication Data
Poirier, Richard.
Robert Frost: The work of knowing.
Includes index.
1. Frost, Robert, 1874–1963—Criticism and
interpretation.
PS3511.R94Z87   811'.5'w   76-57259
ISBN 0-19-502216-5

Acknowledgement is made
for permission to quote from the following works:
The Poetry of Robert Frost edited by Edward Connery Lathem. Copyright
1916, 1923, 1928, 1930, 1934, 1939, 1947, 1949, © 1967, 1969 by Holt, Rinehart and Winston. Copyright 1934, 1936, 1942, 1944, 1945, 1951, 1953,
1954, © 1956, 1958, 1960, 1962 by Robert Frost. Copyright © 1964, 1967,
1970, 1973, 1975 by Lesley Frost Ballantine. Reprinted by permission of
Holt, Rinehart and Winston, and Jonathan Cape Ltd.

"In White" by Robert Frost. Reprinted by permission of The Estate of Robert Frost.

"The Constant Symbol," "Education by Poetry," "The Figure a Poem
Makes," "Poetry of Amy Lowell," and "Preface to *A Way Out*" from *Selected
Prose of Robert Frost* edited by Hyde Cox and Edward Connery Lathem. Copy-
right 1939, 1954, © 1966, 1967 by Holt, Rinehart and Winston. Copyright
1946, © 1959 by Robert Frost. Copyright © 1956 by The Estate of Robert
Frost. Reprinted by permission of Holt, Rinehart and Winston.

The Letters of Robert Frost to Louis Untermeyer. Copyright © 1963 by Louis Untermeyer and Holt, Rinehart and Winston. Reprinted by permission of Holt,
Rinehart and Winston, and Jonathan Cape Ltd.

Selected Letters of Robert Frost edited by Lawrance Thompson. Copyright ©
1964 by Lawrance Thompson and Holt, Rinehart and Winston. Reprinted by
permission of Holt, Rinehart and Winston, and Jonathan Cape Ltd.

Robert Frost: The Early Years 1874–1915 by Lawrence Thompson. Copyright
© 1966 by Lawrance Thompson. Copyright © 1966 by The Estate of Robert
Frost. Reprinted by permission of Holt, Rinehart and Winston, and Jonathan
Cape Ltd.

Robert Frost: The Years of Triumph 1915–1938 by Lawrance Thompson.
Copyright © 1970 by Lawrance Thompson. Copyright © 1970 by The Estate
of Robert Frost. Reprinted by permission of Holt, Rinehart and Winston, and
Jonathan Cape Ltd.

"September 1, 1939" from *The Collected Poetry of W. H. Auden.* Copyright
1940 by W. H. Auden. Reprinted by permission of Random House, Inc., and
Faber and Faber Ltd.

For my dear friend Lillian Hellman

To the Reader

There ought to be in everything you write some sign that you come from almost anywhere.

Robert Frost, at Bread Loaf, 1958

To some extent any poem is an act of interpretation, an inquiry into the resources of the language it can make available to itself. Reading is an analogous act calling on its own literary resources which may, at times, be greater or less than the poem's. Either form of interpretation is always in danger of becoming systematic, of abridging the possibilities of signification, and of settling for terminal verities when what is called for is the continuing exercise of veri-fication. Emerson in the essay "Nature" sounded the proper alert well over a hundred years before recent critical theory began to do so: "Every end is prospective of some other end, which is also temporary."

There has yet to be a thoroughgoing assimilation of what Emerson or William James, Frost's two most potent American forebears, have to offer, and in consequence criticism, and intellectual practices generally, still rest within a situation which Frost recognized sixty years ago—and wisely exploited. "You get more credit for thinking," he wrote to Louis Untermeyer on January 1, 1917, "if you restate formulae or cite cases that fall easily under formulae." But for Frost, "all the fun is outside, saying things that suggest formulae but won't formulate—that almost but don't quite formulate. I should like to be so subtle at this game as to seem to a casual person altogether obvious."

Frost is a poet of genius because he could so often make his subtleties inextricable from an apparent availability. The assumption that he is more easily read than are his contemporaries, like Yeats and Eliot, persists only in ignorance of the unique but equally strenuous kinds of difficulty which inform his best work. He is likely to be most evasive when his idioms are so ordinary as to relax rather than stimulate attention; he is an allusive poet, but in a hedging and off-hand way, the allusions being often perceptible only to the ear, and then just barely—in echoings of earlier poets like Herbert or Rossetti, or in metrical patternings traceable to Milton; he will wrap central implications, especially of a sexual kind, within phraseologies that seem innocent of what they carry. The conclusion of "The Need of Being Versed in Country Things"—"One had to be versed in country things / Not to believe the phoebes wept"— sounds like a formula ready made for the delectation of critics who can then talk, as indeed I do, about poetry in nature, nature in poetry. But the proffered interpretation is compelling enough to mask other possibilities which would greatly enrich it, like the lovely Shakespearean pun in the phrase "country things." The sexuality of the phrase results from the gentle pressures bearing down upon it from the rest of the poem: the chimney, which is all that is left of a house that has burned down, is said to stand "like a pistil after the petals go"; the barn, though it escaped the flame, is no longer "open with all one end" to take the "summer load"; but the birds, nevertheless, "rejoiced in the nest they kept," oblivious in their home-making to the destruction of a once-productive human household. We "need" to be "versed in country things" for the sake of certain realities that belong specifically to human consciousness—the differences between human love and home-making and the mating of animals. Not just a farm but a human nesting place is gone; we can "dwell" only on "what has been," and the feeling of deprivation is one which phoebes, even if they were "versed" in poetry, could not possibly share.

Frost seems to me of vital interest and consequence because his ultimate subject is the interpretive process itself. He "plays" with possibilities for interpretation in a poetry that seems "obvious" only because it is all the while also concerned with the interpretations of what, in the most ordinary sense, are the "signs" of life itself, particular and mundane signs which nonetheless hint at possibilities that continually elude us. "We might never get another vast philosophy," he once remarked in an appreciative aside about Whitehead. His poetry is especially exciting when it makes of the "obvious" something problematic, or when it lets us discover, by casual inflections or hesitations of movement, that the "obvious" by nature *is* problematic. In his talk "On Extravagance" he says of his poems: "So many of them have literary criticism in them—*in* them. And yet I wouldn't admit it. I try to hide it." He does so out of a decorum about the limits of poetry which are also, for him, the provocations to poetic "extravagance." The "literary criticism *in*" Frost's poems helps direct us to larger questions about

the kind of linguistic play in which they engage. His reit-
erations about the limits of metaphor and the boundaries of form are evidences not of fastidiousness or fear—
though he shows instances of both—so much as an effort to promote in writing and in reading an inquisi-
tiveness about what cannot quite be signified. He leads
us toward a kind of knowing that belongs to dream and
reverie on the far side of the labor of mind or of body.

A poetry often designed "to seem to the casual person
altogether obvious" is therefore, philosophically speaking, extraordinarily, purposefully evasive. Entailed in
this process are disciplines and flexibilities of mind that
make Frost the reverse of Yvor Winters' "spiritual
drifter" and exonerate him from any suspicion that he
was merely contriving to win a variety of audiences,
some of them presumably ill-read. His practices derive
from his passionate convictions about poetry as a form
of life. Consider that his "obviousness" results in part
from his having written out of a celebratory, eager, healthy indebtedness to poetic tradition; consider also that
when we read him we are never allowed to forget that it
is poetry and not some other thing that has been written
and is being read. Metrically and by other formal de-
vices, he insists on our acknowledging in each and every
poem, however slight, that poetry is a "made" thing. So,
too, is truth. Thus, the quality which allows the poetry to
seem familiar and recognizable as such, that makes it
"beautiful," is derivative of a larger conviction he shares
with the William James of *Pragmatism*. "Truth," James
insisted, "is not a stagnant property. . . . Truth is *made*,
just as health, wealth and strength are made, in the
course of experience."

Frost has been essential to my own practices as a critic,
here and elsewhere, because he derives energy and excitement from the fact that literature is most "natural"

when it is most self-aware of its status as a "made" or performed object, and when it reveals thereby some pathos and wonderment about its claims to existence. The pathos and wonder belong to existence of any kind which is conscious of existence. It acutely impinges on that form of life which is literature because, more than any other kind of discourse, literature has the capacity to acknowledge in the most positive ways its obligations to a more general, historically recurrent, and mythological will that is somehow never satisfied, the will to achieve meaning. Frost is a formalist poet who finds much of his direction and vitality in conventions created by that will, especially in classical literature, the Bible, English poetry since the seventeenth century, Emerson, Thoreau, William James, and a variety of scientific writings. He is emphatic about the performative thrust of his work as it moves in and through the pre-existent languages of poetry as well as the languages of the rest of life. "The whole thing," he says in his *Paris Review* interview, "is performance and prowess and feats of association. Why don't critics talk about those things—what a feat it was to turn that that way, and what a feat it was to remember that, to be reminded of that by this."

The extent to which Frost's poems differ one from the other is a matter, in part, of how much he wants this concern for signification brought forward or disguised. In a poem like "The Silken Tent" it is very much to the fore, and from the very first line: "She is as in a field a silken tent." What is striking here is that the voice usurps the centrality only apparently given to the figures it lays down. Not the placement assigned to her or a tent so much as the *act* of placement, with the implicit promise of more such actions to follow—it is this act which imposes itself, by the authoritative peculiarity of syntax, as the subject of compelling interest. The elic-

ited suspense waits upon how this voice, with a power
of formulation at once flexible, scrupulous, and grand,
will conduct itself through the rest of the poem. The
suspense becomes embodied in the structure of the
single sentence which gradually shapes itself into a sonnet:

> She is as in a field a silken tent
> At midday when a sunny summer breeze
> Has dried the dew and all its ropes relent,
> So that in guys it gently sways at ease,
> And its supporting central cedar pole,
> That is its pinnacle to heavenward
> And signifies the sureness of the soul,
> Seems to owe naught to any single cord,
> But strictly held by none, is loosely bound
> By countless silken ties of love and thought
> To everything on earth the compass round,
> And only by one's going slightly taut
> In the capriciousness of summer air
> Is of the slightest bondage made aware.

From the outset it is apparent that of her nothing more
will be directly said than is initially offered: "she is"; this
purity of being is one aspect of her loveliness. About the
tent, however, all manner of details are forthcoming: "it
sways at ease" when "its ropes relent"; it has a "central
cedar pole"; it is "loosely bound / By countless silken
ties"; it only feels the "slightest bondage" when one of
the ties "goes taut," and so forth.

In its inversions, its relaxations into a more conventional syntax, its buttressings, the sentence which is the
sonnet has the qualities ascribed to the tent's own
grounded elasticity. The whole poem is a performance,
a display for the beloved while also being an exemplification of what it is like for a poem, as well as a
tent or a person, to exist within the constrictions of

space ("a field") and time ("at midday") wherein the greatest possible freedom is consistent with the intricacies of form and inseparable from them. The poem "is" and "she is," but the tent to which each is obliquely compared exists as a metaphor of a metaphor. She is not "like" a tent; she is "as is a tent when"—"when" it is in motion in such a manner as to appropriate to itself words like "relent" and "gently." By the time we learn that its "silken ties" are "countless" we have been readied also to accept the information that these are "ties of love and thought" and to guess that this is much more than a real tent, silken or otherwise. The characteristics of litany which can be heard in the first line might of themselves suggest that if the tent belongs in "a field" it also belongs in "The Song of Songs," where the bride says that she is as comely "as the tents of Kedar, as the curtains of Solomon." The field itself eventually encompasses "everything on earth"; it is the "field" of the Lord or the "courts of our God" in Psalm 92, where the righteous "shall grow like a cedar in Lebanon."

Both tent and poem are constructs of comparisons that do not completely settle anywhere; each comparison refers us to others in a self-supporting web of connections. Thus, the tent's "supporting central cedar pole," which roots it in the field, is also its highest physical projection. But that wonderfully curious phrase "pinnacle to heavenward" suggests that the "pinnacle" is not only a point of terminus but a pointer, that it induces a kind of probing so anxious as to be repetitious or redundant—"to heavenward." And what's more, that "central cedar pole" maintains its earthy and latently sexual implications, wholly appropriate to a love poem in which the speaker talks of "one's going slightly taut / In the capriciousness of summer air." The sexuality is there, as naturally as in "The Song of Songs" and is a necessary ingredient of that blur of sensation where physical and spiritual realities meet in the poem, sharing in the human exigencies of time and space, and in its delights. Earth, we all remember, is the right place for love. The sonnet "reads" itself, works and mines its own properties in the most critical manner possible. Frost is a poet without pieties, a negotiator between terms of possibility set up with daring, risk, and a truly marvelous poise. With the James of *The Will to Believe,* he would propose that "there is really no scientific or other method by which men can steer safely between the opposite dangers of believing too little or of believing too much. To face such dangers is apparently our duty, and to hit the right channel between them is a measure of our wisdom as men."

To "hit the right channel" between believing too little and too much is to be always more or less in carefully navigated motion. It is the motion in the writing and the reading of Frost that I try to account for in this book, and I hope my interpretations are saved from inflation and summary by his own interpretive restlessness. Sound and metaphor in his best writing, prose as well as poetry, are the loci of energies, not signs of meaning ultimately to be enforced. It was not necessary, even if it had been possible, to deal with all his poems, and the book will have succeeded if it shows not only what he has done in the poems I do discuss but what he is likely to be doing in any of them.

During the writing of this book I was given generous assistance by the John Simon Guggenheim Memorial Foundation and the Graduate Research Council of Rutgers University. I have thought often of G. Armour Craig, who first introduced me to Frost and to his poetry, and I have been helped toward a renewed understanding by some of the graduate students at Rutgers who studied the poems with me. In teaching and in writing I am indebted to Reuben Brower who, at Harvard, created and sustained Humanities 6, a course in interpretation which I can now recognize as distinctively Frostean. Bridget Gellert Lyons and C. F. Main made it a pleasure for me to call on them for advice, and Elizabeth Durkee gave all kinds of essential help, including indications, while she typed the manuscript, that certain parts of it needed more attention. Newton McKeon kept me from some loose bibliographical speculations, but I have probably managed, since then, to introduce some others. My good friend John Hollander has been loyal, generous, and encouraging from the very beginning. I have incorporated nearly all of his many suggestions, and they now seem so essential that I cannot imagine the book without them. To Richard Santino, the artist reponsible for the collage on the dust jacket, I owe some of the life I was able to find in Frost and in myself while this book was being written, and I will always be grateful to him with love and pleasure.

R. P.

New Brunswick, New Jersey
May 1977

Contents

ROBERT FROST

I
A Preview

Robert Frost's eighty-fifth birthday party in 1959 has since been designated "a cultural episode." It brought into focus certain literary antagonisms having to do with the nature of modernism and it demonstrated the difficulty of placing Frost's achievement within the literature of this century. As the principal speaker that evening, Professor Lionel Trilling of Columbia University chose to call Frost "a terrifying poet." Those who felt they somehow already owned the poet were not grateful for what seemed a compliment. To them it was very late in coming and it suggested, when it did come, not any embarrassment that Trilling and his modernist associates had been tardy in recognizing Frost but rather that most of Frost's supporters had failed, for all their attentiveness, to read their poet the way he ought to be read. There are good reasons for disagreeing with Trilling's characterization of Frost, but no need for the hysterical possessiveness that marked the response to his speech. There was a nagging suspicion that he was simply trying to appropriate Frost to New York. New York meant modernism, construed as a cult in whose eyes the constituents of social and historical reality in America were malignant about half of the time. In fact, that is not what Trilling was doing; much of his work is opposed to this modernist view of reality. It was absurd to suppose that he could be using it as a standard to measure the greatness of anyone.

He was not praising Frost for an ideological stance, unless the attribution of Sophoclean centrality can be called ideological. What he admired in Frost had less to do with the kind of "terrifying" reality created by poems like "Design," "A Servant to Servants," "Out, Out—," "Acquainted with the Night," "The Most of It" than with the literary evidences that Frost had made us *aware* of that reality in a new way. He claimed for Frost a particular kind of literary daring, and though, given the history of American culture, such daring necessarily carries ideological implications, these were not what he principally talked about. Trilling's estimate at the eighty-fifth birthday is worth bringing up now that the hundredth has passed, quite aside from whether it is right or wrong—these are not the only criteria for determining the value of a literary judgment. Rather, he offers a kind of large and crucial argument which calls upon you to decide just how important a poet Frost can be for you. What dimensions can he give your life, what shape can he help you give the time of your life, different as it is from his time? You have, more generally, to decide if Frost belongs in the company with twentieth-century writers of the greatest literary and historical magnitude, and, if he does not, whether this magnitude is not perhaps a form of historical pretension, even historical pretentiousness. Because what Trilling was trying to do was claim that Frost had continued a noble and heroic line of dissent. The line was located in American literature by D. H. Lawrence and, all national differences allowed, enriched by him. Trilling was proposing that Frost was radical in a classic American tradition. That is, Frost was trying to slough off an old inherited European consciousness in order that a new consciousness could come to life from underneath. And this kind of radical enterprise, Trilling added, "is not carried out by reassurance, nor by the affirmation of old verities and pieties. It is carried out by the representation of the terrible actualities of life in a new way."

It is obvious that some of these actualities are present in Frost's poetry; it can be shown that he often represented them in a new way. Granting all that, it still cannot be said, I think, that the consequent experience offered by his work is to any importantly consistent degree the Laurentian experience Trilling claims to find there. Quite the reverse. It is as if the technical genius of Frost, along with an extraordinary originality of mind and force of personality, was meant not to challenge "old verities and pieties" but rather to reinstate them. The whole almost alarmingly intense commitment of psychic and sexual energies to poetic performance turns out in Frost's case to be an effort precisely at the "reassurance" of us and of himself.

If this is true, what can we learn from the fact that in the first quarter of the century Frost was considered—and I think still ought to be—an exponent of the new? We can learn an important cultural lesson, if we do not know it already—that nothing pleases people more than the evidence that, however new the style, however unconventional the sounds, they can carry you nonetheless to conventional meanings. Newness in the arts, when it is popularly acclaimed, almost always confirms the old verities. This was one secret of Frost's success, just as it was a secret, too, of the immense popularity of the 1960's of the Beatles or of Bob Dylan. Their

musical and lyrical styles were new to us and were taken
by some as evidence also of the emergence of a "new
consciousness." After a time, however, it was possible to
recognize how conventional, how even learned and affectionately appropriated some of their musical and verbal phrasing really was.

Frost's popularity tells some essential critical and
human truth about him. There is no point trying to
explain the popularity away, as if it were a misconcep-
tion prompted by a pose. There is a Frost who has been
missed, almost lost, because of the lack of intensity and
expectation brought to his poetry by those who know
him best. In writing this book I found myself sometimes
straining against the familiar in order to reach him
where he most intensely lives in his writing. And yet the
Frost I got to know was always somehow restoring himself to the lineaments of a massively settled official portrait. What then is "new" about his writing and what is in
need of being said about it? Engaging yourself critically
with Frost is like taking a trip with an old neighborhood
friend and discovering under the stress of travel that he
can on occasion be altogether more mysterious than
you'd bargained for; he can be more exalted and exalt-
ing, yet show all the while flashes of a pettiness you had
managed before to overlook; he can be full of wonderful excesses of imagination and generosities of spirit and
yet more satisfied, it seems, by his self-control; a man
ennobling in his centralities of feeling, which he will
nonetheless betray by sudden reversions to formula and
platitude. After the trip, you go home again among old
friends. And there he sits, the same man to all appearances, whom the others know as well as you do. The difference is that now the persona has itself become, for
you, an achievement altogether more powerful, impressive, and interesting in what it includes, the tensions it

resolves, the passions it shapes. The others who have never known him to be any different are not so much wrong about him as simply not right enough. They have not, as it were, made the journey out and back, and such a journey is perhaps the central figure for Frost's own poetic enterprise of voice and vision—off into the sublime, back to the domesticated.

So that while the estimate of the so-called general public is necessarily partial and unsatisfactory, it nonetheless represents a kind of truth which criticism cannot afford to ignore. As in the reading of Wordsworth, it is time for criticism to find some way of showing that the surfaces are as important as the depths. The Frost of the best-loved poems is also the Frost who is simultaneously meditating, in a manner often unavailable to the casual reader, on the nature of poetry itself. "Stopping by Woods on a Snowy Evening" is about a central human experience—the enchantments that invite us to surrender ourselves to oblivion; "Mending Wall" is about the opposite impulse, which is to fence yourself in, to form relationships that are really exclusions. But at the same time and in the same terms both poems propose that these human dilemmas are also poetic ones, in the one case the possibly destructive solicitations of the sublime and in the other the claustrophobias of mechanical forms. The poems are about the will to live asserting itself against invitations either to surrender or to constraint, and these, it is intimated, issue as much from the conventions of poetry as from conventions of feeling. The poetry is always showing its alertness not only to the dangers it confronts but also to those it creates.

Frost's poetry can therefore be said to include terror without being itself terrified; it is for the most part reassuring in that it leaves us feeling more rather than less confident about our capacities. His is unlike the poetry of most of his contemporaries, except Lawrence and Stevens, because while you may make your life more complicated by reading it, you do not make your life more unmanageable. You are not led to believe that life is unintelligible or that your capacity to make sense of it merely proves your triviality. Indeed, in his prose, Frost is anxious to suggest that the ordinary sense-making processes are very much like poetic ones, that the making of sense in ordinary activities is analogous, as an art, to the writing of a poem. In "The Constant Symbol," originally used as the preface to the 1946 Modern Library edition of his poems, he remarks that

> Every single poem written regular is a symbol small or great of the way the will has to pitch into commitments deeper and deeper to a rounded conclusion and then be judged for whether any original intention it had has been strongly spent or weakly lost; be it in art, politics, school, church, business, love, or marriage—in a piece of work or in a career. Strongly spent is synonymous with kept.

In this little passage there is much of the essential Frost. Along with a number of clues to his popular appeal, there is a nice sample of why he promises to be more radical than he turns out to be. There is first of all an initial reassurance, that no matter how imposing the title under which he is writing—"The Constant Symbol"—he is still pretty much our friendly neighbor: "every poem written regular." This country language is then followed by a firm, resolute, but still unpretentious rhetorical mounting: "every single poem written regular is a symbol small or great of the way the will has to pitch into commitments." Note, for the unpretentiousness, that the symbol may be "small" as well as "great" and that the thrust toward expansiveness is cheerfully restrained by figures of speech that suggest we are listening to a quite ordinary man. Because if the commitment proposed is a large, rather operatic one ("the will to a rounded conclusion"), the phrase "to pitch into commitments" suggests something not remote from the simple farmyard willingness to "pitch in." Thus the near-grandiloquence of the subsequent "strongly spent or weakly lost" is braced within the realm of anyone's possible daily experience. And lest we miss the point it is made emphatic by the enumeration of those ways outside poetry in which any one of us can be employed. It is all brought to a close, as are many of Frost's poems, by an epigram, something we can take away with us: "Strongly spent is synonymous with kept."

This is an attractive, and above all an adroit performance, a fair enough example of Frost as a writer of prose. Its own "original intent" is to make us assent to a notion which we might ordinarily find presumptuous, namely that poetry is an heroic enterprise and that a poem is made equivalent to a number of activities which belong, as it were, to that real world—of politics, of business—which usually acknowledges poetry, if at all, by condescension. And yet somehow the passage is not a defense of poesy, as if it needed one. It is rather a bit of flattery bestowed by a man of action in poetry on other men of action who, in their own occupations—in which he, of course, also participates—conduct themselves much the way he does. Poetry is not life, but the performance in the writing of it can be an image of the proper conduct of life. The exercise of the will *in* poetry, the *writing* of a poem, is analogous to any attempted exercise of will in whatever else one tries to do. This position is not asserted, since the whole point, after all, is that nothing can be carried merely by assertion. One can only "pitch" in "deeper and deeper," and in this passage

itself there is a demonstration rather than simply a claim
of the validity of what is being said. The validation is implicit in his inclusive suppleness of voice. As in similar
moments in Thoreau, the voice here manages to show
its facility in the tones and nuances—like the submerged
metaphors of sex and love-making, of farming and
business—that belong to the tongues, the argots of occupations outside poetry. Frost's intention is not "weakly
lost" because it is expended in careful checks and balances of voice by which the reader is convinced that this
poet is in all likelihood more articulate in our business
than we could hope to be in his.

Frost's critical prose, in lectures or letters, has none of
the pretentious deferences by which Eliot communicates
his pontifical responsibilities. Rather it seems to gather
assurances about poetry by the emotive and injunctive
power latent in a vocabulary that is primarily concerned
with life: "every . . . poem written regular is a symbol
. . . of the way the will," etc. Proposing himself as a
master of common as much as of poetic tongues, he
would democratize all of these within the equilibriums
of a poem or a sentence. He would do this convinced
that the authority finally achieved by form in life or in
art will be greater than is the authority of any or all of
the tongues more randomly combined. This helps explain, I think, why critics have had such a difficult time
finding large thematic or philosophical reasons, the reasons of general education and of the humanities, for
calling him a great poet. His poems really do not reward
explication in the way the poems of Eliot and Yeats do.
Criticism works best on him when it gets close, and stays
close, when it tries to monitor what is going on in the
dialectical play of sounds and metaphors. The poem
manages to keep nearly everything to itself—or within
the accumulated funds it shares with other poems—and

is most alive and fresh in the way sounds and images spend themselves with and on one another.

That is why the poem is itself what he calls "a constant symbol." An especially charming example is "Hyla Brook," which is very much about the proposition that "strongly spent is synonymous with kept." The poem is never penurious or restrictive in the expenditure of any sound or voice within it, either poetic tongues or those of country folk, and it is equally speculative about its metaphors, whether they suggest mystery, as in the proposal that when we are looking for a brook it can be "found groping underground," or whether they offer some mixture of the poetic and familiar, as when the brook is casually compared to poetry within the easy vernacular of the first line.

> By June our brook's run out of song and speed.
> Sought for much after that, it will be found
> Either to have gone groping underground
> (And taken with it all the Hyla breed
> That shouted in the mist a month ago,
> Like ghost of sleigh bells in a ghost of snow)—
> Or flourished and come up in jewelweed,
> Weak foliage that is blown upon and bent,
> Even against the way its waters went.
> Its bed is left a faded paper sheet
> Of dead leaves stuck together by the heat—
> A brook to none but who remembers long.
> This as it will be seen is other far
> Than with brooks taken otherwise in song.
> We love the things we love for what they are.

Another take-away ending, too, it seems, though only those not educated by the poem would want to take it away. Still, the line does mean just what it can simply be supposed to mean. If we love at all truly then probably we do "love the things . . . for what they are." Of course the poem, as a whole development, imposes a

weight on the familiar idioms of that line, especially on
the word "things" and on the word "what." Very like
Thoreau again, in the way common idioms are transformed by a context which nonetheless supports the
sounds of those idioms. New England speech is not elevated by this process into poetry; it is shown to *be* poetry
as Emerson said it could be. By the end, the brook is
many different "things" according to the season. It is
even compared to a "faded paper sheet," like something
you might write a poem on. This is not a merely fanciful
reading, since one of the things the brook is also compared to, twice over, is "song." The brook is many different "things," and to love it therefore for "what" it is,
is to love it for being a kind of conundrum.

But we lose the poem, and it is lost to us, if we look
beyond the obvious rather than through it. The poem in
its sound makes us assent to the likelihood that what we
shall have to say about it will belong to the obvious.
Much of it, after all, luxuriates in ordinary speech, a
near banality of sentiment; the last line could find a
place, and probably has, on a sampler. And yet the
poem is powerful enough to absorb into itself the
sounds of other, more elevated stylistic conventions
derived from a kind of poetry Frost knew would be rec-
ognizably poetical. Thus, line 5, "Like ghost of sleigh
bells in a ghost of snow"—Reuben Brower, once an Amherst colleague of Frost's and one of his best critics, says
that this is "the most exquisite line in the poem." It might
well be, if we were encouraged by syntax to read Frost
by the line. But we are asked to read him at the very
least by the sentence. For Frost, the sentence is the basic
unit of voice in a poem. Half or all of some of the
shorter poems are made up of a single sentence, "The
Silken Tent" being perhaps the best example. When we
listen to what Frost calls "the sentence sound," we hear

many tongues, including Wordsworthian and Tennysonian poetic tongues, and that truly "exquisite" poetic line is made to accommodate itself to the ordinary vernacular sound of the sentence in which it appears. By the same token, the ordinary vernacular is in turn required to make room for the conventionally poetic.

The wit by which the brook is said to "flourish" by coming up in so frail and common a plant as "jewelweed" should make us wary of trying to isolate any of the items in this *curriculum vitae* of a brook. We cannot separate any detail from the sound of a man talking to other men and women who are like himself. He is a man who, when he uses a traditional figure (by which if still water or lakes stand for mind, running water stands for eloquence or song), does so in the locution of the neighborhood: "By June our brook's run out of song and speed."

The sound of this poem and the filtering through it of metaphor demonstrate what it means to be "at home in the metaphor," how to make conventionally poetic metaphors and sounds almost casually a part of the ordinary movements of nature and of human speech, how, at last, to tame the extravagant potentialities inherent in any metaphor. It was in this sense that Frost was considered a new poet in 1918, and why he remains still a new, a fresh experience of poetry. He was and is a new poet not, however, because he can be said, in Lawrence's terms, to help us slough off a European consciousness in order to allow the growth of a new one. No such radical consequence can be felt from reading him. Rather, what he does is set about affectionately to make old elements of consciousness—here out of Tennyson and Wordsworth—congenial with the likes of Thoreau, and he then makes all of these live within a humanly simple vernacular which had not, before Frost, been able as easily to accommodate any of them. We will have occasion to see how markedly different he is from these writers, but here there is a distinctly American egalitarian impulse, along with a regularity in the writing, a commitment to form, which seems to have behind it only the most practical impulses. English poetry is let into the vernacular not to save New Hampshire but rather to save poetry from itself. This is principally why he is a New English rather than a merely English writer.

I used the phrase "at home in the metaphor." It is Frost's, from the most important of his critical talks, "Education by Poetry," and he issues a warning along with it:

> Unless you are at home in the metaphor, unless you've had your proper poetical education in the metaphor, you are not safe anywhere. Because you are not at ease with figurative values: you don't know the metaphor in its strength and weakness. You don't know how far you can expect to ride it and when it may break down with you. You are not safe in science; you are not safe in history.

To "know the metaphor in its strength and weakness"— obviously we are being asked to know more than the mere graphic design of a figure of speech. But we have to begin, as in a poem called "Spring Pools," by knowing at least that much. The poem introduces us to the pools which are then compared to something that has the power to "reflect." Initially, all this seems to imply is that nature "reflects" on itself, that it delights in correspondences and likenesses. But soon thereafter it is borne in on us that this metaphor can be pushed further to quite another meaning of "reflect," as in "Let them think twice." The natural elements are treated as if self-conscious, as if they ought to be narcissistically desirous

of freezing or chilling their own "reflected" beauty; as if
they should want a moment of delicate balance wholly
freed from the further exigencies of time.

> These pools that, though in forests, still reflect
> The total sky almost without defect,
> And like the flowers beside them, chill and shiver,
> Will like the flowers beside them soon be gone.
> And yet not out by any brook or river,
> But up by roots to bring dark foliage on.
>
> The trees that have it in their pent-up buds
> To darken nature and be summer woods—
> Let them think twice before they use their powers
> To blot up and drink up and sweep away
> These flowery waters and these watery flowers
> From snow that melted only yesterday.

This is a rather hazardous poem and raises in an
acute way a central and evaded problem about how
properly to read Frost. Quite simply, there is a question
here, and to some degree in all his work, of his willingness *not* to be ironic, his willingness not to slough off responsibility by ascribing his own confusions of feeling to
a "speaker" other than himself or to merely some aspect
of himself that has been entrapped, as it were, in a ludicrous situation. The ludicrousness, in turn, is ignored by
critics who habitually talk about "situations" as if they
were all "dramatic." "Dramatic situation" and "speaker"
are terms which I shall have to use now and then, but
never, I hope, in order to exempt Frost from the per-
plexities, absurdities, and contradictions that belong to
some of his poems. His greatness depends, I think, in
large part on his actually seeking out opportunities for
being in untenable positions. In poem after poem he
defies the nature of things, lets his metaphors take him
too far, and all the while appeals to a kind of decorum

by which his excess becomes admirably an evidence of
his dependence upon us to go along with him. It is
wholly proper that the little poem standing at the head
of his collected poems is "The Pasture," with its invitation that we join him on his sorties into the field where
he will "rake the leaves away" and see "the little
calf / That's standing by the mother." It could be an excursion into poetry, Greek and Latin, and he promises
always to return home with us in a line, repeated twice,
which is probably, as Lowell Edmunds suggested to me,
an imitation of the Greek and Latin metrical phenome-
non called bucolic diaresis: "I shan't be gone long.—You
come too." Unless we are willing to join his extravagances we have to read a poem like "Spring Pools" as
smugly as he, in such a case, would have to perform in
it. The poem would thereby become for us an "education by poetry" but of an unappealingly pre-meditated
kind. We would have been invited merely to watch
someone expose himself to an absurdity because of what
was initially a commendable human desire. But the
poem is not like that. It is instead an exercise of Frostean "will," pitching in against all logic. William James
would have understood the poem in this light.

The speaker—really the mind of the poet going
through a representative consultation with itself—
realizes that he is to be deprived of his platonic, or,
more exactly, eleatic vision of unagitated fusion and
oneness, a vision beautifully expressed in Emerson's
"Xenophenes." His initial vision, in the first four lines, is
of a moment when everything seems in a related state of
balance and stillness; he admits to the precariousness of
the scene only in the casual euphemism that it will "soon
be gone." But then, with the last line before the break
in the poem, he acknowledges, in the phrase "up by
roots," a countervailing, brutal reality in the nature of

things. It is then that he proposes, in tones at once angry and petulant, a vision of apocalyptic obliteration; he seems innocent of the fact that the things he would preserve do not themselves suffer from a consciousness either of their own uniqueness or of any dangers to it. As the next to last line beautifully suggests in its "reflected" phrasing, the pools and the trees are happily part of one another; they *are* what is happening to them. However, their delicate transitoriness is no more or less engaging than is the voice of the man raised in protest against it. In this on-going process in nature, human nature is a kind of noble impertinence by virtue of its very wrong-headedness. A difference between Frost and Wordsworth should be apparent in the way Frost chooses to characterize the seeming irrelevance here of human consciousness—the poem is feisty rather than brooding; a speaker can hardly be called alienated who is also as blusteringly involved as this one.

Of the many Frostean characteristics illustrated by this poem none is so important as the way the voice can be said to be victimized by its own energies. It is betrayed by grammer as much as by the logical implications of the metaphors on which it insists. Thus, both pools and flowers are said to "chill and shiver." This yoking of a transitive and a normally intransitive verb is a grammatical indication of the forced effort to make things identical when they are only to some extent similar. "Flowers" may "shiver" and so may "pools," but only the latter have the power to "chill." Similarly, nature in the form of "pools" may indeed "reflect"—in more ways than one, it would seem. Frost knew his Milton and how in his poetry (as John Hollander brilliantly illustrates in *Vision and Resonance*) a verb at the end of a line will often create a near enjambment, so that for a moment we cannot be sure whether it is transitive or intransitive. In the hesitation, just before turning into line 2, we can allow for the possibility that the "pools" "reflect" in the sense that they "think"; but once we make the turn, the verb grasps its object, and "reflect" means only "mirror." "Pools" cannot "reflect" the way the speaker can: they cannot remember the past in the present or meditate upon a destructiveness which is in any event a part of the spontaneous creative movement in which they participate. His imperative to the trees, "Let them think twice," following on a dash which suggests some shock of recognition on his part, is simply a cry if not in the dark then in woods that will get dark no matter what he says in admonishment.

In offering an "education by metaphor" the poem does not test out a figure of speech in any dispassionate way or probe the inconsistencies to which it ultimately brings us. We are made to care as much or more for a highly personalized human voice responding to a specific situation, the kind of voice mostly missing from Stevens. It refuses to accommodate itself to the evident breakdown of the metaphor of "reflection." Like other such voiced presences in Frost's poetry, it will submit to nothing, even its own inventions, without sounding off. When Frost says that we must "know the metaphor in its strength and weakness," if we are to be "safe in history," he means that we must test the metaphor, contend with the logic and the limits of it, not just "use" it. And this can be done by the "voice" which made up the metaphor to begin with: "These pools that, though in forests, still reflect / The total sky . . ." Why the plural "forests" and why "total sky"? He is speaking not of some pools in particular, but of pools in his mind, pools of such unusual visionary sharpness as to be immediately present to him, *"these* pools."

The voice, then, is not of a man standing in a wood looking at pools. We have here a fine instance, it seems to me, that the most misleading advice Frost ever gave for the reading of his or of most lyric poetry is that "Everything written is as good as it is dramatic. It need not declare itself in form, but it is drama or nothing . . . spoken by a person in a scene—in character, in a setting. By whom, where and when is the question." In 1929, when this was written as part of his preface to his play, *A Way Out,* Frost was, as ever, anxious to insist upon the speaking voice in his poems, on what for fifteen years he had been propagating as "the sound of sense . . . sentence sounds." Probably the easiest way to get people to look for these elements was with such pointers as "whom, where and when." But the questions "where" and "when" are often useless and sophomoric if applied to poems in which we are asked to imagine a grown man talking in the woods about pools, or trying, on another occasion, to convince us that an oven bird "is a bird everyone has heard."

Voice in Frost is itself a metaphor as it is not, say, in Auden ("All I have is a voice / To undo the folded lie"). Different on different occasions, voice is a metaphor of a self, of a mind or temperament that engages those other metaphors it creates out of its need to account for whatever is *not* the self. It responds to these—as if they were reality. Like many of Frost's poems, "Spring Pools" is about a man who discovers that even his metaphors about reality, much less any other "truer" forms of it, will not conform to his desires, will not confirm his visions, and not the least because metaphors are as much inherited as are the forests and pools. He is wedded to his metaphors as he might be wedded to a woman who, while a "reflection," is nonetheless, in the words of "The

Most of It," "someone else additional to him." He stays
with the metaphor, argues with it, for it, against it; he is
"in" it to the very end.

Interactions between "voice" and other forms of metaphor, metaphors of otherness, occur everywhere in
Frost; they constitute the very substance of his work.
Among the forms of interaction can be a tension, noticed in "Hyla Brook," between "voice" which is vernacular, something presumably "taken fresh from talk," and
"voice" which is poetic, taken from the poetry of the
past, Emerson or Wordsworth, Keats or Tennyson or
Shelley. In "All Revelation," for example, Frost shows
his capacity for a Yeatsian accent, almost as if he wants
to show how masterfully he can resist it, just as at the
beginnings of his career in London—at thirty-nine and
forty—he chose, after two visits, to avoid the "Monday
nights" where Yeats sometimes took the privilege of tin-
kering with the lines of visiting poets. "All Revelation" is
a poem about efforts to penetrate the stuff of life—to
discover life through the pleasure of the genitalia, or by
the probings of science, or by the faculties of vision—
and at the end there is a mounting toward a released
largeness of voice not ordinarily heard in Frost:

> A head thrusts in as for the view,
> But where it is it thrusts in from
> Or what it is it thrusts into
> By that Cyb'laean avenue,
> And what can of its coming come,
>
> And whither it will be withdrawn,
> And what take hence or leave behind,
> These things the mind has pondered on
> A moment and still asking gone.
> Strange apparition of the mind!

But the impervious geode
Was entered, and its inner crust
Of crystals with a ray cathode
At every point and facet glowed
In answer to the mental thrust.

Eyes seeking the response of eyes
Bring out the stars, bring out the flowers,
Thus concentrating earth and skies
So none need be afraid of size.
All revelation has been ours.

What is especially impressive here is that a demonstrated grandiloquence is made syntactically inseparable
from an audacious refusal finally to exercise it, to sound
like a Big poet. The resistance can be felt in the next to
the last line: "So none need be afraid of size." That has
the characteristic signature of Frost without which the
whole passage might be called Yeatsian. Though of-
ficially regular iambic the line is largely spondaic. It is
far more compacted than any of the others; its tight
monosyllabic economies force the voice from the prophetic into a slightly mocking accent, an accent congenial to the meaning of the line, with its suggestion that
vision ought to concentrate rather than magnify our experience, ought to make it manageable rather than mag
nificent. So much so that retrospectively we are forced
to concede that the "eyes seeking the response of eyes"
may be not the eyes of romantic lovers searching for one
another but rather eyes in their primitive state, eyes just
beginning to discover their utility, seeking, as do the
hands of a baby, for an ordained function in the contin-
ual exploration of the world.

The human limits proposed in poetry of this kind are
clearly not to be confused with poetic limitations. The
poetry discovers its own restraints through successive

violations of them, so that the achievement in this instance seems to be snatched from the jaws, the voiced cadence, of visionary rhetoric even while leaving that rhetoric its own glory. In Frost the vernacular almost invariably modifies or includes any more ambitious venture of voice. It is an Emersonian effort to hold the miraculous within the embrace of the quotidian. The sexual play in the poem is indicative of this. Sexuality is simply "there," as it is in so much of Frost's writing—the specific sexual act of "putting in the seed"—but it is syntactically and in every other way made continuous with the general human thrust toward penetration and creativity. Thus, "what can of its comings come" is kept from being quite as specific as it might sound by the initial uncertainty about whether in the first stanza a phallus is exploring a vagina or a child's head is emerging to look into the world.

"Voice" in conflict with metaphor or with other voices—the measure of this requires extreme delicacy because it is a conflict inextricable from love. The voice, when it gets anxious about the metaphor it is using, is, again, involved with what it has helped create or evoke, with versions of reality or of poetry or of the "other" in which the self has chosen to find a "reflection." The abrasions can involve the terrible knowingness of love or of what once was love. Perhaps inevitably, Frost is a great poet of marriage, maybe the greatest since Milton, and of the sexuality that goes with it. This is signally true of the dramatic narratives and less directly of all his poetry. His feelings are saturated with what Wordsworth, in his "Preface to the Lyrical Ballads" (1800), calls the perception of "similitude in dissimilitude, and dissimilitude in similitude" upon which depends "our taste and our moral feelings." Poems like "Home Burial" or "The Death of the Hired Man" or "A Servant to Ser-

vants" or "West-Running Brook" dramatize marital differences, of taste and feeling (merely teasing differences
in "West-Running Brook"), expressed as alleged incapacities of one or another of the partners to speak
with adequate sensitivity or in a voice supposedly proper
to a situation. Marital voices can become fixed and entrapped within domestic forms, and imaginative freedom, especially for the wives, finds expression in lying
or madness, witchery or suicide.

Frost's criticism, in talks and letters, is almost wholly
given either to metaphor or to sound, the speaking
voice. The first, in its emphasis on the marriage of one
thing to another, implics some necessary limit for anything or anyone; the other, the humanly characterized
voice, suggests, to the contrary, that the individual voice
can have a shaping force, that it can express the will to
exceed the limits imposed by "otherness." His poetry is a
perpetual debate between, on the one side, the inherent
necessity for form in language and in nature, which
requires a dialogue of accommodation, and, on the
other, the equally inherent human need for excursion
beyond form, or (to note how often in Frost the human
actions are equivalent to poetic practice) for taking a
walk beyond the confines of home.

Form, be it of a poem we read or a home where we
live, is, for Frost, all in the making. If it promises security it is only of so relative a kind as to reveal the insecurities around it, insecurities which cannot be made
less real by legislation either of government or church.
It can be said that for Frost the only possible New Deal
occurred in the readjustments immediately after the
Fall. We experience the pleasures and reassurances of
form in the act of having to create it. "All 'homes' are in
finite experience," said William James (*Pragmatism*), a
writer whose works are a treasury of images of which

Frost freely availed himself. But James goes on to observe that "finite experiences as such are homeless. Nothing outside the flux secures the issue of it." Form is a gratifying act of will and also a protective one in a universe where we are otherwise freely exposed to chaos, and it can come into existence as a result of the most ordinary human enterprise, the labor of hands as well as of mind. Performances in poetry and performances in an orchard or a field elicit from Frost, as we have seen, the same rhetoric, and part of his great popularity derived, most likely, from his Emersonian capacity to make people feel that in writing a poem he was being *more* like them rather than less. If he was heroic, then so were they in whatever they did to give form to their lives— making a garden, writing a letter, what have you.

Modernism and liberalism, Eliot and Roosevelt, tended, as he saw them, to weaken the human capacity to shape life by proposing the negligible power of individual enterprise. They posited, in their different ways, a situation in which, in the face of overwhelming deteriorations, individual acts of form were made to seem trivial, where people were therefore encouraged to let the form of their lives depend on the provisions of government—"Provide, Provide"—or even on the formal ending of an Upanishad. Frost's feeling about poetry, the making of form, and the—to him—objectionable movements of contemporary thinking all came together in 1935, appropriately a flourishing time for Eliot and for Roosevelt, when Frost wrote a remarkably eloquent letter in reply to a message of congratulation on his sixty-first birthday from *The Amherst Student:*

> Fortunately we don't need to know how bad the age is. There is something we can always be doing without reference to how good or how bad the age is. There is at least so much good in the world that it admits of form

and the making of form. And not only admits of it, but
calls for it. We people are thrust forward out of the
suggestions of form in the rolling clouds of nature. In
us nature reaches its height of form and through us
exceeds itself. When in doubt there is always form for
us to go on with. Anyone who has achieved the least
form to be sure of it, is lost to the larger excruciations.
I think it must stroke faith in the right way. The artist[,] the poet[,] might be expected to be the most
aware of such assurance. But it is really everybody's
sanity to feel it and live by it. Fortunately, too, no forms
are more engrossing[,] gratifying, comforting, staying
than those lesser ones we throw off, like vortex rings of
smoke, all our individual enterprise and needing nobody's co-operation: a basket, a letter, a garden, a
room, an idea, a picture, a poem. For these we haven't
to get a team together before we can play.

The background in hugeness and confusion shading
away from where we stand into black and utter chaos;
and against the background any small man-made figure of order and concentration. What pleasanter than
that this should be so? Unless we are novelists or econo-
mists we don't worry about this confusion; we look out
on [it] with an instrument or tackle it to reduce it. It is
partly because we are afraid it might prove too much
for us and our blend of democratic-republican-socialist-
communist-anarchist party. But it is more because we
like it, we were born to it, born used to it and have
practical reasons for wanting it there. To me any little
form I assert upon it is velvet, as the saying is, and to
be considered for how much more it is than nothing. If
I were a Platonist I should have to consider it, I suppose, for how much less it is than everything
(Thompson, *Letters,* pp. 418–19).

William James would recognize this as the prose of
what he called "tough-mindedness." Frost casts his lot
with "the truth that," according to James, "grows up inside of all finite experiences." These experiences "lean
on each other, but the whole of them, if whole there be,

leans on nothing" (*Pragmatism*). For Frost, there is a dis-
inclination to "lean" on anyone else even for "co-operation." As he would have it, form is very much a lonely
enterprise of unremarkable or even invisible industry.
And it is perhaps no more lasting than "vortex rings of
smoke"—even blowing *these* can apparently count for
something. There is no yearning in his work for ultima-
tes, none of the desire to "tighten this loose universe"
which James (in a passage that points toward Frost's
poem "Design") ascribed to the "tender minded." What
they want, said James, with persuasive dismissiveness, is

> Something to support the finite many, to tie it to, to
> unify and anchor it. Something *un*exposed to accident,
> something eternal and unalterable. The mutable in ex-
> perience must be founded on immutability. Behind our
> *de facto* world, our world in act, there must be a *de jure*
> duplicate fixed and previous, with all that can happen
> here already there *in posse*, every drop of blood, every
> smallest item, appointed and provided, stamped and
> branded, without chance of variation. The negatives
> that haunt our ideals here below must themselves be
> negated in the absolutely Real. This alone makes the
> universe solid. This is the resting deep. We live upon
> the stormy surface; but with this our anchor holds, for
> it grapples rocky bottom. This is Wordsworth's "eternal
> peace abiding at the heart of endless agitation." This
> is Vivekananda's mystic One of which I read to you.
> This is Reality with the big R, reality that makes the
> timeless claim, reality to which defeat can't happen
> (*Pragmatism*).

We come closest to the spirit of Frost's work whenever
as readers we get into the action, the performance of the
poem, joining him especially in those movements by
which he keeps a poem from "tightening up." There are
disclaimers embedded in assertions ("For once, then,
something"); conciliating understatements that call for

correction ("And to do that to birds was why she came," he says of Eve in "Never Again Would Birds' Song Be the Same"); evasive tactics in the use of words like "almost" and "somehow," of "unless" and especially "as if" ("As if the earth in one unlooked-for favor / Had made them certain earth returned their love," in "Two Look at Two"); predilections for negatives which evoke the reality being denied ("Not bluebells gracing a tunnel mouth— / Not lupine living on sand and drouth" in "A Passing Glimpse"); ascriptions of perception or capacity where none exist ("The aim was song—the wind could see" in "The Aim Was Song"); open-ended endings ("If design govern in a thing so small," "Design"). He is wonderfully exciting in the daring with which he chooses to show that a poem is "less than everything" because, given the nature of things and language, it is difficult enough to be "more than nothing." Frost's is a profound, philosophical use of language, an ultimately austere one which nonetheless provides for its own opportunities of excess. He succeeds in being closer to certain aspects of twentieth-century philosophy—he would have appreciated such a title as Stanley Cavell's *Must We Mean What We Say*—than to the literary modernism of Eliot and Yeats.

II
Beginnings

1. A ROAD NOT TAKEN:
FROST—ELIOT AND JOYCE

In 1913–14 James Joyce, at thirty-two, and Robert Frost, at thirty-nine, each published a "portrait of the artist as a young man." The title of Frost's book, his first, was *A Boy's Will*. Readers are probably more familiar with the career of Joyce's young artist than with the career of the young poet in Frost's volume. Joyce's Stephen, who in the first chapter is an adolescent playing with words as he hovers on the "fringe" of the athletic field, gradually evolves into a Pateresque artist of the 1890's, anxious by then still to be on the "fringe" by putting himself beyond the rules of other public games sponsored by family, church, and country. By the end of the novel he is speaking only to his diary, and he leaves us with the resolve to "forge in the smithy of my soul the uncreated conscience of my race." The pun on "forge" by which creativity is made inextricable from "feigning" or fabrication is not intended by Stephen, but it is surely meant by Joyce, as one of the many ironies directed at the illusions of his younger self. Stephen at the end is filled with a more articulated yearning for the freedom he has wanted from the beginning, but the language he uses is shown by Joyce's contrivance to have accumulated meanings that betray as well as affirm the promises of escape and power.

Catholicism aside, *A Boy's Will* can be compared to *A Portrait,* even to the inclusion of a wary literary nationalism in such poems as "Pan with Us." The book was put together in 1913 at Beaconsfield in England during Frost's first trip abroad, and it includes work dating back to "My Butterfly," the first of his poems to be commercially published, in 1894. In arranging the poems he wanted to avoid even the appearance of chronology based on dates of composition, something that would have locked him into a self-limiting line of poetic development. He was equally reticent about any arrangement that could be construed as an autobiographical record of his romantic and marital life with his wife Elinor White, even though there is a sequence of poems in the book which, as we will see, suggests a connection between his development as a poet and the development of their relationship. He therefore settled on a structural plan that prevents any very simple autobiographical reading. "He could," writes his biographer Lawrance Thompson, "shape a selected group into a spiral of moods, upward through discouragement and withdrawal to aspiration and affirmation. Such a pattern might be reinforced if he made his responses to the changing seasons of fall and winter and spring and summer reflect different phases of his own spiritual growth through dark moods" (Thompson, I, 396).

Writing some years after the publication of the book, to Gorham B. Munson, who had praised him in 1925 as "the purest classical poet in America today," Frost tries to describe those early years on the farm in Derry, New Hampshire, where most of the poems for *A Boy's Will* were written. There, with Elinor and the four children who so far had been born to them and survived, he lived in a solitude which, although not so complete as he claims, was sufficient to allow him to make the quite remarkable statement that it separated him, during these years of poetic initiation from about 1900 to 1906, from history and a sense of time:

> That's where I got my sense that I have forever for accomplishment. If I feel timeless and immortal it is from having lost track of time for five or six years there. We gave up winding clocks. Our ideas got untimely from not taking newspapers for a long period. It couldn't have been more perfect if we had planned it or forseen what we were getting into. It was the luck. It wasn't even instinct that carried us away—just luck. We didn't even know enough to know how hopelessly lost we must have looked from the outside. We never can recapture that. It was for once in a lifetime. That's roughly what *A Boy's Will* is about. Life was peremptory and threw me into confusion. I couldn't have held my own and done myself credit unless I had been a quitter. My infant industries needed the protection of a dead space around them. Everybody was too strong for me, but at least I was strong enough not to stay where they were. I'm still much the same. What's room for if it isn't to get away from minds that stop your works? And the room is the most noticeable thing in the universe. Even in an atom there's more space than matter—infinitely. The matter in the universe gets together in a few terribly isolated points and sizzles.
>
>   In arranging the poems in *A Boy's Will* I tried to plot the curve from blinking people as if they were the sun to being able to face them with my eyes open. But I wasn't escaping. No escape theory will explain me. I was choosing when to deliver battle.—I'm just amusing myself with all this retrospection. It may help give you the spirit   (Thompson, II, 322–23).

In order to "plot the curve" Frost decided on a three-part division of his book, and, except in two cases, provided glosses for the poems, features which were omitted when *A Boy's Will* was published as part of all collections of his poems after 1934. But the original table of contents, including three poems ("Asking for Roses," "In Equal Sacrifice," and "Spoils of the Dead"), all of which were to be eventually dropped beginning with *Collected Poems of 1939*, suggests some of the similarities to Joyce's "portrait" of Stephen both in the arrangement and in the tendency of the older writer to offer what seemed like ironic characterizations of the younger one.

Part I

INTO MY OWN   *The youth is persuaded that he will be rather more than less himself for having forsworn the world.*
GHOST HOUSE   *He is happy in society of his choosing.*
MY NOVEMBER GUEST   *He is in love with being misunderstood.*
LOVE AND A QUESTION   *He is in doubt whether to admit real trouble to a place beside the hearth with love.*
A LATE WALK   *He courts the autumnal mood.*
STARS   *There is no oversight of human affairs.*
STORM FEAR   *He is afraid of his own isolation.*
WIND AND WINDOW FLOWER   *Out of the winter things he fashions a story of modern love.*
TO THE THAWING WIND   *He calls on change through the violence of the elements.*
A PRAYER IN SPRING   *He discovers that the greatness of love lies not in forward-looking thoughts;*
FLOWER GATHERING   *nor yet in any spur it may be to ambition.*
ROSE POGONIAS   *He is no dissenter from the ritualism of nature;*
ASKING FOR ROSES   *nor from the ritualism of youth which is make-believe.*
WAITING—AFIELD AT DUSK   *He arrives at the turn of the year.*
IN A VALE   *Out of old longings he fashions a story.*
A DREAM PANG   *He is shown by a dream how really well it is with him.*
IN NEGLECT   *He is scornful of folk his scorn cannot reach.*

THE VANTAGE POINT   *And again scornful, but there is no one hurt.*
MOWING   *He takes up life simply with the small tasks.*
GOING FOR WATER

Part II

REVELATION   *He resolves to become intelligible, at least to himself, since there is no help else;*
THE TRIAL BY EXISTENCE   *and to know definitely what he thinks about the soul;*
IN EQUAL SACRIFICE   *about love;*
THE TUFT OF FLOWERS   *about fellowship;*
SPOILS OF THE DEAD   *about death;*
PAN WITH US   *about art (his own);*
THE DEMIURGE'S LAUGH   *about science.*

Part III

NOW CLOSE THE WINDOWS   *It is time to make an end of speaking.*
A LINE-STORM SONG   *It is the autumnal mood with a difference.*
OCTOBER   *He sees days slipping from him that were the best for what they were.*
MY BUTTERFLY   *There are things that can never be the same.*
RELUCTANCE

Putting next to last the poem Frost counted as his first, "My Butterfly," is a reminder (just as are the patterns of repetition in *A Portrait* by which Joyce makes an indirect comment on the entrapment of Stephen's consciousness in the past) that the young artist being characterized by the sequence is acting and thinking at the close in the manner characteristic of the beginning. The difference is that Frost, while he may be ironic about the immaturity of his younger self, is not ironic about the *style* of his younger self. His ironies, such as they are, have none of Joyce's large cultural intention. Indeed it would be misleading to call his glosses ironic at all in the Joycean sense. Frost is mostly an older version of him-

self looking at a younger; Joyce is more distinctly an
older *writer* conjuring up, admiring, loving, but also ex-
orcising some of his earlier intellectual and stylistic
predilections and dependencies. Frost may be using the
glosses to protect himself from the possible charge that
in his late thirties he is indulging in feelings proper to an
adolescent, but even that degree of defensiveness is difficult to locate. Rather, the glosses seem unabashedly in
the mode of early Yeats, as in "He Remembers Forgotten Beauty" in *The Wind Among the Reeds* of 1899. When
Frost, in 1910, helped his students at Pinkerton Academy produce two of Yeats's plays, *Cathleen ni Houlihan*
and *The Land of the Heart's Desire,* he decided that Yeats
was his favorite living poet; and he met him in London
three years later after Pound reported that Yeats had
announced that *A Boy's Will* was "the best poetry written
in America for a long time." Frost gives no evidence
whatever that he is shy of indebtedness or that he wants
to be ironic about the fact that the glosses are Yeatsian,
or that in, say, "Waiting" he is like Rossetti of "Silent
Noon," or that in "Love and a Question" there are lines
that are a cross between Poe and Hardy ("A stranger
came to the door at eve, / And he spoke the bridegroom
fair")

By contrast, the cultural implications of Stephen's language are from first to last what concerned Joyce. Not
adolescent posturings only but posturings in a particular
fin de siècle style; not the relative validity of Stephen's
aesthetic theories but the fact that in his formulation of
them he depends on theological vocabularies from
which as an artist he is at the same time declaring his in-
dependence—it is the literary and cultural after-taste of
certain stylized attitudes more than the immaturities of
them which constitute for Joyce a "portrait of the artist."
Frost never betrays, in any sense of the word, the poetic

styles exhibited by the young man in *A Boy's Will,* either
the young man who wrote them or the young man who
speaks in them as if he were himself beginning his career as a writer. Nor does Frost care, as Joyce so abundantly does, about establishing connections between certain styles, on the one hand, and, on the other, various
literary and cultural institutions from which they derive.
Unlike Joyce, that is, the Frost who insinuates his presence in the ordering and arrangement of the material is
not anxious to demonstrate his freedom from the possible snares and delusions of it. The only detachment he
wishes to emphasize is from the temperamental insecurities that get expressed in the poems. He is rather tenderly watching his younger version progress to some
fuller engagement with the world. As we shall see, certain of the love poems are given to a self-conscious stylistic allusiveness meant to characterize the young man as a
writer aspiring at moments to some of the same poet-
icisms, out of Shelley and the Pre-Raphaelites, of which
Stephen Dedalus is so fond. And yet stylistic parody of a
Joycean sort never accompanies the characterization. If
it is supposed, for example, that the poems coming late
in the volume, like "Mowing"—which he was to call his
first "talk song"—or "The Tuft of Flowers," are meant
by their meditative restraint to provide a context in
which certain earlier poems in the sequence can be
called "mannered" or "less mature," then Frost would
not have chosen "My Butterfly" as the penultimate
poem, of which he would later say, "I only brought that
into my collection for the eight lines or so beginning
'The gray grass is scarce dappled with snow' which was
when I struck the note which was to be mine" (Thompson, *Letters,* pp. 526–27).

These reservations and differences when it comes to
Frost's attitude toward the literature of the past and
toward stylization of feeling are to be borne in mind

when one comes upon unmistakable literary echoings in
A Boy's Will. "The Vantage Point," for example, has resemblances to Rossetti's "The Woodspurge." Both
poems are about the sequestering of the self from
human intimacies; both young men exercise therefore a
freedom of bodily disposition (in the one case "My hair
was over in the grass," in the other "I have but to turn
on my arm, and lo"—a line whose metrical adroitness
has been justly praised in Paul Fussell's *Poetic Meter and
Poetic Form*) which brings them into a peculiarly intense
contact with natural details that nonetheless yield no
metaphorical significance.

The Woodspurge

The wind flapped loose, the wind was still,
Shaken out dead from tree and hill:
I had walked on at the wind's will,—
I sat now, for the wind was still.

Between my knees my forehead was,—
My lips, drawn in, said not Alas!
My hair was over in the grass,
My naked ears heard the day pass.

My eyes, wide open, had the run
Of some ten weeds to fix upon;
Among those few, out of the sun,
The woodspurge flowered, three cups in one.

From perfect grief there need not be
Wisdom or even memory:
One thing then learnt remains to me,—
The woodspurge has a cup of three.

The Vantage Point

If tired of trees I seek again mankind,
    Well I know where to hie me—in the dawn,
    To a slope where the cattle keep the lawn.

There amid lolling juniper reclined,
Myself unseen, I see in white defined
    Far off the homes of men, and farther still,
    The graves of men on an opposing hill,
Living or dead, whichever are to mind.

And if by noon I have too much of these,
    I have but to turn on my arm, and lo,
    The sunburned hillside sets my face aglow,
My breathing shakes the bluet like a breeze,
    I smell the earth, I smell the bruisèd plant,
    I look into the crater of the ant.

That the posture in "The Vantage Point" is remarkably similar to one close at hand in English poetry is no
more the occasion for Frostean irony or satire than is
the fact that "A Prayer in Spring" might bring to mind
the Spenser of the "Epithalamion," as well as the Pope
of the early pastorals: "And make us happy in the happy
bees, / The swarm dilating round the perfect trees."
Rossetti of "The Woodspurge" is an inducement both to
the reclining figure of the "young Poet" in "The Vantage Point" and the more composed and composing figure of the older poet who is putting this volume
together. Indeed its very title might owe something not
only to Longfellow's poem "My Lost Youth" ("A boy's
will is the wind's will, / And the thoughts of youth are
long, long thoughts") but to "the wind's will" alluded to
in line 3 of Rossetti's. More generally, Rossetti displays a
talent for "the speaking voice," for what in a letter of
July 4, 1913, Frost was already calling, though he had
been anticipated in this somewhat by Gerard Manley
Hopkins, "the sound of sense," as it works in and against
the regular iambic line. Rossetti often displays a conver-
sational movement and talkativeness, usually overlooked
in general characterizations of him and of the Pre-
Raphaelites. The last line of "The Woodspurge" gets a

Frostean accent when its iambic regularity gives way, under the stress of a series of monosyllabic words, to an emphatic vernacular, while in such longer poems as "Antwerp to Ghent" there are lines ("Our speed is such the sparks our engine leaves / Are burning after the whole train has passed") strikingly similar to the voice movement in some of Frost's dramatic narratives.

Rossetti is "in" the older as much as in the younger Frost who is the speaker of the poem; so too are Pope and Gray in lines 2 and 3, so is Thoreau in the whole first stanza, or Marvell or even Plato of "Phaedrus." Frost's gloss—"and again scornful, but there is no one hurt"—suggests that the poem may simply be about someone in a pout. But what matters by the end is that the person who chooses to be alone also wants to strike up a relationship with things in nature. This is a major Frostean situation that will be found in nearly all the poems in this volume and which raises certain questions central to all his poetry. How close can anyone who is alone, who does not have a human partner, get to "nature"? How potentially deprived of vision is the isolated viewer no matter how closely he tries to look at anything? This is a theme that will carry past *A Boy's Will* into even more ambitious poems like "The Wood-Pile" and "The Most of It."

From the start Frost is intentionally evasive about the degree to which the human dramas in his work are also poetic ones, about the degree to which creative personal relationships are the prerequisite for creative poetic ones—or vice versa. These early poems are eventually about the achieved condition by which the young man is put into a nourishing connection to persons, nature, and, as consequence or cause, to earlier poetry. Such poetry comes to exist for him and for Frost as a "golden treasury," which includes but extends beyond the

famous anthology of Palgrave's which bore that title and
which was always one of Frost's favorite books. It is a
treasury which can be drawn on by Frost, confidently
strong in the originality and strength of his own invest-
ments, without those twinges of conscience which Joyce
exacts from Stephen. The literature of the past is a
golden treasury for Joyce, too, but he is anxious to show
in *A Portrait* that there are all kinds of entailments at-
tached to the inheritance, especially for anyone who
wants to use it as "a breakwater of order and elegance
against the sordid tide of life within him and without."
Joyce's ironies in *A Portrait* are directed ultimately at
illusions about the organizing power of literature in a
situation where other institutions, like the Roman Cath-
olic Church, have lost it.

These illustrative differences between the procedures
of Joyce and Frost provide an occasion for less obvious
discriminations among the modernisms coming to
prominence in the period when Frost began his career.
Joyce's skepticism about literature, especially its institu-
tional power as a source of value, is central to what is familiarly called modernism. What is perhaps special
about Joyce and Eliot and other twentieth-century modernists resides in the paradox that their skeptical treat-
ments of the power of literature had the effect of en-
dowing it, and themselves, with precisely the enormous
cultural importance which they were calling into question. Such disenchantment as they expressed issued
from, and perpetuated, truly extraordinary claims, not
only about literature as the embodiment of culture but
about the literature which they were themselves in the
process of creating. After all, doubts about the power of
writing are not unique in the history of literature, as any
reading of Diderot or of Seneca would suggest; but the
claims made on the basis of this skepticism by twentieth-

century modernists were, in their conscious presumption and ambition, unprecedented. In proposing, that is, that the literature of the past contributes to rather than helps us sort out the chaos of forms in which contemporary life apparently finds itself, modernist writers of Eliot's disposition or of Joyce's assumed that the writing in which the proposition was being made and the writer who was making it had a synoptic and mediating power with respect to contemporary culture which Frost would not choose to claim or to grant. Condescensions directed at Frost by many admirers of the classical texts in English of twentieth-century modernism derive in part from the assumption that modernist literature was made inevitable by historical realities of the twentieth century. It has been assumed that Joyce and Eliot are therefore closer to the central "significances" of their age than is Frost. Works like *The Waste Land* that originally seemed "incoherent" to the general reader finally, therefore, imposed themselves on consciousness as realistic. They are said to be an image of the incoherent and fractured nature of contemporary reality and also to constitute an effort at transcendence.

The comparison I am making between Frost and Joyce or Frost and Eliot is intended, then, to characterize a species of modernism from which Frost quite consciously excluded himself. I am aware that in another context it would be necessary, as Denis Donoghue rightly insists, to note the differences between the modernism of Eliot and that of Joyce. But for my limited purposes here, their similarities are greater still, especially when Frost is brought into the equation. Frost knew how little a place he would have in it. "I like to read Eliot," Burton Rascoe reported him as saying in 1923, "because it is fun seeing the way he does things, but I am always glad that it is his way and not mine";

and of Joyce, "I have heard that Joyce wrote *Ulysses* as a
joke" (Thompson II, 220–21). Where similarities exist
between the young men portrayed in the early works of
Frost, Joyce, and Eliot—their fastidiousness and isolation, their tendency to make poetic inspiration dependent upon romantic ones, their capacity to transform
sense impressions into visionary experiences, their affec-
tations of poetic language, their immersion in the literature of the past, especially the immediate past—all of
these make us aware of how in dealing with some of
these same materials they are fundamentally and repre-
sentatively different.

Chaos is where you find it; form comes into being
where you decide it is most needed; and the important
difference between Frost and certified modernists like
Eliot and Joyce is that his "chaos" compared to theirs
has no historical localizations. For Frost, the whole of
the background is "in hugeness and confusion shading
away from where we stand into black and utter chaos;
and against the background any small man-made figure
of order and concentration. What pleasanter than that
this should be so?" No such "human figure" appears in
Eliot; and in Joyce, if it be Bloom, then he is a figure we
are invited to love with considerable condescension.
Bloom, to put the matter simply, could not read the
book we must read in order to understand him; he
could not comprehend the structural necessities of *Ulysses*. Frost's speakers usually help create the structurings
that are to include them, and these, as in two poems in
this first volume, "Mowing" and "Tuft of Flowers," are
often equivalent to the structuring of the poems themselves.

In saying that Joyce and Eliot were compelled by historical conditions while Frost, for the most part, was not,
I do not mean that the form of their writings was prede-

termined by historical circumstances except as they and their readers came to *imagine* that this was the case. Temperamental or psychological alienation played a crucial part, so did a disenchantment with inherited literary forms, but both feelings preceded those broader encounters with historical plights which in the later works seem to be the source and justification for these feelings. "Modernist" skepticism about "any small man-made figure of order and concentration" is apparent in the earliest, least historically rooted and least allusive writings of Joyce and Eliot. Joyce's "The Sisters," in the contrast it establishes between the poetic elegance and balance of the young boy's language when he is alone in his bedroom as against the fracturing banalities of all other conversation in the story, could be a case in point. And an extremely beautiful example worth pursuing is Eliot's early "La Figlia che Piange." The poem nowhere attempts to justify itself by implicit claims that historical pressures and conditions have made it what it is. And yet it has all the structural characteristics which are to be found, obviously in more developed form, in the later poetry. "La Figlia che Piange" is as modernist in its exertions of poetic power against recalcitrant "material" as is *The Waste Land* and has, in an untried manner, the technical and experimental resources which in the later poems are brought to bear on cultural fragmentation:

La Figlia che Piange
O quam te memorem virgo . . .

Stand on the highest pavement of the stair—
Lean on a garden urn—
Weave, weave the sunlight in your hair—
Clasp your flowers to you with a pained surprise—
Fling them to the ground and turn
With a fugitive resentment in your eyes:
But weave, weave the sunlight in your hair.

So I would have had him leave,
So I would have had her stand and grieve,
So he would have left
As the soul leaves the body torn and bruised,
As the mind deserts the body it has used.
I should find
Some way incomparably light and deft,
Some way we both should understand,
Simple and faithless as a smile and shake of the hand.

She turned away, but with the autumn weather
Compelled my imagination many days,
Many days and many hours:
Her hair over her arms and her arms full of flowers.
And I wonder how they should have been together!
I should have lost a gesture and a pose.
Sometimes these cogitations still amaze
The troubled midnight and the noon's repose.

The poem manifests itself by its inability to stabilize the items within it, the imperative placements of the opening stanza ("Stand," "Lean," "Weave," etc.) give way to a plaintive petition in the last line that the figure should at least continue a movement which for whatever reason excites the man speaking with the prospect of grasping an elusive significance: "But weave, weave the sunlight in your hair." In line 8 ("So I would have had him leave") and in line 21 ("And I wonder how they should have been together!") he is clearly not the lover; in line 15 ("Some way we both should understand") he may be. By the end, he is merely someone ("I" or "he" or "we") remembering memories. All he is ascertainably is a man—or a medium—who anxiously imagines postures, and metaphorical equivalents for them, of dubious relevance. Having tried them, he then gives up: "I should find / Some way incomparably light and deft." By the end we cannot even place the speaker in time. He is speaking somewhere about "sometimes" when "these cogitations still amaze / The troubled midnight and the noon's repose." "Amaze" because he can no more than try to make sense, or a poem, of the cogitations; and the epigraph from Virgil is only one of these attempts, not any more successful, despite some feeble linkages, than the others. The speaker is a medium for impressions, including literary ones, in search of a form, and in this he is no different from the speaker or medium at the end of *The Waste Land.*

"La Figlia che Piange" is, interestingly enough, usually ignored or brushed aside by critics and interpreters who wholeheartedly ascribe to the historical reality of the waste land image. Holding rigidly to this view, they cannot see that as a performance in the face of the intractable, this slight early poem, in its structural similarities to *The Waste Land,* demonstrates that the dislocations characteristic of Eliot's poetry are not inevitably the result of the cultural and historical conditions. In the resemblance between the earlier and the later poems there is an implicit and perhaps embarrassing question. Are the literary characteristics of modernism prompted necessarily by direct confrontations with historical and cultural crises? Or do they not issue as possibly from mysterious personal ones? The poem is evidence that Eliot was simply not by nature the kind of poet who ever could feel that against any "black and utter chaos"—which Frost did not in any case ascribe to the twentieth century—"any little form I can asert on it is velvet, as the saying is." Eliot's was a courageous masochistic exposure of an incapacity to "assert" form (how different is he here from Joyce as well as Frost!)—an incapacity that must have derived in part from a sense of deficient sexual prowess and sexual adequacy. Frost's heterosexual "assertiveness," his confident masculinity, would have made "La Figlia che Piange" imaginatively (and formally) impossible for him, just as "Putting in the Seed" would have been for Eliot.

However, the fact that certain literary characteristics associated with modernism derive from psychological rather than from alleged historical pressures may only prove that the latter were so potently felt as to have been internalized by writers exposed to them, especially when they were of more than ordinary susceptibility and of exceptional genius. It is not that Joyce or Eliot were mythologizing the century and that Frost was not; it is rather that they exhibit different mythologies about the possibilities and functions of literature *in* the century. Curiously enough, Frost's belief in the personal salvation made possible by the assertion of form was a function of his *dis*belief in the capacity of form to do much more than that. It might be argued that Frost could have read Hawthorne and Melville and gotten a sense of cultural exhaustion and waste, of human essence as itself "an antique buried beneath antiquities, and throned on torsos!" as Ishmael would have it. But no one coming to maturity with Frost or Pound would have been exposed to what have since come to be recognized as the main lines of force in "American literature." Hawthorne was James's pacified version; Melville was so generally ignored as a serious writer, until the 1920's, that *Moby Dick* is given one paragraph in the three-volume *Cambridge History of American Literature* published in 1917. Before college, where Frost read Latin and Greek poetry, his readings in American literature, and in English literature, have to be assessed within the context of what literature was then presumed to be and of the relatively a-historical way in which a writer like Arnold would have been assimilated by an American audience. Frost's reading at age fifteen, as described by his wife in 1935, was in spots quite similar to Stephen Dedalus's in

its liking for romantic adventure and heroic exploits, but
even books of this sort cannot be expected to have had
on him the same kind of cultural impact they would
have had on Joyce's "artist":

> . . . he never read [all the way through] a book of any
> kind to himself before his fourteenth year. His mother
> read aloud constantly. Poe and Shakespeare, George
> Mc Donald [Macdonald]—old fashioned romances, like
> "The Romance of Dollard." In his 14th year he read
> Jane Porter's *Scottish Chiefs*, *Mysterious Island* by Jules
> Verne, *Tom Brown's School Days*, first volume Scott's
> *Tales of A Grandfather*, Prescott's *Conquest of Mexico*, and
> also *The Last of the Mohicans* and *Deerslayer*. . . . Read
> first poetry in 15th year. . . . In that year he read a
> little of Shelley and Keats in Christmas gift books. Al-
> most learned all of Poe by heart. Keats and Arnold
> only other poets he ever found he knew as large a
> proportion of. Didn't like Endymion at the time, and
> never has, but except for Endymion, everything
> (Thompson, I, 500).

What is left out here is that his mother also read aloud
to him from Macpherson's *Ossian*, exhibiting a taste
compatible with those romantic poets, Burns, Wordsworth, Bryant, and Emerson, whose works she quoted
to her children from infancy on.

Frost was an American and his reading of English literature cannot be expected to have in it the Arnoldian—
later to be the Leavisian—sense of English letters: that it
was a carrier of as well as a clue to the state of the culture as a whole, that cultural values depended upon an
alert sense of the function of literature and of criticism.
He read for fun and exaltation. It was for Eliot, with all
the fervor of a recent convert to a culture not natively
his—Frost once remarked to me, in effect, "Eliot has left
us and you know he's never really found them"—to

write the essay in 1930 on Arnold and Pater. Eliot was
anxious to make Arnold responsible for the emergence
of the cult of art for art's sake and, along with it, the
eventual usurpation by art of the place in the culture
formerly occupied by religion. Perhaps it is symptomatic
of a merely acquired and appropriated quality in Eliot's
objection to Arnold that his position is more or less a
paraphrase of what he could have gotten from a reading
of Joyce, about whom he had published his well-known
essay "Ulysses, Order and Myth" in 1923. Any sensitive
reading of the last chapter of *A Portrait* and of the opening chapter of *Ulysses* has to take account of the contribution made by Arnold and Pater to Stephen's problem of artistic self-definition.

By contrast, the Arnold of Frost's impressionable
years was not even the author of *Culture and Anarchy,*
much less an inventor of the modernist dilemma. Frost's
Arnold was the poet of "Sohrab and Rustrum," which
he later read to his own children, or "Cadmus and
Hermione," "my favorite poem long before I knew what
it was going to mean to us" (Letter to Louis Untermeyer,
29 April 1934, Thompson, *Letters,* p. 408). Later he
evokes Arnold as an illustration of liberal intellectual
querulousness about the perils of the age and the terrors of nature. "Adlai Stevenson's Democrats," I once
heard him say, were "Dover Beach boys," and in the
poem "New Hampshire" he weaves quotations from
three of Arnold's poems, "In Harmony with Nature,"
"Sohrab and Rustrum," and "The Scholar Gipsy," into a
sarcastic characterization of what he took to be fashionable, intellectualistic anxiety about the age we live in.

> Lately in converse with a New York alec
> About the new school of the pseudo-phallic,
> I found myself in a close corner where   360

I had to make an almost funny choice.
"Choose you which you will be—a prude, or puke,
Mewling and puking in the public arms."
"Me for the hills where I don't have to choose."
"But if you had to choose, which would you be?"
I wouldn't be a prude afraid of nature.
I know a man who took a double ax
And went alone against a grove of trees;
But his heart failing him, he dropped the ax
And ran for shelter quoting Matthew Arnold: 370
" 'Nature is cruel, man is sick of blood';
There's been enough shed without shedding mine.
Remember Birnam Wood! The wood's in flux!"
He had a special terror of the flux
That showed itself in dendrophobia.
The only decent tree had been to mill
And educated into boards, he said.
He knew too well for any earthly use
The line where man leaves off and nature starts,
And never overstepped it save in dreams.   380
He stood on the safe side of the line talking—
Which is sheer Matthew Arnoldism,
The cult of one who owned himself "a foiled
Circuitous wanderer," and "took dejectedly
His seat upon the intellectual throne"—
Agreed in frowning on these improvised
Altars the woods are full of nowadays,
Again as in the days when Ahaz sinned
By worship under green trees in the open.
Scarcely a mile but that I come on one,   390
A black-cheeked stone and stick of rain-washed charcoal.
Even to say the groves were God's first temples
Comes too near to Ahaz' sin for safety.
Nothing not built with hands of course is sacred.
But here is not a question of what's sacred.
Rather of what to face or run away from.
I'd hate to be a runaway from nature.
And neither would I choose to be a puke
Who cares not what he does in company,
And when he can't do anything, falls back   400
On words, and tries his worst to make words speak

Louder than actions, and sometimes achieves it.
It seems a narrow choice the age insists on.
How about being a good Greek, for instance?
That course, they tell me, isn't offered this year.
"Come, but this isn't choosing—puke or prude?"

That sense of futility expressed in the lines from "The
Scholar Gipsy" which Frost derisively quotes (lines
383–85) are a reference to Goethe as "one / Who most
has suffered" and who "takes dejectedly / His seat upon
the intellectual throne." It is an image wholly consistent
with Arnold's general view of the plight of modern culture. As expressed in an essay on Heinrich Heine written in 1863, Arnold's vision defines the kind of modernism that was to be "discovered" later and used as a
rationale for the formal dislocation in the literature of
this century, the heady mixture of discontinuity and cultural allusiveness:

> Modern times find themselves with an immense system
> of institutions, established facts, accredited dogmas,
> customs, rules, which have come to them from times
> not modern. In this system . . . life has to be carried
> forward, yet [modern people] have a sense that the sys-
> tem is not of their own creation, that it by no means
> corresponds exactly with the wants of their actual life,
> that, for them, it is customary, not rational.

"An immense system of institutions . . . which have
come down to them from times not modern"—this sense
of encroachment, which was anticipated and as strongly
expressed in the American literature of Hawthorne and
Melville, is more important to any true understanding
of modernism, and of Frost's special relationship to it,
than is the feeling of cosmic or other "terror." "Terror"
is no more the property of the twentieth century than of
any other period of history or of literature. Politically

and intellectually, Frost tended to find evidences of "system" and its deleterious effects not in anything that has "come down" to us but in what had been more recently contrived. Darwinism, socialism, the New Deal, Freudianism were all to him the dangerous imposition of "system" upon the free movements of life. It was against these that he directed his sometimes vulgar contempt. He accepted much of the past without even thinking of it as constituting a "system." It was more or less an expression of Nature through human beings as its agent. He chose never to "systematize" the sources of human suffering or anguish. Writing, beautifully, of Edwin Arlington Robinson in his Introduction to *King Jasper*, he says that

> there is solid satisfaction in a sadness that is not just a fishing for ministration and consolation. Give us immedicable woes—woes that nothing can be done for—woes flat and final. And then to play. The play's the thing. Play's the thing. All virtue in "as if." "As if the last of days / Were fading and all wars were done."
> As if they were. As if, as if!

It is clear from this little passage alone that the spirit of resistance was provoked in Frost not by the burden or degeneracy of historical, cultural, or literary "systems." Life itself invites us to give up, and it is in rejecting the offer that the human presence makes itself known. He calls for a kind of "woe" that is Biblical, that belongs to our fate. Being "immedicable" it is a fit cause for grief, an emotion far superior, as he argues in this same preface, to grievance. "Grievances are a form of impatience. Griefs are a form of patience."

2. CHOICES

Frost could never blame the "age" for anything, or even blame what he did himself at a certain age for what might have happened to him subsequently. This was the virtue of his pride. Moral and literary accomplishment are of a piece in his poetry because of his near-mystical acceptance of responsibility for himself and for whatever happened to him. His biographer misses this entirely. In his harsh, distorted, and personally resentful view of Frost's manipulative, calculating use of other people, Thompson sees only the determinations of a man who wanted fully to control his career and his public image. Unquestionably, that was one of the things he was doing. He was also revealing something wonderful about human life, or, if you wish, about his sense of what it was. He was communicating his conviction that, mysteriously, nothing happens to us in life except what we choose to have happen. A conscious "use" of other people, a conscious exploitation of them in order to be lazy, in order to get work done, or to get good reviews— this was at least making yourself, and others, aware of what you were doing. What is conspicuous about Frost's letters when he is asking for a favor is their uncommon forthrightness. There is in them the relish of self-exposure. He tries to make visible the choices he is making for his life, choices which were there anyway, invisibly at work on himself and on others. What he calls "the trial by existence" in the magnificent Dante-esque poem of that title in *A Boy's Will* is "the obscuration upon earth" of souls that have chosen to leave heaven and to accept whatever human life might have in store for them. Even after a soul is saved, even after the "bravest that are slain" on earth find themselves in heaven, they discover another opportunity for bravery and choice, an opportunity all the more daring because the choice will not, once taken, even be remembered

> 'Tis of the essence of life here,
>   Though we choose greatly, still to lack
> The lasting memory at all clear,
>   That life has for us on the wrack
> Nothing but what we somehow chose;
>   Thus are we wholly stripped of pride
> In the pain that has but one close,
>   Bearing it crushed and mystified.

There are two kinds of choice here. We "greatly choose" some things and we "somehow chose" all the things that happen to us. The pride we may take in conscious choices is stripped away not by any obvious predominance of the unconscious ones but rather by our being ignorant of how much more inclusive they are. That is, the individual is denied the *privilege* of knowing that in fact no one else has made his life as it is. Frost was always seeking for the restitution of that lost and diminished sense of responsibility even while he was at the same time exalted by the mystery of not being able fully to grasp it. This divided consciousness helps explain the perplexing ways in which a poet who attaches so much value to form, with all the choice that involves, attaches equal value to freedom in the movement of the poem toward a form. The perplexity is not lessened by the fact that within the freedom there are the elements which he also "somehow chose." Thus he will write, in "The Figure a Poem Makes," that a poem "has an outcome that though unforseen was predestined from the first image of the original mood—and indeed from the very mood." For him, life and poems work in much the same way. In both, there is a wondrous emergence into consciousness of those selections, impressions—and choices—that were not available to consciousness when first made.

> The impressions most useful to my purpose seem always those I was unaware of and so made no note of at the time when taken, and the conclusion is come to that like giants we are always hurling experience ahead of us to pave the future with against the day when we may want to strike a line of purpose across it for somewhere. The line will have the more charm for not being mechanically straight. We enjoy the straight crookedness of a good walking stick. Modern instruments of precision are being used to make things crooked as if by eye and hand in the old days   ("The Figure a Poem Makes").

It is not stretching the point to say that this intimation of the peculiar and mysterious workings of choice is what made him so resolute and even ruthless when choice became incumbent or conscious. It was as if the free movement in his life demanded of him that he then do what had to be done either with his career, with a poem, or with a book. Despite differences, he is in this more like Lawrence than like any other writer of the century. And yet it seems apparent that form, for Lawrence as much as for Frost, the more formalistic of the two, by being necessarily to some degree conscious was also, to some degree, imposed, and that what Frost says about "modern instruments of precision" might sometimes apply to his own work on a poem. His claims, again in "The Figure a Poem Makes," to the "wildness of logic" are apt to strike some readers as disingenuous. The "logic" of even some of the best poems, as illustrated by "Spring Pools," does not, as the reader experiences it, appear to be "more felt than seen ahead like prophecy." Some of that, yes—but also a good deal of premeditation and preplotting. Frost is best appreciated if we let him *try* to do the best he can within the drama of form and freedom, and it is in that light that we can understand the design he gave to *A Boy's Will* using some of the poems he then had available. It is a matter of his using "experience," in this case poems, that he had paved "the future with against the day when [he would want] to strike a line of purpose across it for somewhere."

A Boy's Will is an appropriate place for a poem about choices of lives, like "Trial by Existence." The design of the book—what is put in, what is left out, the groupings of the poems, the headnotes—expresses a "choice" about the portrait of man and poet that Frost wanted to present. Or rather what can be inferred from these "choices" of inclusion and exclusion are three portraits whose details sometimes coincide, sometimes blur, sometimes block one another out. One, the cosiest, most availably public, and closest to the glosses, is of a young man who develops a fulfilling relationship to the world after passing through a period of alienation and trial. Another is of a young man trying to shape the complex tension within himself between sexuality and creative powers, between the calls of love and of poetry. This is a more submerged portrait than the first, and its features will remain both more indelible and more obscure all the way through Frost's work. And then there is a darker version of this second portrait, a kind of *pentimento,* a possible portrait later painted over by an author who "repented" and wanted to block out certain features. He kept this portrait hidden, as it were, by the omission of a poem that could have fitted into this volume (bringing with it a darkening of all that would surround it) with at least as much effectiveness as it did into a later group that includes "Never Again Would Bird's Song Be the Same" and "The Most of It" in *A Witness*

Tree of 1942. I am referring to "The Subverted Flower," the first draft of which had been written so early, if we are to believe what Frost himself told Thompson, that it could have been published in *A Boy's Will* (Thompson, I, 512).

Taken together these three overlapping portraits, while they do not account for all the poems in the volume—two of the best, "Mowing" and "The Tuft of Flowers," will be discussed in the last chapter—do include most of them and the overall "plot" of the book. In discussing the alternate and interwoven portraits I want above all to insist that none of the features come inadvertently into prominence. Frost knew exactly what he was doing; he was never innocent of what his poems imply. His original omissions and discriminations are the result of his loyalty to the complex and mystifying way in which languages appropriate to sexuality, poetic practice, and nature are, in his consciousness of them, not to be separated one from the other. The elements of intentional disguise in any one of the tracings of the poetic self should not, that is, make anyone think that the other disguises, found beneath the obvious ones, were therefore unconscious. Frost was at once too doggedly responsible for whatever he did about himself and too mistrustful of himself and of his imagination ever to have said more than he knew.

Thompson's discussions of how the book was put together are at the outset too vague to be useful and too simple to be true. "Alone one night, he sorted through the sheaf of manuscripts he had brought with him and could not resist the impulse to see if he had enough to make up a small volume . . . [which] would represent his achievement up to the age of thirty-eight" (Thompson, I, 396–97). "Impulse"? For one thing, he had far more than "enough" to make a book, and a better book than the one he put together. For another, what he did pick out for *A Boy's Will* did not begin to represent the variety, much less the size, of his accomplishment up to the age of thirty-eight. Evidence of this is in Thompson's own reserach into the dates of composition (Thompson, II, 540–42). No dramatic narratives are included in the book, for example, though at least three that were to appear the next year, 1914, in *North of Boston* had been written as early as 1905 and 1906—"The Death of the Hired Man," "The Black Cottage," and "The Housekeeper." In addition, he had on hand over a dozen poems, all written before 1913, and including some of his best. "Bond and Free" was written in the period 1896–1900, and twelve more were written (or at least begun) in Derry between 1900 and 1911, including "An Old Man's Winter Night," "The Telephone," "Pea Brush," "An Encounter," "Range Finding," "Loneliness," "The Line-Gang," "The Flower Boat," and "The Subverted Flower." In addition, some of the great sonnets were written during 1906–7: "The Oven Bird," "Putting in the Seed," and the fifteen-line sonnet variant "Hyla Brook." All these were held until the third book, *Mountain Interval,* in 1916.

Of course Frost may not have "brought with him" (the precise meaning, if any, of Thompson's phrase is never made clear) some of the poems destined for later printing. In that unlikely case, there would be a still stronger indication of some prior decision not to put into his first book works that would presumably fit better into some design of a poetic progress which was to be revealed in subsequent volumes. But there is no evidence that he did not have all of his manuscript poetry with him. Obviously he had to have the poems destined for *North of Boston* since this was printed before he left England. In fact, as soon as *A Boy's Will* was out, he began to play

tricks with the whole revered critical notion of chronology and "development," using one of the poems he had
had around since 1905–6. His specifically intended vic-
tim was also his most renowned admirer, Ezra Pound.
Knowing that, when the facts became public, Pound,
and the usual cant about newness, would be made to
look silly, he gave him "Death of the Hired Man" as a
"new poem." After the publication in *Poetry* of his review
of *A Boy's Will*, which Frost and his wife found conde-
scending, Pound promised Harriet Monroe, the editor,
that he would have something new from Frost "as soon
as he has done it." "He has done a 'Death of the Farm-
hand' since the book [*A Boy's Will*]," he wrote his father
on June 3, 1913, and adds with yet another example of
his wholly engaging generosity of feeling, that this poem
"is to my mind better than anything in it. I shall have
that in *The Smart Set* or in *Poetry* before long" (Thompson, I, 437). One thing is sure—that many of the poems
held back were incomparably superior to at least three
that he chose to publish but would eventually delete
from later printings of his poems: "Spoils of the Dead,"
"In Equal Sacrifice," and "Asking for Roses." The last of
these is a fair sample of all three. It is mildly interesting
because it offers an early example of Frost's obsession
with human dwellings that are impoverished and apparently deserted, and because it is a kind of *Lied* with
echoes of Burns and Tom Moore. As the young lovers
pass the house, they notice a garden of "old-fashioned
roses":

> "I wonder," I say, "who the owner of those is."
> "Oh, no one you know," she answers me airy,
> "But one we must ask if we want any roses."

It is astonishing to learn, if Frost's own testimony is to
be believed, that at the time he was willing to see in print

this embarrassing poem about a man, a woman, and flowers, he held back "The Subverted Flower" which makes use of the same three items. The complex dramatic interaction between flowers (which are a symptom in the poems of seasonal fertility), sexuality, and poetry is one of the important but uninsistent lines of coherence in the volume. Frost's own awareness of it and of its implications is best indicated by his omission of a poem whose inclusion would have caused a substantial change of emphasis. It would have suggested very dark psychological shadings in the sexual areas which, by the implications of Frost's language in his poetry and in his prose, provide some of the metaphors for artistic creativity. It would also have indicated that he was to some degree victimized by unrequited love and that his career was not as simple an unfolding of self as he wants to suggest.

From the outset "The Subverted Flower" establishes the powerful authority, the psychotic necessity, of its macabre imagery and the relentlessness of its movement. It is the sexual nightmare of an adolescent blankly registering the descent, through sexual repressions, of himself and the girl he desires into different forms of bestiality. The four-beat lines are rhymed in a staggered way that allows sudden accelerations past one fixation, like a nightmare image being recollected, on to the next, where we are suspended as in a trance until a disyllabic rhyme chooses to complete the frame. Except for a few of Meredith's sonnets in "Modern Love" there is little in any poetry before Frost that can approach the direct and graphic sexual terror of this poem, the first lines of which follow:

> She drew back; he was calm:
> "It is this that had the power."
> And he lashed his open palm
> With the tender-headed flower.

He smiled for her to smile,
But she was either blind
Or willfully unkind.
He eyed her for a while
For a woman and a puzzle.
He flicked and flung the flower,
And another sort of smile
Caught up like finger tips
The corners of his lips
And cracked his ragged muzzle.

The poem could refer to an incident of so-called indecent exposure in Frost's courtship of Elinor White, but the details make it likely that it is an account of a nightmare in which such an incident was symbolically enacted. This would be a good reason for his wanting to withhold it, and the probability that the poem has *something* to do with Elinor White is advanced by Thompson as the sole reason for Frost's delaying publication until 1942, after her death. The subject, Frost was later to say in his *Paris Review* interview, was "frigidity in women."

There are, however, complicated literary as well as personal reasons for his not having printed the poem in *A Boy's Will,* reasons that become apparent when we see that, except for its style, the poem would not have been out of place, and, oddly enough, would have easily fitted in thematically. The problem would have been that the poem excites a kind of autobiographical speculation that would have materially altered the "portrait of an artist" that Frost wanted to project. To begin with, the strangeness of the poem is considerably lessened once it is placed among those in *A Boy's Will* wherein flowers are a token of either a precarious movement toward sexual, seasonal, and artistic fulfillment or the failure of these. Or perhaps one should say that its strangeness informs and significantly alters these other poems. The volume as a whole begins with landscapes that are barren, even funereal, and in which the young man walks forth conspicuously alone. Following on the barren landscapes of the first three poems, "Into My Own," "Ghost House," and "My November Guest," whose name is Sorrow, we come upon the just-married couple of "Love and a Question." The bride and groom are visited by a tramp in need of shelter. The bridegroom turns him away from the door, and yet is peculiarly equivocal as he "looked at a weary road" while his bride sits behind him at the fire: "But whether or not a man was asked / To mar the love of two / By harboring woe in the bridal house, / The bridegroom wished he knew." Then in the next, or fifth poem, "A Late Walk," there is a faint signal of a new vitality. A "flower" is just barely rescued from the desolation which has dominated the scene up to that point. The young man is still, though married, walking alone amidst "withered weeds," bare trees, except for "a leaf that lingered brown." But his walk ends in a gesture of unification with what little is still alive in the landscape and with the life that awaits him at home: "I end not far from my going forth, / By picking the faded blue / Of the last remaining aster flower / To carry again to you."

From this point on, the isolated "I" who has only begun to express the intimacy of his feeling for "her" is replaced with "we" and "our." But the world continues nevertheless to be found cold and threatening. The next poem is "Stars" with its landscape of snow in which the lovers might be lost "to white rest and a place of rest / Invisible at dawn"—an accent of Emily Dickinson unusual for Frost. In the poem that follows, "Storm Fear," the young man still lies alone in his wakefulness, but he is apparently with his wife and fears not for him-

self so much as for her and the children. Following
on these it is proposed in "Wind and Window Flower"
that she is a "flower" and that he is a winter wind "concerned with ice and snow, / Dead weeds and unmated
birds, / And little of love could know."

Even before this we have become aware that the
threat to love has been gradually internalized by the
young poet and that the landscape is an imaginary one
of those moods, depressions, and melancholies which
threaten their love with devastation and aridity. Only
with the next four poems—"To the Thawing Wind"
("Give the buried flower a dream"), "A Prayer in
Spring" ("Oh, give us pleasure in the flowers today"),
"Flower Gathering," and "Rose Pogonias"—does the
young poet escape from "dead weeds and unmated
birds." Along with them the poet has himself been seen
as a force for frigidity working in conjunction with the
most malevolent aspects which he selects or imagines in
the natural environment.

Though thematically "The Subverted Flower" could
obviously belong to this grouping, it would have materially changed the implication of these poems insofar as
they are about the nature of Frost's sexual-poetic imagination. By including it, Frost would have transferred responsibility from the young man to "her," or Elinor. As
a result, he would have obscured the fact that the poems
in this volume are essentially concerned with the connections between his poetic prowess and his power to
find love within a landscape of the mind as well as in
relation to another person. The poems trace out the effort to free his imagination so that it might work toward
some harmony with natural cycles both of the seasons
and of sexuality. With inclusion of "The Subverted
Flower," the interest in the volume would have become
more psychological than literary; it would have placed

greater emphasis on the hazards of sexuality to the confusion of a Wordsworthian subject which more classically includes sexuality: the "Growth of a Poet's Mind." "The Subverted Flower" is not, as are the others, about *his* potentially frigid mind or imagination but about hers. His delicacy about Elinor White Frost was real enough, no doubt, but equally real was the desire to make himself responsible for anything that might have affected his poetry. It was Frost's enormous desire for control, form, design that forbade his including a poem which might imply, even by blaming another, that he was not the master of his literary fates.

The exclusion of this poem helps explain a number of things implied by his also having left out the other poems I have mentioned. First of all, the selection for *A Boy's Will* was not governed in any thoroughgoing way by the novelistic and self-revelatory scheme he himself claimed to have set up: "The psychologist in me," he was to say later on, "ached to call it 'The Record of A Phase of Post Adolescence' " (Thompson, II, xxi, 593). Second, the nature of the volume, and the determination of the order of poems, suggest other reasons for leaving out "The Subverted Flower," reasons having to do with Frost's imagination of a poetic career and with his fierce determination to control the public shaping of his life. He would rather have let at least some people think that part of the structure of *A Boy's Will* was dictated by "the seasons," which is superficially true, than allow most people freely to discover that the seasons are finally only a metaphor for the possible and always threatened perversion or subversion of the poetic imagination by the disasters of love. He would rather have pretended that the volume is about "A Phase of Post Adolescence" than have us ask if the connection in his work between sexuality and the progress of poetry is not far more complicated than he chooses to admit. Which is a way of saying that while he knew everything that was going on in his poetry he was not always anxious that we should know as much as he does.

Many of the early poems, offering some of the psychological and structural sources of all of Frost's poetry, are about this relation of love to poetic making, to making in all other senses of the word. A brief biographical digression might be useful here, a recapitulation of Frost's stormy and passionate courtship of Elinor White, with whom he seems to have fallen in love at first meeting. He was seventeen, she nearly two years older, and they sat next to one another in Lawrence High School (Massachusetts). From the outset, her ability as a poet (she stopped writing poems before she married him and in later life tried to disguise and disown those that had appeared in the *School Bulletin*), her knowledge of literature, her marks in school (they were co-valedictorians, but her average was finally higher), her ability as a painter, her suitors at St. Lawrence University at Canton, New York, all excited his competitive admiration and jealousy. Her attendance at college meant their separation, with Frost going to Dartmouth for a short time, then to teach in the Methuen schools until March 1893, then to act as helper and guardian to Elinor's mother and two of her sisters in Salem, New Hampshire. Before she left for school and on her vacations in Lawrence he courted her with the help of Shelley's poetry, especially "Epipsychidion," with its inducements to ignore the institution of marriage. And of course he wooed her with poems of his own.

Indeed, his first volume, strictly speaking, was not *A Boy's Will* of 1913, when he was thirty-nine, but *Twilight* in 1894 when he was twenty, the one surviving copy of which is in the Barrett Collection at the University of Virginia. Only two copies were printed, one for Frost and one for Elinor. It included, in addition to "My Butterfly" which was later to appear in *A Boy's Will,* four other poems full of literary echoes ranging from Sidney to Keats, Tennyson to Rossetti, as in the opening lines of the title poem:

> Why am I first in thy so sad regard,
> O twilight gazing from I know not where?
> I fear myself as one more than I guessed!

He carried Elinor's copy on an unannounced trip to her college boarding house in Canton. Surprised, bewildered, prevented by the rules from inviting him in or from going out herself, she accepted her copy in what seemed a casual but was perhaps a merely preoccupied way. She told him to return home at once. He did so, but only to pack a bag and leave for a suicide journey that took him to Virginia and through the Dismal Swamp at night, "into my own," so to speak. The danger was very real. "I was," he later said, "trying to throw my life away" (Thompson, I, 521). Through this and subsequent travails, torments, threats, and melodramatic scenes, he convinced her to marry him before she could finish school and before he had any secure means of support.

Such briefly are the biographical elements probably at play in some of the early poems. But the biographical material does not tell us as much about the man as the poetry does. By that I mean that the poetry does not necessarily come from the experiences of his life; rather, the kind of poetry he wrote, and the kind of experiences to which he was susceptible, both emerge from the same configuration in him, prior to his poems or to his experiences. Sex and an obsession with sound, sexual love and poetic imagination, success in love and success in art—these conspire with one another. A poem is an action, not merely a "made" but a "making" thing, and "the figure a poem makes," one remembers, "is the same as for love." It is as if in talking about the direction laid down by a poem he instinctively uses a language of ongoing sexual action:

> No one can really hold that the ecstasy should be static and stand still in one place. It begins in delight, it inclines to the impulse, it assumes direction with the first line laid down, it runs a course of lucky events, and ends in a clarification of life—not necessarily a great clarification such as sects and cults are founded on, but in a momentary stay against confusion. . . . It finds its own name as it goes and discovers the best waiting for it in some final phrase at once wise and sad—the happy-sad blend of the drinking song   ("The Figure a Poem Makes").

Three early poems, "Waiting," "In a Vale," and "A Dream Pang," coming nearly in the middle of *A Boy's Will*, illustrate the connections, implicit in the structuring of the whole volume, between sexual love and poetic making, between the "sounds" of love and a poet's love of sound. None of the three is in any sense considerable. Frost's investment in them is relatively slight; they are shy of the complications which, when they emerge in later poems, are more consciously and subtly managed. And yet the poems are the stranger for *not* showing very much acknowledgment of their strangeness. It is as if initially the imagination of the sexual self and of the poetic self were so naturally, so instinctively identified as not to call for comment.

The three poems are published in sequence in *A Boy's Will,* always an important and calculated factor in Frost. They are all what can be called dream poems, and each suggests a different aspect of the dreamlike relationship between poetic and sexual prowess. In the first, "Waiting," the figure of the poet is "specter-like," as he wanders through a "stubble field" of tall haycocks, a bit like the "stubble-plains" in the last stanza of Keats's ode "To Autumn"; the "things" about which he has waking dreams are mostly the surroundings and their noises. From the outset his condition seems peculiarly vulnerable to sights and sounds, and it is not till the final lines that one can attribute this to the fact that what means most to him in his dream is not anything present to his senses but rather "the memory of one absent most," the girl he loves:

Waiting
Afield at Dusk

What things for dream there are when specter-like,
Moving among tall haycocks lightly piled,
I enter alone upon the stubble field,
From which the laborers' voices late have died,
And in the antiphony of afterglow
And rising full moon, sit me down
Upon the full moon's side of the first haycock
And lose myself amid so many alike.

I dream upon the opposing lights of the hour,
Preventing shadow until the moon prevail;
I dream upon the nighthawks peopling heaven,
Each circling each with vague unearthly cry,
Or plunging headlong with fierce twang afar;
And on the bat's mute antics, who would seem
Dimly to have made out my secret place,
Only to lose it when he pirouettes,
And seek it endlessly with purblind haste;
On the last swallow's sweep; and on the rasp

In the abyss of odor and rustle at my back,
That, silenced by my advent, finds once more,
After an interval, his instrument,
And tries once—twice—and thrice if I be there;
And on the worn book of old-golden song
I brought not here to read, it seems, but hold
And freshen in this air of withering sweetness;
But on the memory of one absent, most,
For whom these lines when they shall greet her eye.

Before the mention of his beloved, in the next to last line, the poem is filled with evocations of natural sounds in the "stubble field" where "the laborers' voices late have died"; there is also the "vague unearthly cry" of the nighthawks who plunge "headlong with fierce twang afar"; there are the "bat's mute antics," the "rasp" of a creature who, "silenced by my advent, finds once more, / After an interval, his instrument." But what is apt to seem most provocative—given its place at the end of the poem and its uniqueness among all the references to natural sound—is an allusion to poetic sound, to the "worn book of old-golden song." It, too, is a carrier of sound, very likely of sound that helped (even more than did the sounds of nature) during his courtship of the one now "absent." But however much our literary-critical dispositions might prompt us to separate this item of sound from others, as being more centrally important, it is necessary to note that the young poet-specter tends merely to put the poetic within the sequence of other items. It is joined to them casually with another of the many "ands" that make up the listing. Apparently he does not intend even to read the book in order to bring her closer to mind. More than that, though the book is "worn" and though the poetry is itself "old," his reasons for holding onto it are that it may "freshen in this air," this Keatsian air "of withering sweetness."

The "old-golden song" is to be freshened, strangely enough, by something that is more apt to dry it, to "wither" it. We are readied by this paradox for the introduction, as in "Pan with Us," of the theme of "new" song, new sounds, something poetic for the future—in short, the very poem we are reading which is destined for her: "for whom these lines when they shall greet her eye." With the vitality of "shall greet her eye" the poet is no longer "specter-like." He has gotten past a number of by-ways: of possible dreams on other sounds, of the invitation to do no more than dream, of losing himself to these sounds—a danger only less intense than that in the later "Stopping by Woods on a Snowy Evening." Past all this, the young lover is able to envision a future in love inseparable from a future in poetry. He has been able to do this because, all the while, as the poem moves along, he has been "making it"; he has been writing "these lines."

One indication of the peculiar nature of Frost's reputation as a poet, when compared to an Eliot or a Yeats, is that few have bothered with poems so clearly not of his best like "Waiting" or the two others grouped with it. His admirers are defensively anxious to show only the favorite things, when some of the lesser ones are often even more revealing of his preoccupations with the plights and pleasures in the life of the poetic self. "In a Vale" is, even more than "Waiting," *fin de siècle* in conception and language. With its "vale," "maidens," "fen," and with words like "wist," "list," "dwelt," there is little going on that predicts the later Frost except the penultimate and best stanza. And yet it is still a most ingratiating poem—like an early picture of someone we have gotten to know only in later years—and it tells us perhaps even more than do more posed sittings:

When I was young, we dwelt in a vale
  By a misty fen that rang all night,
And thus it was the maidens pale
I knew so well, whose garments trail
  Across the reeds to a window light.

The fen had every kind of bloom,
  And for every kind there was a face,
And a voice that has sounded in my room
Across the sill from the outer gloom.
  Each came singly unto her place,

But all came every night with the mist;
  And often they brought so much to say
Of things of moment to which, they wist,
One so lonely was fain to list
  That the stars were almost faded away

Before the last went, heavy with dew,
  Back to the place from which she came—
Where the bird was before it flew,
Where the flower was before it grew,
  Where bird and flower were one and the same.

And thus it is I know so well
  Why the flower has odor, the bird has song.
You have only to ask me, and I can tell.
No, not vainly there did I dwell,
  Nor vainly listen all the night long.

The time scheme of these poems is importantly
suggestive of poetic gestations, of the way past and
present provide the nutrients for a poetic future. In
"Waiting" we are in the present, witnessing the impressions made upon a young poet who holds the past in his
hand—Palgrave's *Golden Treasury*—while composing in
his head the "lines" which will in future "greet" his beloved. "In a Vale" is a dream wholly of the past, but it,
too, looks ahead to a future wherein the past will have

been redeemed by the writing of the poems inspired by
it: "You have only to ask me, and I can tell. / No, not
vainly there did I dwell, / Nor vainly listen all the night
long." The listening, again, is to voices or sounds that he
has managed to supersede: "a misty fen that rang all
night"; the voices that have "sounded in my room" and
that "brought so much to say." The dream is a rather
wet one ("the last went, heavy with dew") and it is from
these nocturnal experiences that he learns what, in the
later daytime of publication, he "can tell." With Lucre-
tius, he can tell that "the bird and flower were one and
the same." However, he can also tell a more American
and Emersonian story: of a world, again, which reveals
itself in forms (odor and song) which have in part been
placed there by the human imagination, including
human dreams.

An absent lover imagined in "Waiting" as a future
reader, ghostly lovers or maidens whose sayings "In a
Vale" will in some future time allow him to "tell" readers
about birds and flowers—these figurations are brought
together in the last of the three poems, "A Dream
Pang." There the poet is discovered in bed with his lover
beside him, her very presence proving that his song has
been answered by something more fulfilling than the
echoing sounds of nature. This early poem is thereby a
prelude to laters ones like "Come In" or "A Leaf
Treader," where Frost is in danger of succumbing to the
call of nature, of losing himself, of having his sound in
words absorbed into the sounds made by the natural elements. In this poem he is not learning to "tell" or ex-
pecting the "lines" he is writing to be read; here he is already a poet whose song, in his dream, has been
endangered by her denials and by his proud with-
drawals:

I had withdrawn in forest, and my song
Was swallowed up in leaves that blew alway;
And to the forest edge you came one day
(This was my dream) and looked and pondered long,
But did not enter, though the wish was strong:
You shook your pensive head as who should say,
"I dare not—too far in his footsteps stray—
He must seek me would he undo the wrong."

Not far, but near, I stood and saw it all,
Behind low boughs the trees let down outside;
And the sweet pang it cost me not to call
And tell you that I saw does still abide.
But 'tis not true that thus I dwelt aloof,
For the wood wakes, and you are here for proof.

Now, as she lies beside him ("this was my dream . . .
you are here for proof") the poem can come to articula-
tion; before, while they were alienated from one another, "my song / Was swallowed up in leaves." Without
her, he and his song are lost to the vagaries of nature
and its noises; with her, nature, or the "wood," comes to
a more orderly life outside their place: "the wood wakes,
and you are here." The implications take us to a variety
of poems in which Frost can feel momentarily and ter-
rifyingly included, as he says in "Desert Places," in the
loneliness of nature "unawares." Cut off from the communion of human sex and human love, he is answered
either by random, accidental, teasing responses, like that
of the little bird in "The Wood-Pile," or by evidences of
brutish indifference such as greet the speaker of "The
Most of It":

> He would cry out on life, that what it wants
> Is not its own love back in copy speech,
> But counter-love, original response.
> And nothing ever came of what he cried
> Unless it was the embodiment that crashed
> In the cliff's talus on the other side. . . .

The failure of love, of love-making, the failure to elicit "counter-love" means, as in "The Subverted Flower," that the young poet cannot finally be joined to that human communication with nature which Emerson promised might be found there. Here as elsewhere Frost's Emersonism is grounded in certain basic actualities, especially the sexual relations of men and women, which Emerson himself tended to pass over with little more than citation. Within this sequence of three poems, "A Dream Pang" looks ahead to the implications of a more considerable sequence of three poems, already mentioned, that includes "The Most of It," "Never Again Would Bird's Song Be the Same," and "The Subverted Flower." The implication, briefly noted also in "The Vantage Point," is that a man alone ("he thought he kept the universe alone') cannot see or hear anything in nature that confirms his existence as human. If he is alone, he cannot "make" the world; he cannot reveal himself to it or in it; he becomes lost to it; it remains alien. He cannot make human sound. In "The Subverted Flower" he can at first hope that the impasse " 'has come to us / And not to me alone.' " But even this proposition falls on deaf ears, or essentially deaf ears. It is something "she thought she heard him say; / Though with every word he spoke / His lips were sucked and blown / And the effort made him choke / Like a tiger on a bone."

In the early, as in the later sequence, Frost is concerned in various ways with the possibilities of the sounds of the man-poet-lover in situations where there are competing sounds and where, if he cannot "make it" with his beloved, he cannot "make it" either in competitions with sounds in nature or in other poetry. He cannot "make it" with words so shaped as to reveal his participation in poetry, and—equally important—that such participation is "natural." He is not content to have *"his song"* swallowed up in leaves either of a tree, merely, or of a book, merely. His poetry, his song, must include both.

In the light of this ambition we can best understand Frost's life-long commitment to certain theories of sound and poetic form. The commitment is implicit in all of the poems and in the structural organization of *A Boy's Will.* It was to find theoretical expression somewhat later, in letters written at the time of the publication of the book, and later still in essays and talks. In a letter to the black poet-critic-anthologist William Stanley Braithwaite, on March 22, 1915, for example, Frost said:

> It would seem absurd to say it (and you mustn't quote me as saying it) but I suppose the fact is that my conscious interest in people was at first no more than an almost technical interest in their speech—in what I used to call their sentence sounds—the sound of sense. Whatever these sounds are or aren't (they are certainly not of the vowels and consonants of words nor even of the words themselves but something the words are chiefly a kind of notation for indicating and for fastening to the page) whatever they are, I say, I began to hang on them very young. I was under twenty when I deliberately put it to myself one night after good conversation that there are moments when we actually touch in talk what the best writing can only come near. . . . We must go into the vernacular for tones that haven't been brought to book. We must write with the ear on the speaking voice. We must imagine the speaking voice   (Thompson, *Letters,* pp. 158–59).

"Sentence-sounds" does not refer to the meaning the words give to a sentence but to the meaning the sound of the sentence can give to the words, which is why Frost is so difficult to translate into any other language. It is a matter of stress patterns. Thus, the line "By June our

brook's run out of song and speed" is arranged so that
the potential of the word "song"—as a possible allusion
to "poetry"—is markedly diminished by putting it immediately after the quickly paced vernacular phrase "run
out of." The word "song" would be far more potent, but
altogether too archly so, if it traded places with the word
"speed": "By June our brook's run out of speed and
song." Some of these distinctions are clarified in a letter
written over a year before, February 22, 1914, to his
friend John Bartlett, a newspaper man who was one of
his favorite students at Pinkerton Academy:

> I give you a new definition of a sentence:
>   A sentence is a sound in itself on which other sounds
> called words may be strung.
>   You may string words together without a sentence-
> sound to string them on just as you may tie clothes
> together by sleeves and stretch them without a clothes
> line between two trees, but—it is bad for the clothes.
> . . . The sentence sounds are very definite entities.
> (This is no literary mysticism I am preaching.) They
> are as definite as words. It is not impossible that they
> could be collected in a book though I don't at present
> see on what system they would be catalogued.
>   They are apprehended by the ear. They are gath-
> ered by the ear from the vernacular and brought into
> books. Many of them are familiar to us in books. I
> think no writer invents them. The most original writer
> only catches them fresh from talk, where they grow
> spontaneously.
>   A man is all a writer if *all* his words are strung on
> definite recognizable sentence sounds. The voice of the
> imagination, the speaking voice must know certainly
> how to behave [,] how to posture in every sentence he
> offers   (Thompson, *Letters,* pp. 110–11).

When Frost refers to the "vocal imagination" (in the
essay "The Constant Symbol") he makes it synonymous
with what he calls "images of the voice speaking." Frost

listens for these images as much in nature as in human
dialogue. But there is an important difference in what
he wants and expects to hear from these two different
places: only in human dialogue can such images emerge
as "sentence-sounds" rather than as mere echoes, or vagrant, only potentially significant noises, like ⸢The
sweep / Of easy wind and downy flake,⸥ or what
Thoreau calls "brute sounds." Furthermore, Frost's capacity even to find "images of the voice speaking" in nature depends upon human love; it can be crippled or
thwarted by the lack of it. The matter might be put in a
three-part formula: (1) the "artist as a young man," if
doomed to "keep the universe alone," can only call
fourth from it alien and terrifying sounds, and is in
danger of becoming either a mere passive receiver of
these sounds or himself a brute; (2) the "artist as a
young man" in a reciprocal relationship of love with
another human can, as a result, also find "images of the
voice speaking" in some rudimentary form in nature,
though it is important to know that what he finds is only
an image, nothing wholly equivalent to the human voice
speaking: "The Need of Being Versed in Country
Things" is that one is thereby allowed "Not to believe
the phoebes wept." This brings up the third and most
important point: (3) that the clearest, but not only, differentiation of human sound from sounds in nature is
poetry itself, the making of a poem, the capacity literally
to be "versed" in the things of this world. Any falling—
of leaves, of snow, of man, of the garland of roses which
Adam is holding when he first sees Eve in her fallen
state—can be redeemed by loving, and the sign of this
redemption is, for Frost, the sound of the voice working
within the sounds of poetry. It could even be said that
the proper poetic image of the Fall and of the human
will continually to surmount it is—given accentual-

syllabism's unique role in the handling of English rhythm—the mounting from unstressed to stressed syllables in the iambic pentameter line. Thus, the oven bird can "frame" the question of "what to make of a diminished thing" in "all but words." The words are at the call of the poet; the "making" is in his power. It consists precisely in his showing how the verse form works with and against mere "saying":

He sáys | thĕ eaŕ|lў pét|ăl fáll | ĭs pást,
Whĕn peár | ănd cheŕ|rў bloóm | wĕnt dówn | ĭn shów | eı̊s.

The glory of these lines is in the achieved strain between trochaic words like "early" and "petal," "cherry" and "showers," and the iambic pattern which breaks their fall. The meter is a perfect exemplification of what the poem is about, of the creative tension between a persistent rising and a natural falling—a poise of creativity in the face of threatened diminishments.

3. VISIONS IN RESERVE

Frost needed to imagine a freedom of movement in his own poems as they found their way to a form, to "the figure a poem makes," and he needed also to rely on evidences of such movement in the literature of the past—on voices with which his own voice could be crossed. Above all he needed to confirm his power over these movements and precedents; this was the precondition for any indulgence, on his part, in extravagance. For him poetry did not include but was in itself an extravagance. He often seems afraid even of his own poetry unless he can supervise just when, where, and how it is

to appear, a subject that takes up a good deal of his correspondence. And the tapes and accounts of his talks
and readings, a revealing sample of which can be found
in Reginald Cook's *Robert Frost: The Living Voice,* offer
persistent evidence of the endless public appearances in
which large audiences were told what to get from his
poems and also what not to take. They were told in effect (and the effect was in part a matter of tone and
shaggy appearance) that they need not worry that he
would carry them too far into the unfamiliar. There is
therefore a kind of truth behind the obvious factual
inaccuracies in a letter he wrote to Louis Untermeyer on
May 4, 1916. The "truth" is that he wanted to believe
what he was saying:

[4 May 1916, Franconia]
Dear Old Louis
    When I have borne in memory what has tamed Great
Poets, hey? Am I to be blamed etc? No you ain't. Or as
Browning (masc.) has it:

        That was I that died last night
        When there shone no moon at all
        Nor to pierce the strained and tight
        Tent of heaven one planet small.
        Might was dead and so was Right.

    Not to be any more obvious than I have to be to set
at rest your brotherly fears for my future which I have
no doubt you assume to be somehow or other wrapped
up in me, I am going to tell you something I never but
once let out of the bag before and that was just after I
reached London and before I had begun to value myself for what I was worth. (Toop.) * It is a very damag-
ing secret and you may not thank me for taking you
into it when I tell you that I have often wished I could
be sure that the other sharer of it had perished in the
war. It is this: The poet in me died nearly ten years
ago. Fortunately he had run through several phases,
* Two-penny.

four to be exact, all well-defined, before he went. The
calf I was in the nineties I merely take to market. I am
become my own salesman. Two of my phases you have
been so—what shall I say—as to like. Take care that
you don't get your mouth set to declare the other two
(as I release them) a falling off of power, for that is
what they can't be whatever else they may be, since they
were almost inextricably mixed with the first two in the
writing and only my sagacity has separated or sorted
them in the afterthought for putting on the market.
Did you ever hear of quite such a case of Scotch-
Yankee calculation? You should have seen the look on
the face of the Englishman I first confessed this to! I
won't name him lest it should bring you two together.
While he has never actually betrayed me, he has made
himself an enemy of me and all my works. He regards
me as a little heinous. As you look back don't you see
how a lot of things I have said begin to take meaning
from this? Well . . .

But anyway you are freed from anxiety about my
running all to philosophy. It makes no difference what
I run to now. I needn't be the least bit tender of myself.
Of course I'm glad it's all up with Masters, my hated
rival. He wasn't foresighted enough, I'll bet, to provide
against the evil day that is come to him. He failed to
take warning from the example of Shelley who philos-
ophized and died young. But me, the day I did The
Trial by Existence (*Boy's Will*) says I to myself, this is
the way of all flesh. I was not much over twenty, but I
was wise for my years. I knew than that it was a race between me the poet and that in me that would be flirting
with the entelechies or the coming on of that in me. I
must get as much done as possible before thirty. I tell
you, Louis, it's all over at thirty. People expect us to
keep right on and it is as well to have something to
show for our time on earth. Anyway that was the way I
thought I might feel. And I took measures accordingly.
And now my time is my own. I have myself all in a
strong box where I can unfold as a personality at discretion. Someone asks with a teasing eye, "Have you
done that Phi Beta Kappa poem yet?" "No, I don't

know that I have, as you may say." "You seem not to be particularly uneasy about it." "Oh, that's because I know where it's coming from, don't you know." Great effect of strength and mastery!

Now you know more about me than anyone else knows except that Londoner we won't count because he may be dead of a lachrymous.

And don't think mention of the war is anything to go by. I could give you proof that twenty years ago in a small book I did on Boeme [Boehme] and the Technique of Sincerity I was saying "The heroic emotions, like all the rest of the emotions, never know when they ought to be felt after the first time. Either they will be felt too soon or too late from fear of being felt too soon."

Ever thine

R.F.

(Thompson, *Letters,* pp. 201–2)

Quantitatively the claim is absurd that in 1916 he had all the poems that were subsequently to appear; qualitatively, he had by then written some of his best, without printing all of them. But he had not yet displayed the ranges of his style, the remarkable variations that continued through such later poems as "The White-Tailed Hornet," "The Strong Are Saying Nothing Until They See," "A Star in a Stoneboat," and "Kitty Hawk." He could not in any sense, that is, feel confident that he had either the number or the kind of poems on hand which would allow him to "unfold as a personality at discretion."

The letter shows, as Untermeyer observes (in *The Letters of Robert Frost to Louis Untermeyer,* p. 28), a "characteristic blend—perhaps alternation is the better word—of wildness and seriousness, of prankish nonsense and bitter sense." And yet, the real subject of the letter is retentiveness, explained only in part by his sense of public relations and the advisability of controlling the kind of public "figure" he wanted to make. Control and management of the self is expressed in a fantasy that depends on holding back something that he had in store, and for which an imagined trunk full of completed poems is only a metaphor. Thes words—retentiveness, holding back, restraint, deferment, reserve—are not meant pejoratively. Rather they describe what Frost himself needed and wanted to imagine about his own securities before he could let himself go, as he liked to claim he could, with that course of "lucky events" which is a poem in progress, or let himself take a plunge into a poetic career (in his late thirties by way of a first book), or then declare that he was daringly going to look for success not "with the critical few" but with "the general reader who buys books in their thousands" (Letter to John Bartlett, c. 5 November 1913, Thompson, *Letters,* p. 98). He did all of these things, but he had to lie about himself to some extent in order to do them. His tendency to falsification—as in the letter to Untermeyer, or in the quite different story he must have told Thompson about wondering whether he had enough poems around for his first book, or the lie he told Pound about "The Death of the Hired Man" being a "new" poem in 1913—are those of someone who either needs to convince himself that he has more resources than anyone knows or who wants to claim that he does. Above all, it is the conduct of someone for whom the availability of a haven, real or imaginary, is necessary as a provocation to any step into the unknown.

Remarkably enough, what might be called Frost's congenital distrust of the freedom he liked to extol, his ultimate distrust of an imagination set free as it is in Stevens, is less a failing because it is fully recognized in the poetry and elevated there to a major recurrent theme. He is an extremely difficult poet often because it is nearly impossible to believe that he can be so dazzlingly self-knowing about his own reserves and fabrications while remaining nonetheless so determinately what he is. One of the best instances is the first poem of the first book and therefore the first, except for the frontispiece called "The Pasture," of any of Frost's collected poems, "Into My Own":

One of my wishes is that those dark trees,
So old and firm they scarcely show the breeze,
Were not, as 'twere, the merest mask of gloom,
But stretched away unto the edge of doom.

I should not be withheld but that some day   5
Into their vastness I should steal away,
Fearless of ever finding open land,
Or highway where the slow wheel pours the sand.

I do not see why I should e'er turn back,
Or those should not set forth upon my track   10
To overtake me, who should miss me here
And long to know if still I held them dear.

They would not find me changed from him they knew—
Only more sure of all I thought was true.

The gloss for this poem in the first edition of *A Boy's Will* is "The youth is persuaded that he will be rather more than less himself for having forsworn the world." This is an allowable account only to the extent that it is consciously designed to make the poem more accessible than in fact it is. But it also discourages the kind of attentive reading which the poem needs and requests. The young man has actually forsworn nothing. In his language it is clear that he is solidly planted this side of any world elsewhere. Intricacies of grammer alone indicate how little he is "persuaded" that he can "forswear the world" or that he will become "more sure" for doing so. He is safe within his syntax, his form. Like all of Frost's seemingly apocalyptic efforts, this one is full of hedgings. The "trees" do not stretch "unto the edge of doom": it is merely his "wish," and only one of them, that they should do so. Perhaps, given line 4, he wishes to test the proposition in sonnet 116 of Shakespeare: "Love alters not with his brief hours and weeks, / But bears it out even to the edge of doom." His imagination of withdrawal in stanza two is thereby already vitiated by the blurred acknowledgments of reality, and literary posturing, in stanza one. It is further modified by the conditional tense, "I should not be withheld" (line 5), a construction which makes irrelevant the proposal in line 7 that he is "fearless" and throughout stanza three that he is resolute. As a result, the concluding line ("Only more sure of all I thought was true") is less truculent than pathetic. All that he has "thought" in the preceding stanzas is "true" only because it is *only* thought. There can be no verifications for the somewhat plaintive promise that he would continue on a journey that he has never started, a journey which would in any event depend on conditions ("dark trees" that "stretched away unto the edge of doom") that do not exist. The degree to which Frost accepted this situation as one in which he characteristically found himself might be suggested by the fact that the young man who is trapped at home in this first poem of the first volume is still trapped at home—restrained from extra-vagance beyond form even while imagining what it might be like to wander—in the last poem of his third volume, "The Sound of Trees" in *Mountain Interval:*

> My feet tug at the floor
> And my head sways to my shoulder
> Sometimes when I watch trees sway,

From the window or the door.
I shall set forth for somewhere,
I shall make the reckless choice
Some day when they are in voice
And tossing so as to scare
The white clouds over them on.
I shall have less to say,
But I shall be gone.

Year after year, volume after volume, it is a marvel
how Frost arrives at a visionary mode by elaborate forms
of denial and what can best be called poetic four-
flushing: "I shall make the reckless choice / Some day
. . ." "I should not be withheld but that some day / Into
their vastness . . ." It is a poetry in which the reader is
deceived into visions by Frost and by his own pretense,
as he lets the sentences move casually past the subordinated, dependent, muted reservations that are being
made. "Into My Own," and the other poems immediately related to it in *A Boy's Will* have some salient characteristics belonging to this kind of poetry. Disavowal of
the world and pursuit of the otherworldly always seem
to occur, if we look and listen carefully, to someone who
knows how to find his way back home. This is true in
North of Boston with "The Wood-Pile" ("Out walking in
the frozen swamp one grey day, / I paused and said, 'I
will turn back from here. / No, I will go farther—and we
shall see' "); it is true of "Directive" in the book *Steeple
Bush* of 1947 where it is, after all, a "guide" who "has at
heart your getting lost"; and it can be found in the last
volume, *In the Clearing* of 1962, in a poem remarkable
for the clarity and candor with which Frost declares
what he has been about: "How Hard It Is to Keep from
Being King When It's in You and in the Situation." The
king offers a "lesson" about life which, even casually
read, is also a lesson about Frost's poetry:

"The only certain freedom's in departure.
My son and I have tasted it and know.
We feel it in the moment we depart
As fly the atomic smithereens to nothing.
The problem for the King is just how strict
The lack of liberty, the squeeze of law
And discipline should be in school and state
To insure a jet departure of our going
Like a pip shot from 'twixt our pinching fingers."

All of these poems involve departures and journeys and many of them arrive at desolate landscapes. Such a landscape, in "The Wood-Pile," is meant to be "real," something encountered on a walk rather than a conjuration in the mind of a speaker still at home. More often than not in Frost, however, the landscape is of the mind and the imagination either because, as in "Into My Own," it never existed or because, as in the next poem, "Ghost House," it no longer exists: "I dwell in a lonely house I know / That vanished many a summer ago." The phraseology obviously looks forward to the wildly brilliant opening of "Directive":

Back out of all this now too much for us,
Back in a time made simple by the loss
Of detail, burned, dissolved, and broken off
Like graveyard marble sculpture in the weather,
There is a house that is no more a house
Upon a farm that is no more a farm
And in a town that is no more a town.

The pile-up of negatives here, while less conspicuous than in "The Census Taker" or "A Star in A Stoneboat," is effectively matched in "Into My Own," when Frost tries to define a journey which the young man will not take into a place that does not exist: he wishes the trees were "not the merest mask"; and if they were not, then

he "should not be withheld"; and if they were not a
"mask" and if he were not "withheld" than "I do not see
why I should e'er turn back . . . or these [his friends]
should not set forth upon my track" (which we have to
remind ourselves does not exist) "to overtake me."
Scenes of this kind exist by virtue of what we can call
negative designation, as when in a later poem like "A
Boundless Moment" we are told that "he halted in the
wind, and—what was that / Far in the maples, pale but
not a ghost?" Used in this way, negatives are a clue to
the visionary impulse which gets affirmed by an act of
denial. Such a technique is at work in the visionary moments of other realistically minded American writers,
like Faulkner of *The Bear*. But a distinction needs to be
noted. Faulkner uses negatives in anticipation of and in
the hope that he can dispel workaday actualities which
the reader is presumably ready to impose on the story
("that brown liquor which not women, not boys and children, but only hunters drank, drinking not of the blood
that they spilled but some condensation of the wild immortal spirit, drinking it moderately, humbly even, not
with the pagan's base and baseless hope of acquiring
thereby the virtues of cunning and strength and speed
but in salute to them"). Frost uses negatives quite dif-
ferently, closer to the manner of the Stevens of "A Postcard from the Volcano." Frost denies or negates the reality not of local and obvious but of remote possibilities,
as if to reassure his readers that he is not a visionary
poet. But it is in doing this that he allows himself to be
visionary. He is like an attorney who knows that evidence
striken from the record is apt to remain more strongly
in the mind.

   In such a way Frost introduces himself as a poet of
"nature," and his manner of doing so becomes even

more pronounced, and refined, in a little poem later on,
"A Cliff Dwelling" from *Steeple Bush,* 1947:

> There sandy seems the golden sky
> And golden seems the sandy plain.
> No habitation meets the eye
> Unless in the horizon rim,
> Some halfway up the limestone wall,   5
> That spot of black is not a stain
> Or shadow, but a cavern hole,
> Where someone used to climb and crawl
> To rest from his besetting fears.
> I see the callus on his sole,   10
> The disappearing last of him
> And of his race starvation slim,
> Oh, years ago—ten thousand years.

The announcement in the first two lines is of a Spenserian mirage. The restraint of vision in the repetition
of "seems" . . . "seems" is then followed by the negative
designation: "No habitation . . . unless in the horizon
. . . that spot is not a stain / Or shadow, but a cavern
hole." All of these negatives and reservations and conditions in lines 1–6 are the preliminaries necessary to an
avowal of a vision at the very center of the poem—the
cavern hole of line 7 from (or into) which all the details
of the last six lines can be gathered. It is an exercise in
contrivance, in lying that is meant to be found out by
the very eagerness with which it lays claim to the truth.
The poem responds at last to a quizzical audience this
side of vision. When did all this happen? "Oh, years
ago"—the vagueness quickly corrects itself with an absurd exactness, "ten thousand years," that more or less
comically explodes the visionary claims hesitant enough
to begin with.

With the later poem we are in the same world as "Into

My Own," and the similarity reveals the disguised sophistication of *A Boy's Will* and the degree to which
Frost's own placement of the poems and his glosses have
encouraged far too simple a reading. He was a poet who
might from the beginning have said of his work—and it
bears repeating—what he only casually said in 1962 in
his talk "On Extravagance": "So many of them have literary criticism in them—*in* them. And yet I wouldn't
admit it. I try to hide it." Even here, we might quickly
note the by now familiar manner—saying that he tries to
hide the very thing that he is declaring; that he wouldn't
"admit" the admission he is making.

Much of the literary criticism implicit in his poetry is
Keatsian in its light parody of the "egotistical sublime."
His concern for such excesses indicates, as Geoffrey
Hartman observes of Keats, that "He could not give up
the sublime. He feared that poetry without enthusiasm
was no longer poetry" (*The Fate of Reading*, p. 81). Understandably, Frost was fond of the poetry of Smart,
whose work shows the alternations, to a schizophrenic
degree, between neo-classical modes and a visionary one
that is made to seem aware of its own possible excesses.
For Frost, "extravagance" in poetry depends on saying
what is only possibly, or even what is only unlikely to be,
the case. "But I look on the universe as a kind of exaggeration anyway, the whole business. That's the way you
think of it: great, great, great expense—everybody trying to make it mean something more than it is" ("On Extravagance").

III
Outward
Bound

1. HOME AND EXTRA-VAGANCE

I fear chiefly lest my expression may not be extra-vagant *enough, may not wander far enough beyond the narrow limit of my daily experience, so as to be adequate to the truth of which I have been convinced.* Extra vagance! *it depends on how you are yarded. The migrating buffalo, which seeks new pastures in another latitude, is not extravagant like the cow which kicks over the pail, leaps the cow yard fence, and runs after her calf, in milking time. I desire to speak somewhere* without *bounds; like a man in a waking moment, to men in their waking moments; for I am convinced that I cannot exaggerate enough even to lay the foundation of a true expression. . . . We should live quite laxly and undefined in front, our outlines dim and misty on that side.*

Thoreau, "Conclusion," *Walden*

Frost was fond of saying that Emerson was a great poet of freedom. What he apparently meant, thinking of "Uriel," was something importantly different—that

Emerson was the great poet of rebellion. The wonder of
Emerson is that his admissions of restriction are consistent, as Frost's are not, with a continuous if sometimes
thwarted thrust toward a grandeur of rhetoric and vision. For him the visions had as their prerequisite *only*
the limitations imposed by nature itself. "Exaggeration is
in the course of things," he writes in "Nature" (*Essays,
Second Series*), and the remark is not qualified by his adding later that "every act hath some falsehood of exaggeration in it." We act knowing that we cannot attain what
nature seems to promise, so that when he goes on to say
that "all things betray the same calculated profusion," he
means "betray" in a number of senses and that "calculation" characterizes both the profusiveness of nature and
of our expectant, anticipatory response to it. By its
prodigality, nature encourages in a child at play or in an
adult at work imitative "performances" which can never
have the hoped-for results. "We are made alive and kept
alive by the same arts" which beguile a child who looks
upon the "opaline luster [that] plays round the top of
every toy."

What Harold Bloom says of "strong" poets can be said
of Emerson and Frost—they are "deceived deceivers" in
respect to the prior text which includes nature as well as
books and their "readings" of both. Frost, much less
Thoreau, cannot for me be as great a writer as Emerson
because he is often too comfortable with derived percep-
tions about exaggeration, extravagance, and waste, as
when he talks in the terms quoted at the conclusion of
the last chapter—of the universe trying to make "the
whole business . . . mean something more than it is"
and of the "great, great, great expense" of doing so.
These remarks are more cautious than they initially
sound, and there is in them a touch of satisfaction, as if
he is happy that reality is in collusion with his own in-

stinctive predilections for restraint or for the kind of
extra-vagance or extravagance—I use the terms often
interchangeably to mean both a physical or mental wandering and a verbal or rhetorical one—that always finds
its way home with or without the spoils. Frost knew what
it was to be "yarded," in Thoreau's sense, both like a cow
and like a buffalo. The "yarding" could be close by, such
as an unhappy or impoverished household, social confinements, aloneness, or it could be the "universe" itself,
as in "The Most of It," the many poems about stars, or
the durations of the seasons. He was "yarded" also by
his ideas of the desirability of form, of metaphor, insofar as it tames "enthusiasm," and of sound, whereby
constraints of meter and of voice work upon one another.

Wandering beyond boundaries of a household or a
field is, in Frost, often the enactment of any search for
possibilities greater than those already domesticated. His
many poems of walking are thus poems of "extravagance" in the most pedestrian sense while also being
about the need, and advisability, of poetic "extravagance"; they are about going out to poach on the excesses of nature, an act which in Frost causes none of
the admixtures of pain shown by Wordsworth, as in, say,
"Nutting" and in David Ferry's fine analysis of it. An
ingratiating example of a "walking poem" in Frost is
"Good Hours." Though written in 1911–12, it is the
final poem in *North of Boston,* a volume where the image
of "home" predominates, sometimes as the initial condition or form from which it is necessary to wander, sometimes as the only form available that can be either saved
or doomed by "extra-vagance." The concluding position
of "Good Hours" in the volume is evidence, I think, of
Frost's intention that his poetry of "home" and "extravagance" should be read with some tactful allowance

that the terms may, in the one case, be translated into "form" or "decorum," and, in the other, into poetic or metaphoric "extravagance," or even into the "sublime," though the latter describes a state too extreme for the poem that follows:

> I had for my winter evening walk—
> No one at all with whom to talk,
> But I had the cottages in a row
> Up to their shining eyes in snow.
>
> And I thought I had the folk within:
> I had the sound of a violin;
> I had a glimpse through curtain laces
> Of youthful forms and youthful faces.
>
> I had such company outward bound.
> I went till there were no cottages found.
> I turned and repented, but coming back
> I saw no window but that was black.
>
> Over the snow my creaking feet
> Disturbed the slumbering village street
> Like profanation, by your leave,
> At ten o'clock of a winter eve.

This is an unassuming poem. And yet, like "Into My Own" or "The Pasture," with its delicate classical allusiveness, "Good Hours" hovers on the edge of poetic allegory. The walker here imposes himself on the sleeping scene and on the other people as a poet living within, escaping from, and then returning to certain decorums. With no one to talk to, his company consists of images by which he takes Emersonian possession of the town and its inhabitants, as in the curious phrasings of "I had the cottages . . . ," "I had the sound . . . ," and the evidence that these are more than picturesque locutions in his saying that "I thought I had the folk within." But once he moves beyond decorums of space he "repents," only to discover that his "extra-vagance" has meanwhile violated the decorums of time. He returns to find black-ness and silence; his being awake and in motion is "like profanation." A big word, in this context. It can carry from Latin the suggestion that he is "outside the temple or consecrated place." But if that is what he means he is joking, as also with the elaborate politeness of "by your leave." Any sanctities being violated are of the most triv-ial, social sort—to bed by ten. This is a way, too, of reminding us that any true sanctification of the place is the work of the poet. He walks beyond limits and then returns to them with a freedom that asks "leave" of others only in so easy a way as to indicate that his free-dom is a consequence of his complete inwardness with the place and its people, a violation of neither.

It would be snobbish to call such "extra-vagance" as is being exercised here either tame or safe. It is meant to show the local, accessible forms of extravagance in com-mon life; it is an instance, so to speak, of how the gran-deurs of Emerson can be accommodated to routine. With what seems to me an admirable evidence of human sympathy and poetic daring, "extravagance" in Frost can be made to reside often in the most quiet of those idi-omatic phrases by which, in ordinary speech, we un-knowingly talk a visionary language. In commenting on "Once by the Pacific," for example, he remarks that

> The extravagance lies in "it sometimes seems as if"; that would be a good name for a book: "it sometimes seems as if." Or it says "if only you knew." You could put that on the cover of a book. "If only I could tell you," you know. "Beyond participation lie my sorrows and beyond relief"—and yet you're harping on 'em, you see, in that way   ("On Extravagance").

Such deceptions, wrought by the language of poetry and inherent in the language of daily life, are in Frost

licensed by the deceptions practiced upon us—for the
benefit of human existence—by nature itself. The need
and desire for "extravagance" becomes a part of consciousness because even the weather is given to excesses,
to momentary splurges. Thus, he wonders from whence
"I get the lasting sense / Of so much warmth and light,"
and does so in a poem, "Happiness Makes Up in Height
for What It Lacks in Length," whose title is probably
derived from Santayana: "The length of things is vanity,
only their height is joy," he writes in the penultimate
paragraph of *Soliloquies in England*. Characteristically,
Frost's way of putting it is a good deal more wry than
Santayana's. It is close to parody cliché, and in a stun-
ningly casual refusal to ascribe "the lasting sense" to the
imagination only, as Stevens might have done, he
suggests that "If my mistrust is right / It may be altogether / From one day's perfect weather." In that
word "mistrust" is a symptom of the "great expense" of
exaggeration and what Frost means, in "The Constant
Symbol," when he proposes that "Strongly spent is synonymous with kept." "Mistrust" prompts the kind of
tight bargaining, the shrewd tough-mindedness, which
makes more lastingly precious whatever is earned for
memory or consciousness. "Extravagance" is most mea-
surably worthwhile when, out of impoverishment, we
learn the cost of it, as in the sturdy little poem "The Investment":

> Over back where they speak of life as staying
> ("You couldn't call it living, for it ain't"),
> There was an old, old house renewed with paint,
> And in it a piano loudly playing.
>
> Out in the plowed ground in the cold a digger,
> Among unearthed potatoes standing still,

Was counting winter dinners, one a hill.
With half an ear to the piano's vigor.

All that piano and new paint back there,
Was it some money suddenly come into?
Or some extravagance young love had been to?
Or old love on an impulse not to care—

Not to sink under being man and wife,
But to get some color and music out of life?

"An old, old house renewed with paint," a "man and wife," an "impulse not to care," "extravagance," the lonely figure of "a digger" in a desolate landscape, "the plowed ground in the cold"—the terms of the poem pretty well set the agenda for what will be looked into in the three sections of this chapter. First, in this section, we will consider the relation between the security of "home" and the desire to enhance it by spending more than you have. The expenditures can involve simply caring for someone or something, romantic responsiveness, or some combination of mental and physical vagrancy, of walking beyond the confines of "home" in search for something new that might be brought back. We will then, in the second section, "Women at Home," consider a less profitable and reassuring way of living in this complex of possibilities. In these instances "home" becomes synonymous with confinement, usually of a man and wife trapped in a loveless marriage. They can "spend" nothing in an "extravagant" way except anger and depression; their wanderings on foot, or in the mind, become an attempt to run away, to escape from repression, often into hallucinations and madness. And a third, final variation, "Soundings for Home," will bring Stevens and Frost into an inevitable conjunction, especially where the poems show the "home" or "house" in a state of dilapidation, as a place which neither prompts nor profits from "extravagance." Even the surrounding landscape yields very little, and there is a question of whether or not it is possible to create any kind of habitation.

The title of the whole chapter, "Outward Bound," is meant to pick up the implication in "Good Hours," the poem from which it is taken, that there is an inexorable restraint, perhaps even an involuntary one, in all of Frost's gestures of "extravagance." Having just argued that the restraint has a commendable result in that it induces in him a saving taste for "extravagance" even in the least exciting aspects of human life, I want to look ahead by saying that it also works to Frost's disadvantage in poems where he becomes genteel rather than ordinary. There is always in him this tendency to the genteel. Perhaps it is understandable that he should want, now and then, to seek the calm of what might be called the middle voice, where the very issues that give him his urgencies and power—the need of restraint and yet the imaginative reactions that follow from it; the need for extravagance, with all the costly deceptions it can engender—are pacified or numbed in a flaunting respectability of manner. But then, it is not his giving way to this but his more general refusals to do so that make him so remarkable. He escaped the fate of being the laureate of Academe or of the country-weekending professional types. He did so by always being somehow where he wasn't. During his early years in America, while teaching or trying to work a farm, he immersed himself in English and in classical literature in order to know thereby how to be an American poet; in his middle years he went to England—"I had come to the land of *The Golden Treasury*" (Cook, p. 110)—and there worked harder to gain a public recognition back home

as an American poet than to become like Pound, a "devoted American Europeanist," in Donald Davie's phrase.
And while writing poetry of enormous literary sophistication throughout his life, he worked to promote it not
with the critical "few" but with a general audience and
with an academic one, both of whom were made to
think that he offered an easily understood alternative to
the difficulties of Eliot and the élitism of Pound. He
was always in some sense running away in the expectation that the road would somehow lead him back to a
more acceptable "home." Such is the point, essentially,
of the first poem in his first book, "Into My Own," and
also of the last poem in the book, "Reluctance." Significantly, "Reluctance" is about his *inward* possession of the
theme of exile and return: published in 1912, it could
have had no reference at all to his having gone to England and come back to find himself an established poet:

> Out through the fields and the woods
>   And over the walls I have wended;
> I have climbed the hills of view
>   And looked at the world, and descended,
> I have come by the highway home,
>   And lo, it is ended.
>
> The leaves are all dead on the ground,
>   Save those that the oak is keeping
> To ravel them one by one
>   And let them go scraping and creeping
> Out over the crusted snow,
>   When others are sleeping.
>
> And the dead leaves lie huddled and still,
>   No longer blown hither and thither;
> The last lone aster is gone;
>   The flowers of the witch hazel wither;
> The heart is still aching to seek,
>   But the feet question "Whither?"

> Ah, when to the heart of man
>   Was it ever less than a treason
> To go with the drift of things,
>   To yield with a grace to reason,
> And bow and accept the end
>   Of a love or a season?

Frost was particularly fond of this early poem and read it often in public; it was, he said, "a young one that I love" (Cook, p. 136). It faces up to the twin and contrary necessities of his own nature which generated a good deal of his need to write and his power as a writer. Given such lines as "I have climbed the hills of view / And looked at the world, and descended" it could be called a parable about coming "home" out of reason and necessity; and it is also about the self-betrayal of doing so. To be prompted by necessity and reason is to go with the "drift of things." This drift could be of "leaves"—here, not leaves of grass but Sibylline leaves or the "barren leaves" of Shelley with their portent of imaginative aridity. Frost and Frost's travelers manage always to resist the seeming invitation to join in the process of "drift," be it of dead leaves in the fall, the inexorable movements of a brook, or the flood of received opinion; their resistance, in a poem like "West-Running Brook," or in his political poems, is equivalent to the *élan vital* of Bergson or to what he himself liked to call "passionate preference." Indeed, "the figure a poem makes" and the poetic "making" presence in a poem are themselves obstructions to the "drift of things." And yet the opposition can never be absolute. Nature itself seems to authorize those "drifts" and to give them enough force to extinguish the outlines of any counter-assertive shaping. Because if there is a desire in human life not to become part of the "drift" there is also some desire to join it, to "go" with it and thereby find rest and security, however

deadening. Expressions of the will to resist, like expressions of the will to believe, are no more than that—an
act of body or voice or mind that shows a purpose, as in
the lifting of a knee, or what he calls, in an interview
with Braithwaite, "sound-posturing" (Thompson, II,
34). Here we find both gestures: the man in the poem
remembers climbing, even while he descends with the
falling leaves; and he sounds a prophetic note while
others sleep. Necessity in nature, and sometimes apparently in love, creates a limiting form, and yet the
implication of the poem is that one should have, however unreasonably, a faith in the capacity to create alternative forms. "The heart is still aching to seek, / But the
feet question 'Whither?' "—these feet might be read as a
pun on metrical ones, but only as an unlikely fringe
benefit. Any kind of punning is subordinate to the
serious human need to get beyond not only "drift" but
the equally deadly alternative of stoppage. The only acceptable "stays" are momentary ones.

If, in proposing that poetry is "an escape from emotion . . . an escape from personality," Eliot can be allowed the precondition that "of course only those who
have personality and emotion know what it means to
want to escape from these things," Frost can be allowed
to insist on the necessities of form, and on the moral virtue of there being a limit to any metaphor, and still expect that his readers will see in this very insistence that
he is also congenitally impatient with form and with
limits.

The more so, because Frost locates this dialectical opposition in the most familiar, and familial, of circumstances. That is why, in discussing this matter, I do not
ever want to translate his human and moral preoccupations into exclusively poetic ones. Nevertheless, Frost's
poems about "home" or "houses" do show a great deal

of feeling about associated ideas of poetic form, just as in any poem about marriage there is the pressure of his intense concern with the joinings and separations that are implicit in the nature of metaphor. All of these forms, shapes, joinings exist for Frost not despite differences and tensions but partly because of them. And all imply the possible domestication of the wanderer or of the vagrant; form or "home" must include the desire for what is beyond them. He would have known that "stanza" means "room"—so that when he walks out into the woods, he takes his "room" with him. Poetry for him is the act of reaching out to take in the "extravagant," just as in the eighteenth century it reached out for what was called "enthusiasm," and in the nineteenth, in poems Frost admired by Collins and Keats, for a "star."

Frost could have learned from Collins and Keats some of his own urgency to domesticate whatever is remote, romantic, or even destructively inviting. And if such domestication goes hand in hand with culture, then Frost would, again, be expressing a view sympathetic to these poets in his favorite allegation, both in "Kitty Hawk" and in the Bread Loaf lectures, that culture has always tended to move west northwest. This is a way of saying that the epiphanic states associated with the East (where, as Geoffrey Hartman puts it, the poetic Pantheon contained only Sun and Night) "get moderated by that evening light peculiar to the western hemisphere." Like Hartman's Wordsworth, Frost "knows that his imagination needs a 'star' but he also knows that it must be a 'native star.' It should encompass his own, human destiny from birth to setting" (Hartman, *The Fate of Reading,* pp. 139, 157). Frost might well have worried, along with the English romantics, that his skepticism about "extravagance" and romance, his extraordinary need for the securing power of form, could be a trap for poetry itself.

At the very least it could result in that smugness and cuteness which are the besetting difficulties of some of his poetry, especially in the later books. It is typical of him that he could write a poem archly called "Take Something Like a Star." There is a good deal of witty literary history in the seeming innocuousness of that title. It is as if he is suggesting that since "stars" have already been too much used in poetry, we should choose something "like" one, a new metaphor for a dead metaphor. He tells us, again in the talk "On Extravagance," that by star he means "the Arabian Nights or Catullus or something." He could mean a literature that has been moving west northwest, if only in translation, into the temperate and temporizing zones of England and America where a poetry is to be written that includes his own. And yet at the end of the poem he offers a sly dig—or is it a dig?—at the temperate, cautionary, and conventional way of stabilizing the exorbitant: "We may take something like a star / To stay our minds on and be staid."

Even if these lines should remind us of Frost's preference for "stays" that are only momentary, the distinction is not apt to forestall a suspicion that the kinds of dangers Frost confronts in his imaginary journeys seem at times to have a prepared itinerary. I mean to sound especially critical on this score because in the absence of such criticism mediocre poems have been made to seem more central than much better ones, with the result that his truly great accomplishments have not been sufficiently recognized. The poem "Directive" is a prime example of misplaced adulation. Among Frost's poems of "home" and "extra-vagance" it is for me the culminating example of contrived and stagey imaginative daring that actually involves no daring at all. It is about traveling in order to get "lost" so that you may then find yourself whole again "beyond confusion" by virtue of some quasi-religious ritual. But it is a tricky and devious poem not because it has a lot to say but because it is not sure of what it does want to say, or do. It hints at ironies that cannot be consequential except to those who have enclosed themselves within the circuit of Frost's own work, and for them the ironies ought to be of a claustrophobic self-reference that is at odds with the pretentiously large rhetorical sweeps and presumptuous ironies in which the poem indulges itself. I suppose it is important to wonder whether it is *good* to get "beyond confusion" when, once again, we have to remember that Frost has given such prominence throughout his career to the notion that a poem should only be "a momentary stay against" it. But the poem only titillates on this as on other scores, and there is little in it strongly felt except the landscape. The opening seven lines have been praised earlier in this discussion and will be looked at again later on; they are a pure instance of Frost's descriptive and visionary genius, but after that the poem is an example of his most self-conscious and self-cuddling mode, and it is in fact a less compelling poem than a number of others that claim a good deal less for themselves.

Throughout this part of the book I will be looking at some of these poems, at least at enough of them to suggest how much of Frost's best poetry emerged from a central nervous tension about "home" and "extravagance" before he became programmatic about these matters. I have been arguing that in Frost the various images of "home" exist in relation to the vagrant possibilities of life in much the way that form exists, for him, in relation to visionary experience. His dramatizations of a somewhat perplexed feeling about "home" are symptomatic of his transactions with the disciplines and opportunities of poetic forms. "Home" operates as a temporizing restraint upon rebellious extravagance, but for that very reason also engenders it in the conduct of life and in the conduct of poetry.

For so articulate a champion of form—"There is nothing," he once said, "as composing as composition" (Cook, p. 70)—"home," as the dramatic setting in a poem and also as an image of what the poem offers by way of a secure placement of feeling, nonetheless stimulates the imagination of flight and of liberation. Even when, as in the relevant sequences in *A Boy's Will,* "home" is imagined as "marriage"—the desired destination after the alarms and excursions of adolescence, the attainment of a "natural" place in the scheme of things—Frost has ways of letting us know that he is not likely to become a homebody. Take the small poem in that first volume, "In Neglect," where the lovers are at last together and where the poems, from having been in the first person singular, have now adjusted to the first person plural. They are, as Lawrence might put it, enjoying "freedom together," and this seems to have produced in them, with respect to the rest of the world, a feeling that Frost calls "mischievous." The word "mischief" in Frost is a very potent one. It suggests any tendency to upset the stodgy and settled, and to do so out of the best natural impulses. "Spring is the mischief in me, and I wonder / If I could put a notion in his head—" so says the speaker in the first poem of the next volume, "Mending Wall." Like the speaker in that poem, the two lovers in "In Neglect" are also intent upon dissociating themselves from routine practice. They are treated as ever so slightly eccentric:

> They leave us so to the way we took,
> As two in whom they were proved mistaken,
> That we sit sometimes in the wayside nook,

With mischievous, vagrant, seraphic look,
And *try* if we cannot feel forsaken.

It is likely that this poem has some autobiographical reference to the family response when Frost and Elinor White were married without any evident means of support except Frost's intention to be a farmer, his more or less losing avocation. It also seems likely that by the phrase "the way we took" the poem means his chosen but equally precarious vocation as a poet, a "neglected" one. It will be apparent from what has already been said about the terms "vagrant" and "mischievous" that the lovers are displaying precisely the capacities for imagination that can be released in Frost by the achievement of some dialectical, in-and-out relationship to decorum, but the final attribute ascribed to them, their "seraphic look," ought really to be a "cherubic" one, unless Frost intends to suggest that they are a bit genteel without knowing it. Otherwise, their mischievousness and vagrancy are a bit like Uriel's in the poem by Emerson which is called "the greatest western poem yet" in *A Masque of Reason*. Uriel in Emerson's poem withdraws into a cloud, they to "the wayside nook," and both exude that "cherubic scorn" which Frost, in a talk at Bread Loaf in 1959, called "the whole of Emerson":

> Now cherubic scorn is the scorn a really eager spirit has for people who are older people, the old guard, older people who are lost in the difficulty of betterness. Betterness is hard, you know, and the old guard are all people who have given up on it, you know. And they deserve cherubic scorn, Emersonian scorn. He stayed cherubic all his days; he knew it; he knew that he had the feeling of contempt for a person that had aged to the point where he had given up newness, betterness, you know   (Cook, p. 130).

The actively if temperately rebellious sense of place expressed by the lovers in this poem resembles that of "A Drumlin Woodchuck," who boasts:

> One thing has a shelving bank,
> Another a rotting plank,
> To give it cozier skies
> And make up for its lack of size.
>
> My own strategic retreat
> Is where two rocks almost meet,
> And still more secure and snug,
> A two-door burrow I dug.
>
> With those in mind at my back
> I can sit forth exposed to attack,
> As one who shrewdly pretends
> That he and the world are friends.
>
> . . .
> If I can with confidence say
> That still for another day,
> Or even another year,
> I will be there for you, my dear,
>
> It will be because, though small
> As measured against the All,
> I have been so instinctively thorough
> About my crevice and burrow.

In some early poems, like "Storm Fear," it is implied that the home can be a haven surrounded by an antagonistic environment, but in others it is a kind of redoubt from which one can make raids, if only in the imagination, on anything that seems hostile. It provides the security, that is, for playful subversiveness. The woodchuck can "shrewdly" pretend that he and the world are friends; the lovers "in neglect" can "mischievously" pretend that they and the world are somehow at odds. But in neither case is the tone an embattled one.

The limits, boundaries, or customs which define a "home," a personal property, are often taken, that is, as an occasion for freedom rather than for confinement. The real significance of the famous poem "Mending Wall" is that it suggests how much for Frost freedom is contingent upon some degree of restriction. More specifically, it can be said that restrictions, or forms, are a precondition for expression. Without them, even nature ceases to offer itself up for a reading. Forms of any sort have been so overwhelmed in "Desert Places," for example, that the prospect is for "a blanker whiteness of benighted snow / With no expression, nothing to express," the world as a blank sheet of paper enveloped in darkness.

Natural forces in "Mending Wall," having each year to encounter the human imposition of a freshly repaired wall, tend to become expressive in a quite selective way. Whatever it is "that doesn't love a wall," "*sends* the frozen-ground-swell under it / And *spills* the upper boulders in the sun, / And *makes* gaps even two can pass abreast" (my italics). More important, this active response to human structurings prompts a counter-response and activity from people who are committed to the making and remaking of those structures. And who are such people? The point usually missed, along with most other things importantly at work in this poem, is that it is not the neighbor, described as "an old-stone savage armed," a man who can only dully repeat, "Good fences make good neighbors"—that it is not he who initiates the fence-making. Rather it is the far more spirited, lively, and "mischievous" speaker of the poem. While admitting that they do not need the wall, it is he who each year "lets my neighbor know beyond the hill" that it is time to do the job anyway, and who will go out alone to fill the gaps made in the wall by hunters: "I

have come after them and made repairs / When they
have left not one stone on a stone." Though the speaker
may or may not think that good neighbors are made by
good fences, it is abundantly clear that he likes the
yearly ritual, the yearly "outdoor game" by which fences
are made. Because if fences do not "make good neighbors" the *"making"* of fences can. More is "made" in this
"outdoor game" than fences. The two men also "make"
talk, or at least that is what the speaker tries to do as
against the reiterated assertions of his companion, which
are as heavy and limited as the wall itself. So hopeless is
this speaker of any response, that all his talk may be
only to himself. He is looking for some acknowledgment
of those forces at work which are impatient of convention and of merely repeated forms; but he is looking in
vain:

> He only says, "Good fences make good neighbors."
> Spring is the mischief in me, and I wonder
> If I could put a notion in his head:
> *"Why* do they make good neighbors? Isn't it
> Where there are cows? But here there are no cows.
> Before I built a wall I'd ask to know
> What I was walling in or walling out,
> And to whom I was like to give offense.
> Something there is that doesn't love a wall,
> That wants it down." I could say "Elves" to him,
> But it's not elves exactly, and I'd rather
> He said it for himself.

However arrogantly self-assured, his interrogations
should, ideally, have an effect on his neighbor comparable to the effect of ground-swells on stone walls. Voice
and nature are thus potentially allied. Just as early
spring "sends" or "spills" what is firmly placed, so the
"notions" of the speaker are meant to displace the settled ideas in his presumably blockheaded friend. He

wants to convert him to subversion, empower him to get
"under" or go "behind his father's sayings." And yet
being as vain of his language as any ill-read poet might
be, the neighbor cannot recognize the "saying" as having
come from his father: "And he likes having thought of it
so well / He says again, 'Good fences make good neighbors.' "

Frost was of many minds about "fences," "homes," or
"yards." His genius as a narrative poet is in part his capacity to sustain debates between people about the nature of the "homes" which they very often occupy
together. But it is a dangerous subject for him. It can
encourage his tendency to wax idyllic about the possibilities of marital relationships, and this, in turn, sometimes reduces those possibilities for dramatic confrontation and for tension in dialogue that help make
"Mending Wall" not only a humanly interesting but an
intellectually rigorous poem. A dramatic narrative
wherein differences of interpretation about "home" are
more tenderly evoked is, of course, the poem which
follows "Mending Wall" in *North of Boston*, "The Death
of the Hired Man." It is significant that the poem was
written in 1905–6, a period when Frost was often ro-
mantically persuaded that "home" and "marriage" were
the antidotes to poetic as well as to personal sterility.
Crucial to the poem is the discussion between the young
husband and wife about whether or not a truant old
field hand should be allowed to stay in their house now
that he has decided to return, sick and probably unable
ever to work again:

> Part of a moon was falling down the west,
> Dragging the whole sky with it to the hills.
> Its light poured softly in her lap. She saw it
> And spread her apron to it. She put out her hand
> Among the harplike morning-glory strings,

Taut with the dew from garden bed to eaves,
As if she played unheard some tenderness
That wrought on him beside her in the night.
"Warren," she said, "he has come home to die:
You needn't be afraid he'll leave you this time."

"Home," he mocked gently.

                    "Yes, what else but home?
It all depends on what you mean by home.
Of course he's nothing to us, any more
Than was the hound that came a stranger to us
Out of the woods, worn out upon the trail."

"Home is the place where, when you have to go there,
They have to take you in."

The ambitious lunar sweep of the first two lines of this
quotation is brought into a human and domestic focus
in the third line, when the light of the moon "poured
softly in her lap." "She saw it,"—the sharpness of that
clause, the more emphatic for its adding an extra accented syllable to the line, suggests that the wife is alert
to the support she is getting from remote influences. It
is a support she needs in her efforts to induce a benign
mood in her husband toward the old man. Her gestures
embrace these influences while they simultaneously
reach out to play upon domestic artifacts—or may we
call them props?—which are of her own making: the
"morning-glory strings" that stretch from the "garden
bed" to the eaves under which, most likely, is their marital "bed."

The tenderness that "wrought on him beside her in
the night" can therefore be said to emanate not from
her alone but from an environment, both natural and of
her own creation. And it is this shared environment
which is "their home." Since the issue of what to do

about a difficult old man is in every way made subordinate to what is essentially a marriage idyll, there is no
doubt about how the poetry wants the issue to be resolved. There is a Miltonic tinge here, both in the scene
and in the wife's way of arguing with her husband. She
is assisted by the tender seductiveness of the world
around them and assured of success by her prior knowledge of the inward disposition which has already put
him there, "beside her in the night."

I am describing rather than promoting this kind of
poem. Like "Directive," whose undoubted felicities of
expression have already been sufficiently commended
by Randall Jarrell, it belongs to Frost's elevated mode.
And when Frost decides to be elevated he very often betrays to mere social commendability the more strenuous,
aristocratic, courageous, visionary possibilities called into
being by poems like "After Apple Picking" or "The Most
of It." His tone is of one anxious to please those who
want their elevation in an easy chair, and it is no accident that a remark as sententious as the wife's—that
home is "something you somehow haven't to deserve"—
should have become proverbial. Frost is close to selling
out to his popular audience when he, or his characters,
speak as if the environment around them adequately
sustains their aspirations to hygienically fine feelings.
"The Death of the Hired Man" has that touch of gentil-
ity which is even more obnoxiously at work, for me, in
the dramatic narrative "The Generations of Men." The
letter is about a family reunion held where "Someone
had literally run to earth / In an old cellar-hole in a
byroad / The origin of all the family there," and where a
sample bit of dialogue runs

> "You poor, dear, great, great, great, great Granny!"
> "See that you get her greatness right. Don't stint her."

The only likely audience for this would be the prosperous academic weekenders who have notoriously laid claim to southern New Hampshire. Much the same sort of thing can be found, as we will see presently, in a far more considerable poem like "West-Running Brook." Such poems are characterized by an aphoristic dialogue long staled by rehearsal. It is a kind of dialogue bad enough (but acceptable for other reasons) in the lesser Wordsworth, and it somewhat vitiates the claim in a letter of Frost's to Thomas Mosher that in *North of Boston* "I dropped to a level of diction that even Wordsworth kept above" (Thompson, *Letters,* pp. 183–84).

There are many other poems that would support this claim, but in those under consideration the dialogue registers mere differences of opinion and not differences of speech, not differences in the *way* something gets said. Meanings, that is, are not generated out of sentence sounds as they are, so remarkably, in the best of Frost. And even when he wants consciously to center his drama in speech rhythms he can sometimes do so with only the crudest sorts of differentiation. As examples, "The Code" and "A Hundred Collars" are about cultural confrontations over the way things ought to be said. In the first, the town-bred farmer learns how the tone of his remarks, however innocently made, can be taken as an insult by country workers. In the second, Frost pretends to satirize the kind of well-bred summer people to whom he caters in "The Generations of Men," but in fact he only gives them, as readers, an always welcome opportunity to disown caricatures of themselves, as embodied in the person of the distinguished scholar:

> Lancaster bore him—such a little town,
> Such a great man. It doesn't see him often
> Of late years, though he keeps the old homestead

And sends the children down there with their mother
To run wild in the summer—a little wild.

Missing a train on his way to Lancaster for the week-
end, the "scholar" has to share a bed in a rooming house
with a bill collector named Lafe. Lafe's teasing loquacity
and generosity in offering the doctor a hundred collars
that have grown too small for him reduces his highly
educated bedmate to inarticulateness and the prospect
of a sleepless night. Mainly because their rendering of
culturally differentiated tones of speech is so broadly
and fatuously obvious, poems like "The Code," "A
Hundred Collars," and "West-Running Brook" are especially clear illustrations of one of the central themes or
motive forces in Frost's longer dramatic narratives. Very
often these trace the gradual accumulation of tensions
about acts of speech, about *how* things are or were being
said. Typically, each of the characters wants to lay claim
to a "home" territory by the power of speech, whether
this be through some idiomatic coloring or with some
anecdotal capacity, like that shown in "The Mountain"
by the Wordsworthian old man "who moved so slow /
With white-faced oxen, in a heavy cart, / It seemed
no harm to stop him altogether." The speaker, a visitor
in the neighborhood, wants to know about the mountain which shadows the village. In reply the old man is
especially anxious to promote interest in "a brook"

> That starts up on it somewhere—I've heard say
> Right on the top, tip-top—a curious thing.
> But what would interest you about the brook,
> It's always cold in summer, warm in winter.
> One of the great sights going is to see
> It steam in winter like an ox's breath,
> Until the bushes all along its banks
> Are inch-deep with the frosty spines and bristles—
> You know the kind. Then let the sun shine on it!"

His excitement ("one of the great sights") produces metaphors ("like an ox's breath") that then propel him into obvious excesses (the "inch-deep" frost). The freedom of imagination has the qualities of a country tall-tale, and is a clue to a later admission of fact—the old man has never seen the brook. Neither apparently has anyone else, though everyone is sure it exists, including, by the end, the interlocutor, who can now be treated as if he were himself willing to join in a community mirage:

> "Warm in December, cold in June, you say?"
>
> "I don't suppose the water's changed at all.
> You and I know enough to know it's warm
> Compared with cold, and cold compared with warm.
> But all the fun's in how you say a thing."

Maybe it is fun—until in that last line we are asked to compliment Frost for his efforts. It is like asking for gratuities after a display of country quaintnesses and native sentence sounds. Sometimes Frost so wants to be old New England, poor boy from California that he is, that here and in a mostly embarrassing poem entitled "New Hampshire" he can surrender himself, as A. Alvarez notes, though with too complete an indictment, to the delusion that to have lived in New Hampshire or Vermont is to have become philosophically enabled in an especially ingratiating way.

2. WOMEN AT HOME

Frost is often at his best when "home" is at its worst. "Home" could not be much worse than in most of his

poems about women in the country. In a peculiar way,
his treatment of women recalls a nineteenth-century
novelistic convention in which the repression of women,
and the restriction on their active participation in the
outdoor world, force them into exercises of free imagination and fancy. Men can busy themselves with affairs
outside the "home," and women are sometimes to be
gratified with what is brought back to them, as in
"Flower-Gathering." But when in Section V of "The Hill
Wife" the woman has an "extra-vagant" impulse, it is not
to bring back flowers but to escape altogether:

> It was too lonely for her there,
>   And too wild,
> And since there were but two of them,
>   And no child,
>
> And work was little in the house,
>   She was free,
> And followed where he furrowed field,
>   Or felled tree.
>
> She rested on a log and tossed
>   The fresh chips,
> With a song only to herself
>   On her lips.
>
> And once she went to break a bough
>   Of black alder.
> She strayed so far she scarcely heard
>   When he called her—
>
> And didn't answer—didn't speak—
>   Or return.
> She stood, and then she ran and hid
>   In the fern.
>
> He never found her, though he looked
>   Everywhere,

And he asked at her mother's house
    Was she there.

Sudden and swift and light as that
    The ties gave,
And he learned of finalities
    Besides the grave.

Frost's sense of the plight of women who have nothing but a home to keep—with too little work if childless, too much if there are boarders or workers on the farm—is responsible for a series of remarkable poems about the frustrations of imagination and its consequent expression in the distorted forms of obsession, lies, or madness. Very often "home" is the prison of madness, recognized as such by the keepers and so acknowledged by the victims, like the woman in "A Servant to Servants," who has been to an insane asylum and who is not afraid of the men who board in her house "if they're not / Afraid of me. There's two can play at that. / I have my fancies: it runs in the family. / My father's brother wasn't right."

The poem is a long soliloquy delivered to outsiders. In the many poems where one finds them listening to Frost's isolated country talkers these outsiders usually say nothing or so little that what pretends to be dialogue makes us at a certain point nervously wonder if it is not really only soliloquy, or an expression of mad loneliness searching through an interior monologue for a listener. These particular outsiders are supposedly camping on the land rented out by the woman's husband Len. Understandably, she is glad to have someone to talk to; she is worried at the end that they may not stay very much longer; and both feelings make her admission of madness, along with her account of her uncle's insanity, also an attempt simply to make herself interesting. Everything she says is touched with a possibility that it may not be wholly true. As in all of Frost's poems about isolated women who indulge in lying, or so we suspect, the lies are more than a form of country exaggeration. They are also, to remember a line from "The Investment," an attempt to "get some color . . . out of life" which otherwise is intolerably, hopelessly drab. Her account of the mad uncle's imprisonment is full of a powerful and self-frightening inventiveness:

> And just when he was at the height,
> Father and mother married, and mother came,
> A bride, to help take care of such a creature,
> And accommodate her young life to his.
> That was what marrying father meant to her.
> She had to lie and hear love things made dreadful
> By his shouts in the night. He'd shout and shout
> Until the strength was shouted out of him,
> And his voice died down slowly from exhaustion.
> He'd pull his bars apart like bow and bowstring,
> And let them go and make them twang, until
> His hands had worn them smooth as any oxbow.
> And then he'd crow as if he thought that child's play—
> The only fun he had. I've heard them say, though,
> They found a way to put a stop to it.

Like the old man in "The Mountain" who describes the spring on the summit only then to say that he has never seen it, her description is especially interesting because, in the very next line, she admits "I never saw him." He was before her time. But she did live long enough in the house where her uncle was kept till "It got so I would say—you know, half fooling—/ 'It's time I took my turn upstairs in jail.' " In the new house to which Len moves her, her imagination feeds again on pictures, fictions, things that are extraordinary. Only now these are excited by the long views from her kitchen window. She resembles the woman in "The Hill Wife" who at last "didn't answer . . . didn't speak" about the thwarted intensities of feeling within her:

> It seems to me
> I can't express my feelings, any more
> Than I can raise my voice or want to lift
> My hand (oh, I can lift it when I have to).
> Did ever you feel so? I hope you never.
> It's got so I don't even know for sure
> Whether I *am* glad, sorry, or anything.
> There's nothing but a voice like left inside
> That seems to tell me how I ought to feel,
> And would feel if I wasn't all gone wrong.
> You take the lake. I look and look at it.
> I see it's a fair, pretty sheet of water.
> I stand and make myself repeat out loud
> The advantages it has, so long and narrow,
> Like a deep piece of some old running river
> Cut short off at both ends. It lies five miles
> Straightaway through the mountain notch
> From the sink window where I wash the plates,
> And all our storms come up toward the house,
> Drawing the slow waves whiter and whiter and whiter.
> It took my mind off doughnuts and soda biscuit
> To step outdoors and take the water dazzle
> A sunny morning, or take the rising wind
> About my face and body and through my wrapper,
> When a storm threatened from the Dragon's Den,
> And a cold chill shivered across the lake.

Near the end of this passage, which might bring anyone to tears, there are indications of a romantic and highly erotic inclination, and, elsewhere in the poem, of sexual frustration in this childless marriage. Love has been exhausted by drudgery, and her marriage is now much like her mother's: "Father and mother married, and mother came / A bride to help take care of such a creature, / And accommodate her young life to his. /

That was what marrying father meant to her." She is married to someone incapable of more than the platitudes of accommodation. As against the wondrous care and passion of her language about the water and the waves in storm, Len's language is an echo of what is heard from the "old-stone savage" in "Mending Wall," the same sort of mindless compliance with the least that life has to offer: "Len says one steady pull more ought to do it. / He says the best way out is always through." The poem is a frightening and pitiable dramatization of how a "home," deprived of emotional fulfillments of any kind, can prompt a woman to perverse and beautiful extremities.

The poem anticipates the equally remarkable, somewhat later (1922) "The Witch of Coös":

> I stayed the night for shelter at a farm
> Behind the mountain, with a mother and son,
> Two old-believers. They did all the talking.

The talking involves a good deal of humbugging, though again to an extent we cannot surely determine, by a woman who wants to maintain her neighborhood reputation as a witch: "Summoning spirits isn't 'Button, button, / Who's got the button,' I would have them know." The story is of a skeleton who, in the words of the son,

>   left the cellar forty years ago
> And carried itself like a pile of dishes
> Up one flight from the cellar to the kitchen,
> Another from the kitchen to the bedroom,
> Another from the bedroom to the attic,
> Right past both father and mother, and neither stopped it.
> Father had gone upstairs; mother was downstairs.
> I was a baby: I don't know where I was.

Once more we have an account of something by somebody who did not see it and who, perhaps for that reason, extemporizes in vivid and show-off metaphors,
such as the memorable skeleton that, according to the
son, "carried itself like a pile of dishes." Understandably, the mother, in her account, chooses a metaphor no less inventive but somewhat more romantic—
the bones are put together "like a chandelier":

> I had a vision of them put together
> Not like a man, but like a chandelier.
> So suddenly I flung the door wide on him.
> A moment he stood balancing with emotion,
> And all but lost himself. (A tongue of fire
> Flashed out and licked along his upper teeth.
> Smoke rolled inside the sockets of his eyes.)
> Then he came at me with one hand outstretched,
> The way he did in life once; but this time
> I struck the hand off brittle on the floor,
> And fell back from him on the floor myself.
> The finger-pieces slid in all directions.

The telltale keepsake bone cannot be found in the
button box, and even if it could it would not prove that
the skeleton was a former lover killed by her husband,
Toffile. All Toffile does, even by her account, is act like
an unusually indulgent mate, willing to believe his wife's
claim that a skeleton has come up from the basement,
though he cannot see it or hear it. He is then willing to
bolt the attic, never to open it again, as if to support her
further claim, never more substantiated than any of the
others, that the skeleton has chosen to go there.

A pattern seems to emerge from these poems. In
"The Witch of Coös" as in "A Servant to Servants" we
have a woman imagining a figure of insane, frustrated,
and obscene sexuality caged in a house with a married

couple. And this married couple, too, is ever so subtly characterized as possibly sexless, possibily frigid, and therefore potentially obscene. On the night of her vision

> The bulkhead double doors were double-locked
> And swollen tight and buried under snow.
> The cellar windows were banked up with sawdust
> And swollen tight and buried under snow.

The repetitions give an emotional intensity that might be expected from a woman who wants to interpret the always unsteady movements of a skeleton, reputed to be her former lover, as a "balancing with emotion." This is the same women who, before she offers her images of "something swollen tight and buried under snow," admits that

>   The only fault my husband found with me—
> I went to sleep before I went to bed,
> Especially in winter when the bed
> Might just as well be ice and the clothes snow.
> The night the bones came up the cellar stairs
> Toffile had gone to bed alone and left me,
> But left an open door to cool the room off
> So as to sort of turn me out of it.

A widow now, with a son who seems surprised at her willingness to tell a stranger that the skeleton was of a man who once had his way with her, she at least has the pleasure, having also put her husband in the grave, of a bed to herself and some distraught bones that at night sometimes come down from the attic to "stand perplexed / Behind the door and headboard of the bed / Brushing their chalky skull with chalky fingers."

"Extravagance" of imagination such as is found in "The Witch of Coös" and "A Servant to Servants" derives from characters who react vigorously against quite specifically portrayed domestic confinements of "home." Their ghoulishness is very different from that imagination of expanded possibility, of greater domestic inclusiveness, such as we find in the woman of "The Death of the Hired Man" when she holds out an apron to the moon, but it is more characteristic of what is to be found in the best of Frost's domestic narratives. Especially when a woman is the speaker in such poems the bursting out of imagination comes in the form of images at once terrifying, comically macabre, and sexually charged. These are poems of the mind's extravagance not supported by the feet, of women stuck at home rather than of men wandering beyond the boundaries of the homestead.

There are instances of actual wanderings away from home, as in "The Hill Wife," and in "The Fear" of a woman who feels she must go forth to confront some presence, some Other, possibly an intruder, possibly a lover, and possibly no one. "The Fear" is about a woman's efforts to validate the imaginations that haunt a home and deprive it of its ascribed function as a place in which to live and to love. "Home" in "The Fear" is a place over which the couple seems to exercise only the most tentative and harassed authority. The opening, like the opening of "Home Burial," locates the essential characters, objects, lighting, and movement with a kind of cinematic genius:

> A lantern light from deeper in the barn
> Shone on a man and woman in the door
> And threw their lurching shadows on a house
> Nearby, all dark in every glossy window.
> A horse's hoof pawed once the hollow floor,
> And the back of the gig they stood beside
> Moved in a little. The man grasped a wheel.
> The woman spoke out sharply, "Whoa, stand still!—

I saw it just as plain as a white plate,"
She said, "as the light on the dashboard ran
Along the bushes at the roadside—a man's face.
You *must* have seen it too."

                              "I didn't see it.
Are you sure——"

                         "Yes, I'm sure!"

                              "—it was a face?"

"Joel, I'll have to look. I can't go in,
I can't, and leave a thing like that unsettled.
Doors locked and curtains drawn will make no difference.
I always have felt strange when we came home
To the dark house after so long an absence,
And the key rattled loudly into place
Seemed to warn someone to be getting out
At one door as we entered at another.
What if I'm right, and someone all the time—
Don't hold my arm!"

The light "deeper in the barn" shines on the man and
wife as if spotting them as intruders. The poem refers to
them even on the familiar terrain of their own lives,
only as "a man and woman in the door." In some sense
they are strangers to a territory they are supposed to
share, and for the reason that so much of the life of the
wife is obsessed—owned, so to speak—by someone else,
some haunting presence. Metrically, the dialogue is
managed so that her alienations from her husband are
given an especially painful stress. It is implied that there
have been many other instances similar to the present
one where her sense of pursuit and intrusion have had
to go unconfirmed:

> "I didn't see it.
>
> Are you sure——"
>
> "Yes, I'm sure!"
>
> "—it was a face?"

This little exchange is a stunning example of the dramatic and characterizing significances that can emerge from Frost's versification. "My versification," he wrote in a letter to John Cournos on July 8, 1914,

> seems to bother people more than I should have expected—I suppose because I have been so long accustomed to thinking of it in my own private way. It is as simple as this: there are the very regular preestablished accent and measure of blank verse; and there are the very irregular accent and measure of speaking intonation. I am never more pleased than when I can get these into strained relation. I like to drag and break the intonation across the meter as waves first comb and then break stumbling on the shingle. That's all but it's no mere figure of speech though one can make figures enough about it   (Thompson, *Letters*, p. 128).

The splitting of the few lines quoted above allows, by the process Frost describes, such variations of voice that the "strained relation" between the man and the woman is inseparable from the "strained relation" between the regular measure of blank verse and the irregular accent of speaking intonation. The range of metrical options is but one sign of the wondrous suspensions of possibility that Frost allows to anyone who reads with an attentive ear. " 'Are you sure' " can be read in an iambic combination with the previous line (" 'Í did│n't sée it. / Áre│yóu súre' ") or, allowing a trochaic first foot with the equiva-

lent of an unstressed syllable for the dash (and interrup-
tion) after "sure——," it can be read with its ascertain-
able conclusion ("'Áre yòu|súre——| . . . it wàs à
faće?' "). Either way the line indicates some doubt about
the accuracy of her report (e.g. "Are you sure it was a
face and not something else"). But the stress on "sure"
in " 'Are you sure——' " followed by the trochaic opening of the next line, with the comma counting as an
unaccented syllable ("'Yés ;|I'm sure!' ") leaves three
possibilities for a reading of " 'I'm sure!' " It could be a
spondaic ("'Yés ;|I'm súre!' ") or an iambic foot ("'Yés
;|I'm súre!' "), either constituting, especially with the
exclamation point, an emphatic, tight-lipped response to
his query. It could also be a trochee, however ("'Yés, |
I'm sùre!' "), with the suggestion, *"I* am sure, but of
course you, as is your habit, are not sure that it was a
face." The fact that these and other metrical possibilities
are simultaneously available in this brief exchange is itself an indication of the frustration, impatience, and uncertainty in the relationship between the man and the
woman. And her exclamation at the end of the passage,
" 'Don't hold my arm!' " is, by the same means, powerful
enough to call for a stress on every word, but is almost
equally strong if we let our voices follow the regular
iambic beat. The poem thereby sustains all the possibilities of feeling in the kind of explosive equilibrium
which is at work between the speakers themselves.

The woman's very determination to validate her fear
makes it seem all the more like a psychotic conjuration.
And when, in an eerie confrontation on the road, they
do meet a man who turns out to be only a stranger giving his young son the experience of a country walk at
night, the genius of the poem resides in Frost's letting us
see that far from being reassured she is thereby made
even more terrified:

We're stopping for the fortnight down at Dean's."

"But if that's all—Joel—you realize—
You won't think anything. You understand?
You understand that we have to be careful.
This is a very, very lonely place.—
Joel!" She spoke as if she couldn't turn.
The swinging lantern lengthened to the ground,
It touched, it struck, it clattered and went out.

Her call for "Joel" goes unanswered. Possibly, though we cannot know, he has impatiently turned round and gone home. But his disappearance, and the extinguishing of the lamp, are meant to suggest something more terrifying to her even than the possibility that the man she has seen on the road is a former lover come back to haunt them. The effort to externalize her "fear" has proved ludicrous; there was indeed nothing "out there" to be exposed by the lantern, and we might at this point remember that at the outset a lantern "shone" on them. At the end "the fear" is in them, or in her, the result of imaginings that have been betrayed. She is left calling in the darkness of the night on a husband for help he will not give her, and it is a darkness now deprived of any objectification for her dread.

Frost's poetry recurrently dramatizes the discovery that the sharing of a "home" can produce imaginations of uncontrollable threat inside or outside. "Home" can become the source of those fears from which it is supposed to protect us; it can become the habitation of that death whose anguish it is supposed to ameliorate. And this brings us to one of Frost's greatest poetic dramatizations of the theme, "Home Burial." Here, as in "The Fear," the pressure is shared by a husband and wife, but once again the role of the husband is ambiguous. Though he does his best to comprehend the wife's difficulties, he is only partly able to do so. The very title of the poem means something about the couple as well as about the dead child buried in back of the house. It is as if "home" were a burial plot for all of them.

The opening lines of Frost's dramatic narratives are usually wonderfully deft in suggesting the metaphoric nature of "home," the human opportunities or imperatives which certain details represent for a husband or a wife. In "The Fear," the couple is already outside the house, which is described as a place unoccupied, and so compelling is the wife's "extra-vagance" of imagination that they do not enter the house in the course of the poem; in "Home Burial," the couple are trapped inside the house, which is described as a kind of prison, or perhaps more aptly, a mental hospital. Even the wife's glance out the window can suggest to the husband the desperation she feels within the confines of what has always been his family's "home"; it looks directly on the family graveyard which now holds the body of their recently dead child: *

> He saw her from the bottom of the stairs
> Before she saw him. She was starting down,
> Looking back over her shoulder at some fear.
> She took a doubtful step and then undid it
> To raise herself and look again. He spoke   5
> Advancing toward her: "What is it you see
> From up there always—for I want to know."   [always?]
> She turned and sank upon her skirts at that,
> And her face changed from terrified to dull.
> He said to gain time: "What is it you see,"   [see?]   10
> Mounting until she cowered under him.
> "I will find out now—you must tell me, dear."

*For reasons that will become apparent my quotation of lines 1–30 of this poem is taken from the 1949 edition of *Complete Poems of Robert Frost,* editorially supervised by the author himself. Certain emendations made by Lathem in his 1969 edition, *The Poetry of Robert Frost,* are indicated in the margin in brackets.

She, in her place, refused him any help   [help,]
With the least stiffening of her neck and silence.
She let him look, sure that he wouldn't see,   15
Blind creature; and awhile he didn't see.
But at last he murmured, "Oh," and again, "Oh."

"What is it—what?" she said.

        "Just that I see."

"You don't," she challenged. "Tell me what it is."

"The wonder is I didn't see at once.   20
I never noticed it from here before.
I must be wonted to it—that's the reason.
The little graveyard where my people are!
So small the window frames the whole of it.
Not so much larger than a bedroom, is it?   25
There are three stones of slate and one of marble,
Broad-shouldered little slabs there in the sunlight
On the sidehill. We haven't to mind *those*.
But I understand: it is not the stones,
But the child's mound—"

      "Don't, don't, don't, don't," she cried.   30

The remarkable achievement here is that the husband and wife have become so nearly inarticulate in their animosities that the feelings have been transferred to a vision of household arrangements and to their own bodily movements. They and the house conspire together to create an aura of suffocation. For a comparable sense of divorcement communicated mostly by silent uses of space in a "home," a supposedly shared area, perhaps the best analogy is not to be found in literature but in film, such as the opening of Antonioni's *La Notte*. But of course Frost's special genius is in the placement of words. The first line poses the husband as a kind of spy; the opening of the second line suggests a habituated

wariness on her part, but from that point to line 5 we
are shifted back to his glimpse of her as she moves ob-
sessively again, as yet unaware of being watched, to the
window. Suggestions of alienation, secretiveness, male
intimidation ("advancing toward her") within a situation
of mutual distrust, a miasmic fear inside as well as outside the house—we are made to sense this before anyone speaks. Initially the fault seems to lie mostly with
the husband. But as soon as she catches him watching
her, and as soon as he begins to talk, it is the grim mutu-
ality of their dilemma and the shared responsibilities for
it that sustain the dramatic intelligence and power of the
poem.

I have indicated in the margin a number of the emendations made by Lathem in his edition—which is assumed to be "authoritative"—because his version substantially loses the poignant delicacy with which Frost
treats the estrangement between husband and wife.
Lathem chose to make two emendations wholly on his
own: he added a question mark after "always" in line 7,
and he put a comma after "help" in line 13. He also ar-
bitrarily chose to follow early editions by allowing a
question mark at the end of line 10, though Frost had
deleted it in all the editions he supervised after 1936,
including the 1949 *Complete Poems*. These textual matters are worth considering, because while Lathem's
choices hurt the poem, they make us aware of punctua-
tion in ways that considerably increase our appreciation
of nuances which might otherwise go unremarked. We
can note, for example, the scrupulous justice with which
Frost tries to locate, even through the use of a comma,
the sources of conflict in this "home." There is a marvelously managed shifting in the apportionment of blame.
Thus the man's initial speech, while impatient, is meant
to be more gentle than it is in the assertively interroga-

tive form that Lathem's question mark gives it. Without the question mark, there is the implication that the husband has learned, after many trying experiences, not to expect an answer to his questions. And the strength of her obstinacy with regard to him is then confirmed by the fact that instead, of showing fear at his "advancing on her," her face, on his near approach, changes from "terrified to dull." Nonetheless, the choice of "until" and "under" in the phrase "mounting until she cowered under him" suggests that there indeed is a calculated masculine imposition of will in the way he acts, though this possibility is as quickly muffled by his then speaking more gently still (" 'I will find out now—you must tell me, dear' ") with its allowable lack of stress on the word "now" and the especially strong beat, after a comma, on the word "dear." Frost did not choose to put a comma after the word "help" ("She, in her place, refused him any help / With the least stiffening of her neck and silence"), and its absence is crucial to our recognition of how perverse and stubbornly uncompliant she can be. With the comma added, the line suggests that her stiffness and silence merely *accompanied* her refusal to tell him what she had seen out the window; without the comma, we are allowed to infer that she would choose *not* to stiffen her neck lest she thereby give him any clue at all about what she has been staring at: "Sure that he wouldn't see / Blind creature . . ." These surges of surreptitious feeling between the two of them obviously result not from their immediate juxtaposition on the stairs but from a customary incapacity to share any feelings with one another.

Of course he does see what is out there, the child's grave. And her challenge then to " 'Tell me what it is' " is merely the first of many instances in which differences are defined, as they so often are in Frost, as differences

in the use of words, in the way one speaks or hears
things, in the uses to which a metaphor is put, be it sane
or crazy, brutal or insensitive: " 'You don't know how to
ask it' " (line 43), she complains, and he—" 'My words
are nearly always an offense. / I don't know how to
speak of anything' " (lines 45–46); or, again (line 70),
" 'A man can't speak of his own child that's dead,' " to
which in the next line she replies, " 'You can't because
you don't know how to speak.' " Her lengthy indictment of him near the end of the poem begins with her
claim, " 'I can repeat the very words that you were saying . . . think of it, talk like that at such a time!' " (lines
91, 94). One of the husband's initial mentions of the
graveyard does betray a certain tactless predominance
and possessiveness (" 'The little graveyard where my
people are!' "), but this is immediately followed by a
metaphor of diminishment that somewhat restores a balance (" 'So small the window frames the whole of it' ").
However, this in turn gives way to yet another metaphor
of dangerously thoughtless implication: " 'Not so much
larger than a bedroom, is it?' " In its very casualness, really a kind of stupidity, the husband's comparison of the
graveyard to a bedroom is a sign that, having been made
so nervous about the inadequacy of his language, he has
to double or triple his illustration of anything he wants
to communicate. He seems unaware of his tastelessness,
which is of course all the more reason to think that his
bedroom metaphor reveals some of his deepest feelings
about what has happened to their marriage. But if the
bedroom is like a graveyard, the reason has as much to
do with her excessive (possibly neurotic) sensibility as
with the obvious deficiencies of his. And if he is insensitive, he is at least not without gentleness. When he asks
her " 'Don't—don't go. / Don't carry it to someone else
this time' " (lines 56–57), he is less peremptory than is

she: " 'Don't, don't, don't, don't' she cried" (line 29), a
line that is as remarkably powerful in its effect as a similar one in Hemingway's "Hills Like White Elephants":
"Will you please please please please please please please
stop talking?" She is asking him not to speak; he is asking her not to leave him.

Out of some terrible fastidiousness she seems to want
to abridge even what is left of their relationship, while
he, because of love, and some incipient pride of place in
the community, is doing his best to maintain some sort
of contact:

"My words are nearly always an offense.   45
I don't know how to speak of anything
So as to please you. But I might be taught,
I should suppose. I can't say I see how.
A man must partly give up being a man
With womenfolk. We could have some arrangement   50
By which I'd bind myself to keep hands off
Anything special you're a-mind to name.
Though I don't like such things 'twixt those that love.
Two that don't love can't live together without them.
But two that do can't live together with them."   55
She moved the latch a little. "Don't—don't go.
Don't carry it to someone else this time,
Tell me about it if it's something human.
Let me into your grief. I'm not so much
Unlike other folks as your standing there   60
Apart would make me out. Give me my chance.
I do think, though, you overdo it a little.
What was it brought you up to think it the thing
To take your mother-loss of a first child
So inconsolably—in the face of love.   65
You'd think his memory might be satisfied—"

"There you go sneering now!"

                                    "I'm not, I'm not!
You make me angry. I'll come down to you.

God, what a woman! And it's come to this,
A man can't speak of his own child that's dead."   70

Sexuality in Frost has been noted, when at all, with a
kind of surprise. And yet in a very great number of his
poems it figures, as it does here, as a submerged metaphor for his all-consuming interest in the *relational* and
transitional nature of poetry, of thinking, of talking itself.
The husband and wife here cannot "ask" anything of
one another or "tell" anything without giving offense
partly because they both are flawed in their sense of
time and of timing. With her desire to stop everything
in the interest of mourning the death of an infant, she
cannot understand his apparent incapacity to mourn at
all and his choosing to talk, instead, of everyday concerns. She does not see that this is his only way of man-
aging grief, of not letting it consume his or her life. And
the words she accuses him of using as he sat there talking on the day he buried his child—" 'Three foggy
mornings and one rainy day / Will rot the best birch
fence a man can build' "—form themselves without his
knowing it, but with complete appropriateness, into a
metaphor for the way nature, if only by some accident
of weather, will erode whatever human beings might
make to protect themselves from the reality of change
and death. The wife sees and then describes her husband's actions on that day with an angry exactitude, a
kind of novelistic passion for detail, characteristic of
country women in the poems we have been looking at:

If you had any feelings, you that dug
With your own hand—how could you?—his little grave;
I saw you from that very window there,
Making the gravel leap and leap in air,   75
Leap up, like that, like that, and land so lightly
And roll back down the mound beside the hole.

I thought, Who is that man? I didn't know you.
And I crept down the stairs and up the stairs
To look again, and still your spade kept lifting.   80
Then you came in. I heard your rumbling voice
Out in the kitchen, and I don't know why,
But I went near to see with my own eyes.
You could sit there with the stains on your shoes
Of the fresh earth from your own baby's grave   85
And talk about your everyday concerns.
You had stood the spade up against the wall
Outside there in the entry, for I saw it."

There is a genius here of a sort found in the brilliantly right sentence in Joyce's "The Dead" when Gretta
remembers how her dead lover of long ago stood under
her window in a cold that was to chill him to his death:
" 'I can see his eyes as well as well!' " she says to Gabriel.
" 'He was standing at the end of the wall where there
was a tree.' " Allen Tate remarks on how a vision of the
past is framed with startling immediacy by the mention
of that "tree," how it lets us share a reality vividly
present to the person speaking. The same peculiar con-
vergence of past and present occurs here, thanks to
Frost's keen sense of the power of variation and repetition: " 'Making the gravel leap and leap in air, / Leap
up, like that, like that, and land so lightly.' " Her charge
continues, and with the same haunted exactness of recollection:

"I can repeat the very words you were saying:
'Three foggy mornings and one rainy day
Will rot the best birch fence a man can build.'
Think of it, talk like that at such a time!
What had how long it takes a birch to rot   95
To do with what was in the darkened parlor?"

It is important here to notice the comparative
bareness of the attendant language when she quotes the

metaphor of the "birch fence." His inability to respond
effectively to her charges is understandable: an indictment cannot be answered when it is only more or less a
description, as if certain words and acts are inherently
contemptible. " 'I'm cursed. God, if I don't believe I'm
cursed,' " he says, and indeed he is being "cursed": there
is no word more apt for what she says to him. It is worth
recollecting here something that Frost wrote in a letter
to Wilbert Snow, a poet and professor of English at
Wesleyan University, in 1933:

> My mind goes back to how true Turgeneff holds the
> balance between protagonists and antagonists in the
> death of Bayarov in *Fathers and Sons.* He is perfect in
> his non-partizanship. I never quite like to hear a wife
> turned on against her husband or vice versa. They
> know too much about each other and they are not dis-
> interested. They lack, what they should lack, detach-
> ment. Maybe it bothers me as a breach of manners
> (Thompson, *Letters,* p. 393).

On the chance that the wife's accusations might prove
more persuasive than they should, Frost corrects the
flow of our sympathies by allowing for a curious imbal-
ance in that part of the poem (lines 97–107) given to
her complaints about the brevity of all human sorrow. It
is as if even the proportions of the poem—its form and
decorum—much less those of mourning, must be
swelled out of proper shape by the wife's obsession with
her grievances. The catalogue of her complaints is a
symptom of how for her they have become a way of
deadening a deeper grief too painful to be borne. Her
list of grievances is no adequate metaphor, that is, for
the grief she feels. All she can do is insist that " 'I won't
have grief so,' " won't have it, that is, dissipated by the
passage of time. In response, one might think of a poem

called "Good Relief" never collectied by Frost in any volume, in which he says that "No state has found a perfect cure for grief / In law, in gospel, or in root or herb." *
"Grief without grievance"—this, we have seen, was a dictum for Frost; the limits of sympathy were no less prescribed by the nature of things than were the limits of metaphor. A bit like the wife here was his sister Jeanie, as described in a letter of April 12, 1920, to Louis Untermeyer:

> She has always been antiphysical and a sensibilitist. I must say she was pretty well broken by the coarseness and brutality of the world before the war [World War I] was thought of. . . . She was willing to go almost too far to show her feeling about it, the more so that she couldn't find anyone who would go far enough. One half the world seemed unendurably bad and the other half unendurably indifferent. She included me in the unendurably indifferent. A mistake. I belong to the unendurably bad.
>
> And I suppose I am a brute in that my nature refuses to carry sympathy to the point of going crazy just because someone else goes crazy, or of dying just because someone else dies. As I get older, I find it easier to lie awake nights over other peoples' troubles. But that's as far as I go to date. In good time I will join them in death to show our common humanity (Thompson, *Letters,* p. 247).

The experience in the reading of the poem is that the wife's talk in this long peroration has a driven and dissociated quality with respect not only to the form of the poem but to the conversation going on in it. That is why the husband feels that she has somehow purged herself

* The poem can be found in Lathem and Thompson, eds., *Robert Frost: Poetry and Prose,* pp. 362–63.

and that the "talk" will of itself have relieved her and
the situation of a kind of swelling:

> "There, you have said it all and you feel better.
> You won't go now. You're crying. Close the door.
> The heart's gone out of it: why keep it up?   110
> Amy! There's someone coming down the road!"
>
> *"You*—oh, you think the talk is all. I must go—
> Somewhere out of this house. How can I make you——"
>
> "If—you—do!" She was opening the door wider.
> "Where do you mean to go? First tell me that.   115
> I'll follow and bring you back by force. I *will!*—"

Clearly, she cannot say "it all" because her grievances
are not and cannot be the equivalent of her grief, and so
she necessarily rejects what to her cannot help but
sound like condescension. Her movement out of the
house, out of discord, and into a literal "extra-vagancy"
on the road leads again to his assertion of masculine
threat and will, though this is now so tempered by an evident love and toleration and concern that the threat
sounds more like a plea and an admission of helpless-
ness.

Besides being a moving and powerful human drama,
"Home Burial" is about the limits, as revealed through
the consciousness of these two unique people, of "home"
as a place, a form, a mode of discourse in which often
unmanageably extreme states of feeling occur. But if the
limits are sad and terrifying, Frost seems nonetheless
sure of their necessity. His decorums, he would have it,
are consistent with reality and, if respected, can make
life at least manageable. Violations of decorum in a
poem or in any other formed relationship are a cause as
well as a symptom of induced terror. "Poetry is measured in more senses than one," Frost wrote to Sidney

Hook in September 1929. "It is measured feet, but more important still it is a measured amount of all we could say an we would. We shall be judged finally by the delicacy of our feeling of where to stop short" (Thompson, *Letters*, p. 361). It could be said that the central subject of this poem is poetic form seen in the metaphor of domestic form—a debate between a husband and wife about how each "shall be judged finally by the delicacy of our feeling of where to stop short." She claims that he has violated any possible decorums of grief by his lack of expressiveness. Hence, she "must get out of here" (line 37), "somewhere out of this house" (line 113)—this poem, too. He insists that she restrict her expression of grief to the house and to the boundaries of their marital contract, but he is in all this too peculiarly willful for her or for his own good. The poem ends on his exclamation " 'I *will!*' "—our only sure indication that she has by then gone through the door she has been gradually opening while they talk.

3. SOUNDINGS FOR HOME

Frost's poetry of "home" is a dramatization of the human costs and human benefits of decorum. As a reader becomes more intimate with the poems, however, it is hard to resist what seem like solicitations to think of social or psychological or domestic decorums as somehow synonymous with poetic ones. How much "extravagance" is possible within decorum; how much can be mediated by it; what extremities are induced by the constraints or failures of mediation; and what, in case of failure, are the prospects beyond decorum or mediation except nothingness or madness? These are issues central to English poetry, especially since 1800, and to the great Americans, Whitman and Stevens. One of the reasons Frost has not been taken as seriously as Stevens is in part explained by the fact that though he can be found working within some of the same dialectical oppositions, he chose resolutely, even defiantly, to work also within the circumstantially or topically familiar, as if from a list of the hundred most famous poetic and novelistic situations. So insistently ordinary, so particularized is the domestic drama of his work that it appears to be written *against* that kind of poetry which is an interpretation of itself and of its potentialities. Of some importance, too, when it comes to the understandably Anglophilic bias of literary critics, is the fact that Frost chose a landscape— for the early poems it is the intervales of the White Mountains and the countryside around Derry in southern New Hampshire; for the later ones, the Taconic Mountains around Shaftesbury and the Green Mountains around Ripton in central Vermont—which does not have anything storied about it. Even Emerson complained in his "Ode Inscribed to W. H. Channing" (and Frost repeats the complaint in his poem "New Hampshire") that "The God who made New Hampshire / Taunted the lofty land with little men." It was a landscape without poetic or sublime associations and Frost got credit for being able even to report on a region and a people so uninspiring.

Frost was treated mostly as the brilliant poet of the average human lot, and that attitude continues (despite earlier recognitions from Robert Graves and Edwin Muir, from Allen Tate, Robert Penn Warren, and especially Jarrell, and also from a more recent critic like James Cox) to stand in the way of efforts to give him credit for being a great poet precisely because it was

within that human lot that he found the glories and
plights of poetry itself.

It is difficult even now to get accustomed to this combination, no matter how many precedents are brought
to bear from Wordsworth or Coleridge. Whenever there
is a poem by one of these three involving "home" and
"extra-vagance," there is provision for a place where
the poet or central figure belongs, a kind of home base,
and for something beyond, on which the figure gazes
while he is out walking or while he is sitting on a hillside.
Both the viewer and the view are made to seem at least
latently mythological either by being put in a recipro-
cally enhancing relationship to one another or by
suggesting the degree to which human consciousness
prevents rather than assists such a relationship.

And yet it is obvious that Wordsworth and Coleridge
have proved far more accommodating than has Frost to
critics who like their poems to be about poetry. The
reason, I think, is that while it is possible, as we have already seen, to infer from Frost's poems an interest in
the drama of poetic "making," he is some of the time
even tiresomely determined not to surrender the human
actuality of his poems to a rhetoric by which action is
transformed immediately into ritual, as in the account of
the boy stealing the boat in *The Prelude*. Where such en-
largement of rhetoric occurs in Frost, it redounds almost invariably to the disadvantage of the speaker; he
must face the opposition both of nature and of the decorum, however pliant, which Frost establishes between
himself and the reader. There are "over-reachers" in
Frost, like Meserve in "Snow," but Meserve is never allowed to *"sound"* like one, and the "extra-vagance" of his
conduct is accepted by his neighbors with an admiration
that is both begrudging and impatient, until they can get

him safely back home. Frost sets up obstacles to his own capacities for transcendence, and I can think of no poem in which he allows himself (without all kinds of subtle vernacular modulations and deflations) the sustained rhetorical eloquence he admired in a poem like Shirley's "The Glories of Our Blood and State." Having met the challenge that no one can turn certain kinds of New England and especially household experience into metaphor, he then, with an exquisite pride, wants to show that he does not choose ostentatiously to extend his metaphor into a fashionable literariness. A great poem like "Home Burial" thus has to win its way, with a lean and sinewy and finally irresistible necessity, to a reading that tells us not only about lives but about Frost's own life in the writing of poetry and about his rescue of a life for poetry out of his own desperate need for circumscriptions.

He is a poet who finds his freedom of movement out of a sense of restraint: the movement to one extreme is provoked by the imminence of the other. "The Wood-Pile" is like a sequel to "Home Burial," with the man in this instance wandering from a "home" that seems little more than an abstraction to him and to us. More a meditation than a dramatic narrative, it offers the soliloquy of a lone figure walking in a winter landscape. It is a desolate scene possessed of the loneliness of "Desert Places." Attention is focused on the activity of consciousness in this isolated wanderer, and nothing characterizes him as a social being or as having any relationships to another person. While the poem has resemblances, again, to Wordsworth's "Tintern Abbey," or Coleridge's "Dejection: An Ode," it is more random in its structuring and has none of the demarcations of the descriptive-reflective mode. A better way to describe the poem is suggested in a talk by A. R. Ammons, "A Poem as a Walk." "A walk involves the whole person; it is not reproducible; its shape occurs, unfolds; it has a motion characteristic of the walker" (*Epoch,* Fall, 1968, p. 118).

The man in the poem is not, like Stevens' Crispin, "a man come out of luminous traversing," but more like the "listener" in Stevens' "The Snow Man." In each poem is a recognition of a wintry barrenness made more so in Frost by a reductive process by which possibilities of metaphor—of finding some reassuring resemblances—are gradually disposed of. At the end, the speaker in Frost's poem is as "cool" as is the listener in Stevens, and also as peculiarly unanguished by the situation in which he finds himself. It is as if the wintry prospect, the arrival at something like Stevens' First Idea, a cold clarity without redeeming deceptions, has in itself been an achievement of the imagination. It is something won against all such conventional blandishments as the "misery" of what Harold Bloom calls the "Shelleyan wind" in "The Snow Man" or the flirtatious bird in "The Wood-Pile."

The persistent difference between Frost and Stevens applies here, too, however. It resides in the kind of context the reader is asked to supply for each of the poems. Thus, despite the absence of characterizing detail, the speaker in "The Wood-Pile" shapes, from his very opening words, a human presence for us in his sentence sounds, his voice; he makes us imagine him as someone in a human plight "far from home." By comparison, the "voice" in "The Snow Man" belongs not to a person but to a quality of rumination, and Bloom is succinctly generalizing about the poem—he calls it Stevens' "most crucial poem"—when he remarks of its author that "the text he produces is condemned to offer itself for interpretation as being already an interpretation of other interpretations, rather than as what it asserts itself to be, an interpretation of life" (*Poetry and Repression,* p. 270).

"The Wood-Pile" is about being impoverished, being on the dump—to recall two related states of consciousness in Stevens—with no clues by which to locate yourself in space. All you can assuredly know about "here" is that you are far from "home":

> Out walking in the frozen swamp one gray day,
> I paused and said, "I will turn back from here.
> No, I will go on farther—and we shall see."
> The hard snow held me, save where now and then
> One foot went through. The view was all in lines
> Straight up and down of tall slim trees
> Too much alike to mark or name a place by
> So as to say for certain I was here
> Or somewhere else: I was just far from home.

If this is a *situation* that resembles winter visions of Stevens, the *sound* resists any effort to bring visionary possibilities into being. The voice of this man ("So as to say for certain I was here / Or somewhere else") cannot be expected to test the poetic potentialities of what is seen and heard and can even less be expected to cheer itself up by indulging in the hyperbolic or the sublime vocabularies. There is an informality even in the initial placements—"out walking . . . one gray day"—of the spondaic effect of "gray day," as if it were a scheduled occurrence (like "pay day") and of the possible metaphoric weight in what he says, as in the allusion (but not really) to the lack of adequate support he can expect in this landscape ("The hard snow held me, save where now and then / One foot went through"). Such anxious and innocuous precision about the relative hardness of the snow or the size and contour of the trees is humanly

and characterologically right. It expresses the kind of
paranoia that goes with any feeling of being lost and of
losing thereby a confident sense of self. Paranoia, displaced onto a small bird chancing by, becomes the motive for metaphor: the bird is endowed with the characteristics being displayed by the man observing him:

> A small bird flew before me. He was careful
> To put a tree between us when he lighted,
> And say no word to tell me who he was
> Who was so foolish as to think what *he* thought,
> He thought that I was after him for a feather—
> The white one in his tail; like one who takes
> Everything said as personal to himself.
> One flight out sideways would have undeceived him.
> And then there was a pile of wood for which
> I forgot him and let his little fear
> Carry him off the way I might have gone,
> Without so much as wishing him good-night.

There is a combination here of yearning, competi-
tiveness, and resentment that threatens to become ludicrous, a parody of the romantic search for associations
and resemblances. And the parodistic possibility is increased by the syntax of the lines about the bird's tailfeathers. They could mean that the bird was foolish to
think that the man had this particular design upon him.
But the lines could also be the speaker's rendition or imitation of what he thought the bird was thinking, i.e.,
"Who does that man think he is to think that he can get
hold of my tailfeathers?" In any event, there is more
"thinking" proposed than could possibly or profitably be
going on. That the paranoia and self-regard confusingly
attributed to the bird are really a characterization of the
man who is observing the bird is further suggested
by the accusation that the bird is "like one who
takes / Everything said as personal to himself"—a jocu-

lar simile, given the fact that there is only "one" person
around to whom the comparison might apply. If all this
is to some degree comic, it is feverishly so, the product
of intense loneliness and displacement. From its opening moment the poem becomes a human drama of dis-
possession, of failed possessiveness, and of the need to
structure realities which are not "here," to replace, in
the words of Stevens, "nothing that is not there" with
"the nothing that is."

   The only probable evidence of structure that he does
find, already put together, is the "wood-pile," a forgotten remnant of earlier efforts to make a "home" by people who, when they did it, were also away from home.
The pile of wood, which lets the speaker promptly
forget the bird, once more excites his anxious preci-
sions. He still needs to find some human resemblances,
evidences in zones and demarcations for the human capacity to make a claim on an alien landscape. What he
discovers is sparse indeed, his reassurance equally so, as
we can note in his rather pathetic exactitudes:

>   It was a cord of maple, cut and split
>   And piled—and measured, four by four by eight.
>   And not another like it could I see.
>   No runner tracks in this year's snow looped near it.
>   And it was older sure than this year's cutting,
>   Or even last year's or the year's before.
>   The wood was gray and the bark warping off it
>   And the pile somewhat sunken. Clematis
>   Had wound strings round and round it like a bundle.
>   What held it, though, on one side was a tree
>   Still growing, and on one a stake and prop,
>   These latter about to fall. I thought that only
>   Someone who lived in turning to fresh tasks
>   Could so forget his handiwork on which
>   He spent himself, the labor of his ax,
>   And leave it there far from a useful fireplace

To warm the frozen swamp as best it could
With the slow smokeless burning of decay.

The poem here could be read as a commentary on the
earlier "The Tuft of Flowers" where, instead of a bird, a
butterfly acts as a kind of pointer who "led my eye to
look / At a tall tuft of flowers beside a brook" and where
these flowers, in turn, direct his attention to signs of
work having been done by another man with "A spirit
kindred to my own; / So that henceforth I worked no
more alone." "The Wood-Pile" is obviously a much
starker poem. The "tuft of flowers" was left as a kind of
signature, a greeting and communication; the pile of
wood was simply forgotten by the man who cut and
carefully stacked it, as he went on to the distractions of
other things. The wood-pile cannot therefore prompt
the gregarious aphorisms which bring "The Tuft of
Flowers" to a close: " 'Men work together,' I told him
from the heart, / 'Whether they work together or
apart.' " Remnants of a human presence in the swamp
only remind the walker that he is completely alone in a
place that has been deserted. And his aloneness is the
more complete because there are no alternatives outside
the present circumstances which give him any comfort.
Even when he thinks of a fireplace it is not with images
of conviviality but only with the observation that it
would be "useful." The wood burns of itself, with a
warmth that cannot be felt and without giving any evidence whatever that it belongs in the world of men and
women. "With the slow smokeless burning of decay" is a
line whose sound carries an extraordinary authority and
dignity because it has emerged out of the more saunter-
ing vernacular movements at the beginning of the
poem. It induces a kind of awe because it is the acknowledgment of nature as a realm wholly independent of

human need or even human perception, and it belongs not only in what it says but in its very cadence with Wordsworth's evocation at the end of his sonnet "Mutability" of "the unimaginable touch of Time."

If the speaker "resembles" anything at the end of the poem, it is the wood-pile itself, something without even a semblance of consciousness; it is wholly self-consuming. As in "Desert Places," another poem about a lonely man walking in a landscape of snow, the man in "The Wood-Pile" could say that "The loneliness includes me unawares." This line is a little poem in itself. It has a syntactical ambiguity more common in Stevens than in Frost. It can mean both that the loneliness includes him but is unaware of doing so, and that the loneliness includes him and *he* is not aware of its doing so by virtue of his near obliteration. In either case he is not so much included as wiped out; he is included as if he were inseparable from, indistinguishable from, the thing that includes him. He is on the point of being obliterated by the landscape, rather than allowed to exist even as an observer of it, much less a mediating or transcending presence.

Despite Frost's devotion to Emerson, it was impossible for him ever to feel that to become "nothing" on a "bare common" is also to become, as in the opening paragraphs of *Nature,* a "part or parcel of God." For Frost's lonely walkers, far from "home," nothing can come from such nothing, and they therefore must try to speak again and in such a way as to make known an ordinary human presence. Frost in this mood is bleaker than Stevens. He resists the transcendentalist willingness to disentangle the self from the ties of "home" and from any responsibility to domesticate whatever might be encountered while one is "extra-vagant." Stevens, but not Frost, could say with Emerson that on that "bare common," faced with evidences of a primal and impoverished reality of "snow puddles at twilight under a clouded sky," it is possible by the power of heightened imagination so to transform reality that

> the name of the nearest friend sounds then foreign and accidental: to be brothers, to be acquaintances, master or servant, is then a trifle and a disturbance. I am the lover of uncontained and immortal beauty. In the wilderness, I find something more dear and connate than in streets or villages. In the tranquil landscape, and especially in the distant line of the horizon, man beholds somewhat as beautiful as his own nature.

Frost's whole theory of "sentence sounds" is implicitly a way of taking an exception to transcendental vision and to the Sublime as an alternative to the discovery of barrenness: "I cultivate . . . the hearing imagination rather than the seeing imagination though I should not want to be without the latter" (Thompson, *Letters*, p. 130). Barrenness, poverty, the mind of winter are posited as conditions of life and of poverty by both Frost and Stevens. But while in Stevens these exist in a tradition that passed from Emerson through Santayana, with a dialectic weighted toward sublimity and supreme fiction, in Frost, following a tradition that passed from Emerson through William James, these same conditions are held within a quite different dialectical tension. "Home" exerts such a simultaneous restraint on and incentive to "extra-vagance" that anyone who feels it must become pugnacious in the expressed need for ventilation, for some degree of imaginative license. Hence the sharply more individuated and personalized tone of Frost's poems. In that respect, "The Wood-Pile" is perhaps more quiescent than "Desert Places," in that it does not, or cannot, go on to some final combative assertion of a confronted self, the sort of thing we hear in

They cannot scare me with their empty spaces
Between stars—on stars where no human race is.
I have it in me so much nearer home
To scare myself with my own desert places.

The self-assertion here is implicit in the slangy school-yard tone of "They cannot scare me" as it applies itself to something akin to Eliot's "vacant interstellar spaces." It is typical of Frost that he would bring, without any signaling, a fashionable-sounding phraseology of self-diminishment into combination with that kind of vernacular voice which draws its strength from a sense of rootedness, no matter how unfertile the soil. "Home" is the place where one might hear a phrase like "they cannot scare me"; the anxious tension that goes into that sound is what induced Frost to change the second line of this passage from its original form in the first printing (*The American Mercury*, April, 1934), where it read "Between stars—on stars void of human races." Frost settled on a sound altogether more vernacular and idiomatic and which got rid of the literarily portentous word "void."

Voice is the most important, distinguishing, and conspicuously insistent feature of Frost's poetry and of his writing about poetry. There is scarcely a single poem which does not ask the reader to imagine a human character equivalent to the movement of voice, and there is no other poet in English of whom this is so emphatically the case. Behind the theory of "voice" and "sentence sounds" that he presented wholly as a literary choice, behind his related insistence that poetry was as good as it was "dramatic," there is a psychological and moral imperative. It can be most simply described as a revulsion against the idea of human transparency. Under any and all circumstances he would resist becoming a "transpar-

ent eyeball." It would mean getting lost. This was never
an agreeable prospect for him, despite little hints to the
contrary in "Directive," and there are therefore no
poems by him of visionary afflatus. There are, however,
close to terrifying poems about wandering off, losing
the self, or belonging nowhere. That is the plight of the
men in the poems we have been considering and of the
man in "Acquainted with the Night" who has "out-
walked the furthest city light."

> I have stood still and stopped the sound of feet
> When far away an interrupted cry
> Came over houses from another street,
>
> But not to call me back or say good-by. . . .

The deprived figure in "Desert Places" is faced with
another threat of the same kind: of disappearing without any record of his having been there or any protest at
his going. He is confronted with "a blanker whiteness of
benighted snow / With no expression, nothing to express." We hear their voices in a kind of wilderness. The
situation in which these Frosty figures find themselves
does have an equivalence in Stevens where the observer
in "The Snow Man" "listens in the snow, / And, nothing
himself, beholds / Nothing that is not there and the
nothing that is." But the very suppleness of syntactical
maneuverings in these lines, and in much of Stevens'
poetry, with its intricate patterns of repetition and echoing, is meant to dissuade any reader from finding evidences in the voice of an imaginable speaker. Both poets
propose a similar plight, but in one it is of life and in the
other of the poetic imagination.

Stevens and Frost part company at the point where
Stevens exercises his belief, with Santayana, that the
power of the imagination can create realities in a poem

that can exist in defiance of the evoked realities of a "fact." Truth was not required, as it was for Frost and the William James of *Pragmatism,* to "grow up inside of" finite experiences; rather, it was something that imagination could *create* as an alternative form of experience. Stevens himself very beautifully argues the case, using metaphors of "home" and "extra-vagance," in Part One of "Three Academic Pieces":

> . . . the intensification of reality by resemblance increases realization and this increased realization is pleasurable. It is as if a man who lived indoors should go outdoors on a day of sympathetic weather. His realization of the weather would exceed that of a man who lives outdoors. It might, in fact, be intense enough to convert the real world about him into an imagined world. In short, a sense of reality keen enough to be in excess of the normal sense of reality creates a reality of its own. Here what matters is that the intensification of the sense of reality creates a resemblance: that reality of its own is a reality. This may be going round a circle, first clockwise, then anti-clockwise. If the savor of life is the savor of reality, the fact will establish itself whichever way one approaches it.

True "realization" for Frost occurs *after* the man who went outdoors comes back in. "I opened the door so my last look / Should be taken outside a house and book." Thus Frost begins a poem called "One More Brevity," in his last volume. But the "look," while a perfectly "extra-vagant" one, in that it is beyond both "home" and literature, is really a way of assuring himself that the stars are in place so that he may sleep more securely: "I said I would see how Sirius kept / His watchdog eye on what remains / To be gone into if not explained." "Intensifications" while "out of doors" are not in themselves a true form of "realization," so far as Frost is concerned, since the very nature of metaphor involves for him a constant pressure, *at some point,* against intensifications and the excesses that go with them. Quite charmingly, while the man is looking up at the star Sirius a dog slips by "to be my problem guest: / Not a heavenly dog made manifest, / But an earthly dog of the carriage breed." This is a fine example of what Frost means when he says "I would be willing to throw away everything else but that: enthusiasm tamed by metaphor" ("Education by Poetry").

For Stevens, on the other hand, metaphor, or "re-semblances," *creates* the conditions for enthusiasm:

> . . . it is not too extravagant to think of resemblances and of the repetition of resemblances as a source of the ideal. In short, metaphor has its aspect of the ideal. This aspect of it cannot be dismissed merely because we think that we have long since outlived the ideal. The truth is that we are constantly outliving it and yet the ideal itself remains alive with an enormous life (Part One, "Three Academic Pieces").

In Frost, the ideal aspect of metaphor exists only that it may be tested. Metaphor is an education by which the reader learns to be "at ease with figurative values," at ease not to luxuriate but the better to know "how far [he] may expect to ride" a metaphor "and when it may break down with [him]" ("Education by Poetry"). That is how one becomes "safe in history" or "in" science. Being "safe in" anything is clearly not a condition proposed by Stevens' "Notes Toward a Supreme Fiction." Stevens therefore can write a kind of ecstatically imagined poetry seldom found in Frost:

> Close the cantina. Hood the chandelier.
> The moonlight is not yellow but a white
> That silences the ever-faithful town.

How pale and how possessed a night it is,
How full of exhalations of the sea . . .
All this is older than its oldest hymn,
Has no more meaning than tomorrow's bread.
But let the poet on his balcony
Speak and the sleepers in their sleep shall move,
Waken, and watch the moonlight on their floors.
This may be benediction, sepulcher,
And epitaph. It may, however, be
An incantation that the moon defines
By mere example opulently clear.
And the old casino likewise may define
An infinite incantation of our selves
In the grand decadence of the perished swans.
                    (From "Academic Discourse at Havana")

Stevens' is a poetry of possible impossibility, a poetry of vacation, which is at least as valuable as any "momentary stay against confusion," and bound to be more rapturous.

When Stevens and Frost met, not for the first time, in February 1940 in Key West, Stevens remarked, "Your trouble, Robert, is that you write poems about—*things.*" To which Frost replied, "Your trouble, Wallace, is that you write poems about—bric a brac" (Thompson, II, 666). In an earlier meeting, in Florida during the spring of 1935, Stevens had apparently complained that Frost simply wrote too much. " 'You have written on subjects that were assigned,' is what he meant," Frost remarked in March 1935 in a talk at the University of Miami (Florida) in apparent allusion to Stevens. Frost's answer, if he gave one, can be guessed from what he says a year later, 12 March 1936, in a letter to L. W. Payne, Jr.:

Oh I mustnt forget I wanted to correct you in a matter. Somewhere I found you saying lately that my formula of twenty-five years ago—Common in experience and

uncommon in writing—meant that the subject should
be common in experience but that it should be written
up in an uncommon style. I believe that may be Munson's mistake. [Frost is referring to a book by Gorham
B. Munson: *Robert Frost: A Study in Sensibility and Good
Sense* (New York, 1927).] You're not to blame for it.
The subject should be common in experience and uncommon in books is a better way to put it. It should
have happened to everyone but it should have occurred to no one before as material. That's quite different. I was silent as to the need of giving old themes a
new settings of words. I am silent still (Thompson, *Letters*, pp. 426–27).

What is "common in experience"? Obviously it could
be said that one common experience is "impoverishment," as in a run-down house, and that another is
the attempt at solace, as in painting the house. And it
could also be said that these "experiences" can be found
as frequently in Stevens as in Frost. But the difference is
that in Stevens they are not "common"; it can be said
without disparagement that they are instead literary and
theoretical; they are states of poetic rather than of social
consciousness; they call for actions of mind rather than
actions of bodies. The leaves which fall in Frost's "The
Leaf-Treader" are not the Shelleyan leaves of Stevens'
"Domination of Black," and the response to them, as a
threat of death, is in Frost not a swirling rhetoric of cosmic incantatory fear but rather a pep talk to the
speaker's knee: "But it was no reason I had to go because they had to go. / Now up, my knee, to keep on top
of another year of snow." Similarly, the "dirty house" in
Stevens' "A Postcard from the Volcano" gets at the end
"smeared with the gold of the opulent sun," while the
"old old house" in Frost's "The Investment" is "renewed
with paint" because the man and wife want to "get some
color and music out of life."

So "common" is the experience in Frost that the phrasing of that last line is purposefully clichéd. Or rather it is not so much clichéd as an allusion to cliché. The reader is asked to indulge in a cliché, and to do so without irony, without even the patronizations of compassion. After all, that paint cost money; it truly means something in the life of a couple who share a community of deprivation and respond to it with practical imagination. A reader and writer who conspire in a sympathetic understanding of domestic and social clichés are in a different relationship to one another than are a reader and writer who conspire in the understanding of literary allusions or the pressure of one literary text or tradition on another. Frost asks us to be *both* kinds of readers; and his unique difficulty is in the demand that we be common and literary all at once. Which is a way of suggesting, again, the great difference sometimes between Frost, whose extensive literary allusiveness is always less apparent than are his allusions to clichés, and any of the other great figures of the first half of this century.

West-Running Brook, where "The Investment" appears, has other poems of deprivation, some well known, like "Bereft" and "Acquainted with the Night," but also some little known, like "The Cocoon":

> As far as I can see, this autumn haze
> That spreading in the evening air both ways
> Makes the new moon look anything but new
> And pours the elm tree meadow full of blue,
> Is all the smoke from one poor house alone,
> With but one chimney it can call its own;
> So close it will not light an early light,
> Keeping its life so close and out of sight
> No one for hours has set a foot outdoors
> So much as to take care of evening chores.
> The inmates may be lonely womenfolk.

> I want to tell them that with all this smoke
> They prudently are spinning their cocoon
> And anchoring it to an earth and moon
> From which no winter gale can hope to blow it—
> Spinning their own cocoon did they but know it.

Once again, "a poor house alone," with scarcely a sign of habitation or embellishment; once again, an observer with some admitted limitation of view ("As far as I can see"); once again, a question about the nature of a "home" when there are almost no signs of life around it. The observer is much like the man in "The Census-Taker" who wonders "what to do that could be done— / About the house—about the people not there." "The Cocoon" is a poem of seeing more than of walking, and the extravagance consists in the effort to sustain the metaphor of a "cocoon" when there is so little to support it. The observer is offered some chimney smoke, to be sure—more, at least, than "the smokeless burning of decay" in "The Wood-Pile"—and this is apparently enough to warrant an "investment" of imagination, a kind of poetic imitation of the action of the couple who renew the paint on their old, old home. Nonetheless, the speaker here is bothered—he has been looking at the house "for hours"—by the disparity between his rather modest metaphor, on the one hand, his bit of extravagance about the curling smoke, and, on the other, the lonely obliviousness of the people—if, indeed, there are any inside the house—to the significance of their fire smoke. Clearly, there is nothing extravagant about them; the house keeps whatever life it has "close and out of sight." He "wants to tell them" they are spinning a cocoon, and that in so doing they are making a link between heaven and earth. But this is something that they do not and cannot "know."

There is a desire, not urgent but nonetheless humanly

and poetically challenging, to see what can be "made" of the "poor" house here, the old house in "The Investment," and even the house that has been left behind in "The Wood-Pile," with its merely "useful fireplace." The places and persons in these poems are not so much drab as stripped and bare, and the details given about them dispel rather than suggest any possibility of character or of eccentricity. It is a barrenness that is exemplary or even mythological in tendency, establishing a testing ground for observers who want to make something up about it—not a supreme fiction, perhaps no more than "some color and music" or an encouraging metaphor.

These poems are thus somewhat different from the dramatizations already looked into of marital struggles or of ambulatory itineraries away from home and back again. They are not the kind most commonly associated with Frost and are seldom anthologized or discussed. As a result they have not as yet established a context for themselves by which the familiar Frostean disengagement from any sort of motionlessness or stasis can be seen not only as a moral but as a literary act. In these particular instances, the literary element, the degree to which the poems become a species of literary criticism, is especially strong because the speaker in something like "The Cocoon," even more evidently than in "The Wood-Pile," is a poet as well as a chance observer. But he is a poet about whom Frost, as an overarching presence, exercises some of his most subtle and most gentle discriminations.

Two other poems in this group, "On the Heart's Beginning to Cloud the Mind" and "The Figure in the Doorway," are about houses looked at with some sort of ulterior, "creative" intention by a poet-observer from a passing train. The poems are placed next to one another in *A Further Range,* which also includes "Desert Places,"

"Design," and "Provide, Provide." All these are medita-
tions on bleakness, a subject of increasing frequency in
Frost's work beginning with his fourth volume, *New
Hampshire*. They are different from earlier poems about
the failures of "home" to nourish the imagination in that
the narrator is disengaged and relatively dispassionate.
The houses are discovered by accident, and it is implied
that the viewer is somebody who wanders less in a
search for signs and embodiments than to amuse himself with the possibility of their existence.

The title "On the Heart's Beginning to Cloud the
Mind" admits to something implicit in the other poems
in this group: that because the observer has no active
part in whatever is going on inside the house, he makes
things up which are not only fictitious (that, of course, is
his right) but also wrong-headed and banal. The opening of the poem—"Something I saw or thought I
saw / In the desert at midnight in Utah"—is a possible
allusion to Virgil's *Aut videt aut vidisse putat,* as Reuben
Brower observes, or, as likely, to *Paradise Lost,* where at
the end of Book I, "some belated peasant sees / Or
dreams he sees" some fairy elves. But the comic rhyme
"I saw / Utah" makes the allusion parodistic. We can be
reminded also of "For Once, Then, Something," which is
also a poem about trying to have a vision, trying to see
"something" which is probably only that—"some thing"
and not a metaphor for any thing. Here, the landscape is a barren desert observed from the lower berth
of a fast train. The man sees "A flickering human pathetic light / That was maintained against the night, / It
seemed to me, by the people there, / With a God-
forsaken brute despair." It is this mere supposition ("it
seemed to me") which makes him think that his heart is
"beginning to cloud" his mind. The alternative possibility—that the light is a burning tree kept flaming by

various people at their pleasure—is, he has to admit, only "a tale of a better kind." But his fictionalizing is at least adequate to a further conjuration: he invents a domestic scene wherein a woman in the darkened room of this hypothetical house shares with him a view of the desert scene. She, however, is without fear or suspicion. He guesses that she knows, as he does not, what the lights "really" mean, and as the poem nears its end he manages to "typify" the woman and her husband in a nascently mythological way:

> Life is not so sinister-grave.
> Matter of fact has made them brave.
> He is husband, she is wife.
> She fears not him, they fear not life.
> They know where another light has been,
> And more than one, to theirs akin,
> But earlier out for bed tonight,
> So lost on me in my surface flight.

"Surface flight" necessarily describes more than the train's movement. It reminds us of the unabashed superficiality of the man's vision. The concluding lines are justly critical of the poetic vision or realization that precedes them: the engine smoke abets the sentimentality of his "clouded mind." The claim that he sees "far into" anything suggests distance rather than powers of penetration:

> This I saw when waking late,
> Going by at a railroad rate,
> Looking through wreaths of engine smoke
> Far into the lives of other folk.

The poem is a critical inquiry into itself and its own procedures. It dramatizes the action of a mind attempt-

ing to make metaphorical enhancements, but its language suggests that the action is too casually a violation
of privacies. The kind of mythologizing in which this
man engages is often a "flight" over the surface of reality rather than into it. Lawrence's delighted remark
about Whitman comes to mind: "ALLNESS! shrieks
Walt at a crossroads, going whizz over an unwary Red
Cap Indian."

As if spoken from the same train window, "The Figure in the Doorway" reads like an effort to correct such
poetic "flights" from wobbling off course. Frost's train-
window poems are different from Rossetti's—as in the
series "A Trip to Paris and Belgium"—in that they raise
not merely phenomenological problems but questions of
misreading, of necessary failures of perception:

> The grade surmounted, we were riding high
> Through level mountains nothing to the eye
> But scrub oak, scrub oak and the lack of earth
> That kept the oaks from getting any girth.
> But as through the monotony we ran,
> We came to where there was a living man.
> His great gaunt figure filled his cabin door,
> And had he fallen inward on the floor,
> He must have measured to the further wall.
> But we who passed were not to see him fall.
> The miles and miles he lived from anywhere
> Were evidently something he could bear.
> He stood unshaken, and if grim and gaunt,
> It was not necessarily from want.
> He had the oaks for heating and for light.
> He had a hen, he had a pig in sight.
> He had a well, he had the rain to catch.
> He had a ten-by-twenty garden patch.
> Nor did he lack for common entertainment.
> That I assume was what our passing train meant.
> He could look at us in our diner eating,
> And if so moved uncurl a hand in greeting.

The vision of the "great gaunt figure" filling the cabin door prompts little more than superficial reportage. Four lines in a row begin with the repeated "he had"; the man's possessions are then as dutifully listed. It reads as if the speaker were determined not to make anything out of what he sees. Beyond these measurements, all we learn about the man is the merest guess-work. In an Empsonian sense, the poem has a pastoral inclination: it is "assumed" that the passing train is "common entertainment" for the "grim" figure in the cabin door and that he must sometimes be moved (even though he is not on this one occasion, when the speaker has opportunity to see him) to "uncurl a hand in greeting." As in "On the Heart's Beginning to Cloud the Mind," there is scarcely any scene at all here; there is no material for poetry except what might be guessed *if* the spectator were in a position to watch long enough. This, then, for all its self-discipline, also becomes a "surface flight," and the best he can do with the image of the giant man in the doorway is to make a "tall tale," in a grotesque sense of the term, about what might happen at some future time: "And had he fallen inward on the floor, / He must have measured to the further wall. / But we who passed were not to see him fall." Frost's evident intentions in the poem are pleasantly confirmed in a speech given at Bread Loaf on July 2, 1956, where he said of "The Figure in the Doorway" that "it might not be true of him at all, but there is such a thing. I might have been all wrong about him. He might have been a candidate for the Democratic party" (Cook, p. 110).

These poems are evidence of Frost's congenital circumspection about "extra-vagance"—about making things up while "in flight," about inventing other people's lives without getting intimately involved with them, about the problematics of mere accidental relationships,

mere glimpses of a "field looked into going past"
("Desert Places") or glimpses of a desert or a house from
a fast train, or something so grandly and therefore remotely conceived as is "the universe" by the young man
who cries out at the beginning of "The Most of It":

> He thought he kept the universe alone;
> For all the voice in answer he could wake
> Was but the mocking echo of his own
> From some tree-hidden cliff across the lake.
> Some morning from the boulder-broken beach   5
> He would cry out on life, that what it wants
> Is not its own love back in copy speech,
> But counter-love, original response.
> And nothing ever came of what he cried
> Unless it was the embodiment that crashed   10
> In the cliff's talus on the other side,
> And then in the far-distant water splashed,
> But after a time allowed for it to swim,
> Instead of proving human when it neared
> And someone else additional to him,   15
> As a great buck it powerfully appeared,
> Pushing the crumpled water up ahead,
> And landed pouring like a waterfall,
> And stumbled through the rocks with horny tread,
> And forced the underbrush—and that was all.   20

This is the most powerful of what might be called his
spectatorial poems, those in which a wandering figure
tries to locate a "home" by the exercise of vision, the
making of metaphor, or the making of sound to which
an answering call is expected. Along with the poems
being discussed in this section (and "Neither Out Far
nor In Deep") "The Most of It" is a poem in which
"life" is being asked to do some or all of a "poet's" work.
The request is illegitimate, and it is made not by Frost
but by the speakers or spectators—or would-be poets—
in his poems. If their calls on "life" have a pathos of in-

nocence, they also elicit that Frostean exasperation
which is aroused by anyone who acts politically, or poetically, as if the world owes him a living, or as if it is easy
to be "at home in the metaphors" one contrives about
the world.

Metaphors, like other marriages, are not made in
heaven. About this, Frost and Stevens would agree. Metaphors are made by poets, either by those who write
poems or by the kind of Emersonian poet who is potentially in any one of us. Significantly, the poem following
"The Most of It" is "Never Again Would Birds' Song Be
the Same." There, the world itself has already been
made our "home," partly by the fact that the "birds"
"from having heard the daylong voice of Eve / Had
added to their own an oversound." It is a sound that still
"persists" in the wilderness which is of our present moment. But her "sound," her "voice," was not, we have to
remember, directed to birds at all in any naive expectation that they would answer her in kind or in any other
way. The birds simply heard her voice as it was "carried
aloft" from the intercourse between Adam and Eve, the
"call or laughter" of their daily life together before the
Fall. To the extent, then, that the sound of birds has
been crossed with and become an echo of human sound,
it is not to be confused with the kind of sound the man
in the opening lines of "The Most of It" requests as an
answering call from the wilderness around him. Keeping the universe alone, he is an Adam without an Eve.
To paraphrase a passage from Frost's "The Constant
Symbol" which we have already looked at, it might be
said that he wants to "keep" the universe without spending very much on it. He has not learned the essential lesson that "strongly spent is synonymous with kept." Or,
to make another comparison, he "keeps" the world the
way the old man keeps house in "An Old Man's Winter

Night," forever making sounds, even to "beating on a box," in order to lay some claim to the world around him: "One aged man—one man—can't keep a house / A farm, a countryside, or if he can / It's thus he does it of a winter's night."

The supposed model for this isolate and solitary man, this man who has not entered into or engaged upon any kind of "marriage," was, according to Thompson, a young poet named Wade Van Dore whom Frost met first in Franconia, New Hampshire, in 1922 and later at the University of Michigan in 1925. Frost helped Van Dore with the publication of his first volume of poetry, *Far Lake,* in 1930, and it includes two poems, "The Echo" and "Man Alone," whose superficial resemblances to "The Most of It" encourage Thompson to claim that Frost's poem, especially under its original title "Making the Most of It," was meant as an "ironic reply" to Van Dore's work (Thompson, II, 361). And indeed some passages from Van Dore might easily have provoked Frost, like the following from "The Echo":

> Made mellow by a wall of trees
> My call came swiftly back to me.
> My word the forest would not take
> Came bounding back across the lake.
> Through outer trees to shade grown black
> I peered and saw, like strips of snow
> That form in rocks the ages crack
> The trunks of birches, half aglow.
> Again I called, and now I stirred
> A fearful bird to swiftly fly.
> Far off I heard his angry scream,
> But not a gladdened human cry.
> It seemed I could not overthrow
> The brooding barrier of the trees.
> My voice grew swift, my call more keen,
> But always backward came the word

Of it to me, that seemed to sigh
For him I sought, for all reply.

Or this passage from "Man Alone":

If he should loudly call, then stand and wait
Until the sound had traveled far and made
A voice reply, he'd know the forest held
No mate for him. An echo would reply,
Giving him back his lonely call and word.
A deer might start. . . .

The similarities of circumstance and phrasing between these poems and Frost's "The Most of It" are extensive enough not to need comment, and it seems
probable that Van Dore's poems were an incentive for
Frost's. But to treat "The Most of It" as an ironic "reply"
to Van Dore is to miss the altogether more important
fact that Frost's poem is too powerful for such irony.
Van Dore provided no more than a nudge, if that, push-
ing Frost in the direction of a poem already waiting in
him to be written, a great poem that is a culmination of
the motifs and themes we have been looking into. In
some sense, too, it brings into sharper focus many of his
poems about echoing and shows the degree to which his
poetry absorbs and continually comments upon the
echoing streams, hills, and rocks of pastoral poetry, the
"Sweet Echo, sweetest nymph that lives unseen" of Milton's "Comus," and especially the echoes that greet
Wordsworth's Boy of Winander. The poem exists within
a large poetic context of "echoing" that has been best
located in English poetry by John Hollander and Angus
Fletcher. In that sense, Wordsworth's "There Was a
Boy" must be thought to have had a stronger claim on
Frost than a quite minor poem by Van Dore which itself,
directly or indirectly, derives from passages like the fol-

lowing, taken from the 1805 version of *The Prelude,*
Book V:

> There was a Boy, ye knew him well, ye Cliffs
> And Islands of Winander! many a time,
> At evening, when the stars had just begun
> To move along the edges of the hills,
> Rising or setting, would he stand alone,
> Beneath the trees, or by the glimmering lake;
> And there, with fingers interwoven, both hands
> Pressed closely palm to palm and to his mouth
> Uplifted, he, as through an instrument,
> Blew mimic hootings to the silent owls
> That they might answer him. And they would shout
> Across the watery vale, and shout again
> Responsive to his call, with quivering peals,
> And long halloos, and screams, and echoes loud
> Redoubled and redoubled; concourse wild
> Of mirth and jocund din! And, when it chanced
> That pauses of deep silence mocked his skill,
> Then, sometimes, in that silence, while he hung
> Listening, a gentle shock of mild surprise
> Has carried far into his heart the voice
> Of mountain torrents; or the visible scene
> Would enter unawares into his mind
> With all its solemn imagery, its rocks
> Its woods, and that uncertain heaven, received
> Into the bosom of the steady lake.
>
> This Boy was taken from his Mates and died
> In childhood, ere he was ten years old.
> Fair are the woods, and beauteous is the spot,
> The Vale where he was born: the Church-yard hangs
> Upon a slope above the Village School,
> And there, along that bank, when I have passed
> At evening, I believe, that oftentimes
> A full half-hour together I have stood
> Mute—looking at the grave in which he lies.

Wordsworth's poem is closer to Frost's than its
"echoes loud / Redoubled and redoubled" might super-

ficially suggest. Nature responds, but only with what is initially rejected as inadequate in "The Most of It" and with what becomes inadequate in Wordsworth—with "copy speech." The Boy has to blow *"mimic* hootings," an echo of the echo he seeks, before he hears anything at all, and even this eventually gives way to a "deep silence" that "mocks his skill." During these "pauses" the images "carried far into his heart" may be less awesome but are no less mysterious than "it" or "the buck." The poem ends with a "muteness" confirmed by the Boy's death and by the reflective man who stands as a "mute observer" beside his grave. We are left with a mere chronicler of echoes no longer to be heard; the man can himself call no voices out of silence, even his own. Under circumstances so imposingly mythological (the Boy is dead before the poem but lives in the memory of the man and of the cliffs and islands), "deep silence" is not meant to be *less* than echoing sound, and possibly it is more. So, too, with the "response" in "The Most of It": to be told that "that was all" does not, needless to say, mean that "all" is nothing.

The difference between the Wordsworth and the Frost poems is that in Frost the spectator can draw no sustenance from memories of anyone like "The Boy of Winander," and must face the likelihood that his human presence is altogether an irrelevance. But that does not mean that the "it" at the end should be written off, as it generally is, as a mere terrifying negation of meaning. It is an awe-inspiring and wonderful representation of what we do not know and cannot name—what poets cannot name any more. The final words of the poem, "and that was all," are addressed not to the inadequacy of the buck to live up to the spectator's sentimental expectations but to the incapacity of the spectator, and of us, to find any way to account for the buck, its power and fantastic indifference. If one wants to talk about irony in the poem, then the irony is directed not toward the romantic attitude but toward a naive version of it, one that takes no account of what Wordsworth himself saw as the merely contingent boundaries of the self in the face of undefinable, inarticulable influences.

Of the opening, Frost remarked in "On Extravagance," "It begins with this kind of person: 'he thought he kept the universe alone;' . . . just that one line could be the whole poem, you know." I think Frost wanted to suggest that very likely nothing would be "realizable" from the person from whom the rest of the poem issued, a person who cannot *"make* the most of it." A benighted version of Wordsworth's boy who lets whatever occurs be "carried far into his heart" or "enter unawares into his mind," this man apparently will not let himself be satisfied with anything that comes back to him, echo, silence, or embodiment. But he stands there bathed in a mythological heroism nevertheless. What does happen at the end, in fact or in his mind, is far too awesome and magnificent to have been conceived merely as an ironic commentary on a pathetic but hardly disreputable desire to find "counter-love, original response" in nature. Though the spectator does not get what he apparently wants, he does get, and the reader with him, a vision of some fabulousness beyond domestication.

"The Most of It" is a kind of poem which creates adherents rather than readers. Any "analysis" is resented as reductive, and of course it is. The poem suspends itself brilliantly in such a large but wavering mythological context that its grandeur depends upon our not being able very precisely to answer those questions which, again, Frost himself persistently wanted to put to a poem: "By whom, where and when is the question" (Preface to *A Way Out*). As for "whom," the wholly

elusive "he" is never characterized even by a speaking
voice, and yet "he" is placed over against an immense
"where," the "universe" and later the "boulder-broken
beach" that looks toward a cliff hidden by trees. As for
"when" his calling could have taken place, line 5 hints at
a specific time ("Some morning"), but lines 9 and 10
("and nothing ever came of what he cried / Unless it was
the embodiment . . .") suggest that he "called out"
whenever he felt like it. To specify a specific dramatic
situation here or in other crucial poems by Frost, like
"Spring Pools" or "Hyla Brook" or "The Silken Tent," is
to expose to ridicule both the situation and the person
speaking. By its impressive generality of reference, to
"the universe," to "life," to "counter-love," the poem
implicitly requests us *not* to localize. Indeed, grammatically at least, the evidence is that "life" itself wants an answer as much as does the man: "He would cry out on
life that what it wants / Is not its own love back in copy
speech, / But counter-love, original response." Those
phrases are peculiar; their rather technical angularity
makes it sound as if a prescription were being called
for. And "original response" is close to oxymoronic since
to call for a sound that has an unprecedented origin is
to deny its capacity to be "re-sponsive," a word which in
the Latin sense means to pledge back something that has
once been received. It is as if "life" itself were making
the demand on the world through the demand of this
single man in it, and as if life's demands were inherently
wonderful as well as impossible.

In the best and simplest sense the poem is exciting for
the largeness of its embrace, and because the man is
beautifully anxious that "life" be allowed to exalt and
enrapture itself. So that even without knowing classical
literary analogues in echo literature, and all that is implied therein about man and his relation to the universe,

any reader feels the presence and pressure here of a
great human tradition and a great human predicament.
In the expansive gestures of inclusiveness made at the
outset, in the efforts to bring a universe into the focus of
the self and its immediate environments, the poem is
about the attempt to "make" a home by demanding a
"return," a coming back of sound enriched and transformed by its movements out into the universe. If the
man or "life" asks too much, then the response which
they do get by the end of the poem is at least to that
degree more powerfully informative about the nature of
things than if they had asked for too little. If the aspiration is always to bring "home" what would otherwise be
unseen, an element left to chaos, then at least the effort
should show not only what can but also what cannot be
given house room. Apparently that includes this horny-
hoofed creature, if indeed it even exists, who "lands"
only to "stumble" and "force" its way back into the obscurity from which it came. "The most exciting movement in nature," Frost says in "The Poetry of Amy Lowell," "is not progress, advance, but expansion and
contraction, the opening and shutting of the eye, the
hand, the heart, the mind. We throw our arms wide
with a gesture of religion to the universe, we close them
around a person."

The image of this man throwing his arms "wide," as it
were, "with a gesture of religion to the universe," domi-
nates the poem only to line 10; after that, the poem
more or less ignores him, and devotes itself to the great
buck. It is said to be an "embodiment" but of what? It is
possible to read lines 9 and 10, "and nothing ever came
of what he cried / Unless it was the embodiment that
crashed" so that "it" refers to "nothing." The embodiment in that case becomes his hallucination of—to quote
again the ever-useful phrase from Stevens—the "noth-

ing that is not there and the nothing that is." Even if the embodiment does physically exist, its appearance is wholly fortuitious; it is no necessary "response" at all. Frost's use of the word "unless" is characteristic, as already seen in "A Cliff Dwelling" where "no habitation meets the eye / Unless in the horizon rim . . ." And it functions, as do his frequent uses of "as if" or "something," when talking about presences, to induce in his meditative poems some of the speculative excitement that belongs also to his narratives of haunts or ghosts, like "The Witch of Coös." Symbols are thus poised ready to come into being, but only into the most uncertain kind of significance. The end of the poem, "and that was all," suggests that something happened for which we have no better language. Doubtless Thoreau would have been satisfied, if we are to believe a passage from *Walden,* another example of how various are the writings, including Cowper's "The Castaway," which Frost might have had in mind as he wrote this poem:

> When, as was commonly the case, I had none to commune with, I used to raise the echoes by striking with a paddle on the side of my boat, filling the surrounding woods with circling and dilating sound, stirring them up as the keeper of the menagerie his wild beasts, until I elicited a growl from every wooded vale and hillside ("The Ponds").

But Thoreau, famously, was not looking for someone else additional to him; far from being worried that he "kept the universe alone" he seemed quite happy to be "the keeper of a menagerie" of wild beasts. The man in the poem is not so lucky—or so superficial. He wants more, the "most," but his gesture to the universe does not close even around a person. Rather, we are left with the possibility that the gesture remains open, unless it closes, self-protectively, before an image of vastation or of animal necessity which admits, as the repeated use of the word "and" in the last three lines suggests, of no subordination or modification or taming. This "embodiment" could be in no one's menagerie.

One further way of allowing the poem its proper resonance is to read it as part of the sequence of three poems in which Frost placed it in *A Witness Tree*. It appears first, followed by "Never Again Would Birds' Song Be the Same" and then by "The Subverted Flower." All three suggest, as indeed do Frost's earliest love poems in *A Boy's Will,* that consciousness is determined in part by the way one "reads" the response of nature to human sound. By placing "Never Again Would Birds' Song be the Same" between "The Most of It" and "The Subverted Flower," Frost once again reveals his deep commitment to married love as a precondition for discovering human "embodiments" in nature, for discovering Adam and Eve, whose intercourse included the "call or laughter" that was "carried aloft" where ever since it has been "crossed" with the song of birds:

> He would declare and could himself believe
> That the birds there in all the garden round
> From having heard the daylong voice of Eve
> Had added to their own an oversound,
> Her tone of meaning but without the words.   5
> Admittedly an eloquence so soft
> Could only have had an influence on birds
> When call or laughter carried it aloft.
> Be that as may be, she was in their song.
> Moreover her voice upon their voices crossed   10
> Had now persisted in the woods so long
> That probably it never would be lost.
> Never again would birds' song be the same.
> And to do that to birds was why she came.

Nothing in Frost more beautifully exemplifies the degree to which "tone of meaning" or sounds of voice create resemblances between birds and Eve, between our first parents and us, between the unfallen and the fallen world. On such resemblances as these Frost would have us imagine a habitable world and a human history. This is a poem which establishes differentiations only that it may then blur them. The delicate hint of a possible but very light sarcasm in the first line blends into but is not wholly dissipated by a concessive "admittedly" in the sixth line. This is one man allowing for another's pride of love but unable to resist the suggestion that perhaps his friend is a bit overindulgent. And the other concessive phrasings, "Be that as may be" and "Moreover," are equally delicate in their effectiveness. For one thing, they tend to take the sting out of the possibly ironic statement that the eloquence of Eve "could only have had an influence on birds"; for another, they lighten the force of "persisted"; and they allow for an almost unnoticeable transition by which the reader is moved from the "garden round" of the second line to "the woods" in line 11.

The tone of the poem is of a speaker who is now here with us and of our time and destiny, while it is at the same time full of a nice camaraderie with our first parents. It is loving and responsible all at once, accepting the parentage of Adam and Eve and the necessary consequences of the Fall, along with the acknowledgment of the possibly good fortunes that also attended it. Eve did come—from Adam and with Adam— in order that the song of birds should, by being changed, *mean* more than it otherwise would have. The force of the word "aloft" is ever so discreetly crucial here. Her eloquence had power not indiscriminately but only when it was carried to a "loftiness" that belongs to great love and great poetry, neither of which need be separated from the delights of "call or laughter." The "voice upon their voices crossed" became part of Emerson's fossil poetry, awaiting discovery by future readers, and lovers. The ability to hear the "daylong" voice of Eve in bird song teaches us that our own voices, like the voice in this poem, still carry something of our first parents and their difficult history. Mythological identification in this poem consists of voices finding a way to acknowledge and also to transcend historical differences and historical catastrophes. The birds' oversound in relation to words resembles the "sentence sounds" described in the letter, already quoted, which Frost wrote in February 1914 to John Bartlett: "A sentence is a sound in itself on which other sounds called words may be strung." And a bit later he insists that "the ear is the only true writer and the only true reader . . . remember that the sentence sound often says more than the words" (Thompson, *Letters,* pp. 111, 113).

"Never Again Would Birds' Song Be the Same" is quite properly located between two poems in which human sound fails in an attempted transaction with nature. It is as if the young man and the woman of "The Subverted Flower," the last of the three poems, were in a post-lapsarian world where flowers and sex have the power to transform them into beasts, while the man alone in "The Most of It" is in the world without an Eve of any kind, and where the only form of animal life which can be heard, seen, or imagined in response to a cry of loneliness is so alien as to be called "it." In both poems the world is devoid of love, and consequently, as Frost would have it, of the power to realize a human extension, "someone else additional to him," a metaphor, like Adam and Eve, that would augment the human animal and allow it to make a human "home." These three great poems are profoundly about finding a "home" in the largest sense—by propagating the self through love, through the metaphorical discovery of self in another. "You must have read the famous valentine / Pericles sent Aspasia in absentia," Frost writes at the end of the late poem (1951) "How Hard It Is to Keep from Being King When It's in You and in the Situation." And he then gives his version of the valentine:

> For God himself the height of feeling free
> Must have been His success in simile
> When at sight of you He thought of me.

Simile or metaphor is the act of love, the act of writing poetry, and also evidence in each of these of how something as frighteningly big and potentially chaotic as the "universe" can be "kept" to a human measure. In the disproportion between these two words, "universe" and "kept," is both the pathos of "The Most of It" and a clue to Frost's sense that his own personal and poetic salvation lay in facing up to the full cost, in poetry and in daily living, of the metaphors he makes. "Earth's the right place for love," we are told in "Birches," and while there are times when the speaker of that poem would "like to get away from earth awhile," his aspiration for escape to something "larger" is safely controlled by the recognition that birch trees will only bear so much climbing before returning you, under the pressure of human weight, back home.

IV
Time
and the Keeping of Poetry

"Home," as we have been seeing, is a recurrent image in Frost with various and involuted meanings. Most specifically it is a place, a house or a familiar plot of ground, where someone feels that his or her life is shaped, agreeably or not. It can accommodate aberrations, mental and verbal extravagances, and the psychological dramatic intensities that may develop from the sharing of the same space. Much of what can be said of "home" in Frost can also be said of literary forms, at least in the way he thought of them, as when he writes to L. W. Payne, Jr., that "what makes a piece of writing good . . . is making the sentences talk to one another as two or more speakers do in drama" (Thompson, *Letters,* p. 427). "Home," like any literary form, involves relationships that work themselves out internally and under the aegis of decorums which can contain and therefore even encourage excesses of expression. But in Frost, such limits can and do become stifling; hence, the provocation to an extravagance that seems to break the bounds of decorum. This can mean simply walking or wandering away from a house or a family; or, at the

level of style, it can refer to extensions of consciousness
into visionary sublimities of language.

There is a corollary recognition in Frost about the
possibilities of life in time. Human consciousness of the
passage of time is necessarily agitated, sometimes by the
prospect of limited duration, other times by the reassurance that this limit, as of a storm or winter, can be bene-
ficial. Necessarily, however, consciousness of time is far
more "tensed" and complicated than is any consciousness of "home." It admits of less possibility of choice; it
does not brook defiance. Anyone can, after all, simply
wander off and become lost to the persons and things
that identify him. Frost might conceivably, for example,
have defied his nature and become a writer of free
verse. But the defiance of time is implicitly ridiculed by
biological reality, by the inescapable facts of birth and
death. To defy time is to assume divinity, and this has
never, in the long run, been a promising career. Frost
plays for what he knows are "mortal stakes." And yet his
acknowledgment of the realities of time does not constitute any humble submission to a fate. Time itself, as it
gets expressed in the seasons, allows and even induces
the hope of possible reprieves. Thus "October," the
poem as well as the month, keeps in its "mildness" some
remnants of spring and of summer. Frost's educated
consciousness, when it comes to the power of time, is
expressed in the subtle and cautious wit of the conditional verb in "I Could Give All to Time":

> To Time it never seems that he is brave
> To set himself against the peaks of snow
> To lay them level with the running wave,
> Nor is he overjoyed when they lie low,
> But only grave, contemplative and grave.
>
> What now is inland shall be ocean isle,
> Then eddies playing round a sunken reef

Like the curl at the corner of a smile;
And I could share Time's lack of joy or grief
At such a planetary change of style.

I could give all to Time except—except
What I myself have held. But why declare
The things forbidden that while the Customs slept
I have crossed to Safety with? For I am There,
And what I would not part with I have kept.

Again, we find the familiar word "kept"—"He
thought he kept the universe alone" ("The Most of It");
"One aged man—one man—can't keep a house, / A
farm, a countryside" ("An Old Man's Winter Night");
"Strongly spent is synonymous with kept" ("The Constant Symbol"). "Keeping" is the lovely and loving
human effort to secure something from oblivion; and as
Shakespeare's sonnets insist, poetry is itself a form of
"keeping": "And all in love with Time for love of
you, / As he takes from you, I ingraft you new" (Sonnet
15). Such "keeping" is very subtly expressed here by
Frost's metaphor of the eddy playing round a sunken
reef. The eddy is compared to "the curl at the corner of
a smile." This is a rather determined smile, perhaps
even "brave," which is an attribute denied both to time
and to the rather monumental natural structures which
are nonetheless subject to the erosions of time. In any
case, the image of human bemusement, in its disciplined
plasticity, is to be contrasted to the somewhat pompous
demeanor given to Time by this poem. Whatever the
pathos in the image of the smile, it is offset by pride
in the fact that a human expression so fleeting can yet
be an adequate simile for massive and unhuman force.

Changes of "planetary style" are habitual to the planet
and of no concern to Time. If they are to be recognized
at all it is only by human consciousness; "planetary style"
can only be "kept" by human style, specifically by simile

or metaphor. This is a view of consciousness, of time, and of poetry that is not unique to Frost, but it looks for precedents to Renaissance more than to Romantic poetry. Frost is different from Wordsworth or Coleridge to the degree that he never, even for dramatic purposes, treats human consciousness as a burden. To the contrary, he flaunts it. The poem at hand is as much about the incapacities of Time as about its power. It cannot be "brave"; it cannot feel "joy" or "grief." And the obvious patronizations in the phrasing "Grave, contemplative and grave," make it doubtful that these virtues, if such they be, are to be allowed to "Time" either, except as a way of pointing up the superiority of contrasting human expressions in response to "planetary changes."

Especially at moments when he seems most uncritically banal and where a dead-headed reader might be inclined to trot out a dead-headed phrase like "pathetic fallacy," Frost insinuates in an offhand and sometimes witty manner that human beings have a special prerogative with respect to time. We can be said to have invented it, to have given it a character. No, we are not responsible for its power; but we are responsible for any *measure* of its power, for codifying the pattern of its expenditures. Most simply, we have named and mythologized the seasons in a way that suggests rejuvenation as well as fall—that "other fall we name the fall." "Putting in the Seed," as an instance, dramatizes the discovery, in a man not theoretically conscious about time, that his "seed" can be "kept" if he joins creatively in a process that unites the human body and its transformations with the earth and its changes. Frost, with such metaphors as "like the curl at the corner of a smile," can, in the making of poetry, achieve an analogous kind of creativity and "keeping." Sex and poetry are both potentially ways of "keeping" things from time while also giving things to time. In saying that Frost's remark "Strongly spent is synonymous with kept" is about love-making as well as the making of poetry, we say no more than does Shakespeare when, in addition to his claim that poetry might "ingraft you new," he says that "nothing gainst Time's scythe can make defense / Save breed, to brave him when he takes thee hence" (Sonnet 12).

What happens in nature is in our "keeping" as well as it is in time's "keeping," for the reason that poetic metaphors can embody and transmit these happenings. Still more important, however, is that for Frost human sexual intercourse suggests that the making of metaphor—the finding, to recall Wordsworth again, of "similitude in dissimilitude, and dissimilitude in similitude"—is what nature itself is all about. This is so instinctive a feeling, and exerts a pressure so unselfconsciously transmitted into Frost's writing, that even the most apparently innocuous little poems can be endowed with a peculiar strength by it. "Devotion" is a good instance.

> The heart can think of no devotion
> Greater than being shore to the ocean—
> Holding the curve of one position,
> Counting an endless repetition.

Clearly, the description of geological relations here is meant as a metaphor for human ones, of one person "holding" to someone or "keeping" her or him despite (or is it because of?) counter-surgings or agitations. It is not a logical position to be in, and the phrase "can think of no devotion" has a long-suffering or sardonic impatience about it. Hearts do not "think"; hearts love unreasonably and put up with a good deal, like the "endless repetition" of domestic wrangling. The traditional association of the ocean with the female might imply that the embracing shore is the strong and patient male, a

tolerant, steadfast spouse. But Frost is no kind of chau-
vinist, and such a merely domestic picture does not, besides, account for the sexual overtones of "curve" or the
fact that when the sexes do "curve" into position it is not
the male who customarily receives a repetition of movements sometimes so "endless" as to induce "counting." It
is usually the female who must feel sufficient "devotion"
to stay in "the curve of one position." The sexes in the
poem are interchangeable.

I do not want to argue that the poem is *about* sexual
intercourse. Rather, the way the metaphors move
around in it and "speak" to one another makes human
sexuality a necessary condition of the reader's consciousness. Through "sexuality" we "know" what it means to
be "devoted" or how to "keep" something, and in part
because sex involves learning how to "spend" strongly.
The poem is another example of why Frost's work is
suffused with sexuality and the drama of the sexes. To
talk about nature as a destructive-restitutive force is to
talk about compatible contraries similar to those at work
in relations between the sexes. There is a kind of inevi-
tability of sexual innuendo even in a little poem like
"From Iron (Tools and Weapons)":

> Nature within her inmost self divides
> To trouble men with having to take sides.

The poem is dedicated to a Pakistani friend of Frost's,
Ahmed S. Bokhari, an assistant secretary at the United
Nations, and refers to a great lump of iron ore placed in
the so-called meditation room at the UN Building in
New York by the King of Sweden. Frost lets the poem
mean the obvious—that "Nature" contains in the one
piece either a source for weapons or for tools, for war or
for peace. However, the notion that divisions in nature

"trouble men with having to take sides" admits also of a sexual image too witty to be put aside. After all, a sexual connotation in Frost is always so much more than that. To take a particular side is both the biological option of men and women and also a "trouble" in the sense that men and women do "choose" whether or not to exercise the option. This distinctly human capacity for "trouble" and choice thus makes a further division in nature. It divides human nature from nature as represented in iron ore. "To take a side" is also, particularly at the United Nations, to debate, to talk, to argue national and racial divisions within a oneness which is represented both by the piece of ore and by its symbolic location. Our distinction from other animals is nothing less than the capacity for "trouble," our ability to express a consciousness of the "divisions" in us and in things in nature which cannot themselves attain to consciousness. Like other animals, we have sexual divisions, but unlike others we make divisions by setting up nations and then we try to ameliorate the divisions by setting up leagues or communities of nations. The side one takes, "holding the curve of one position," articulates a part of nature or the world in opposition to some other part. But the division occurs only because, in Frost's view of things, there is the danger otherwise of being included "unawares," absorbed into indivisibility. Division occurs because of a consciousness of the potentially overwhelming power of all that is not the self, especially as this is embodied in the movements of nature and of time. Any effort to resist wholeness, inclusiveness, abstraction in Frost derives from an imagination which has also been stimulated by the pleasures of passivity, the desire simply to give in: "I could give all to Time except—except."

In poems about time as it becomes manifest in the movement of the seasons, Frost makes us most directly

aware of the "I" when he is refusing to give himself up
to some phase of nature, like a storm, even though it
seems to carry in it the irresistible threats of death and
of endings. In defining his own presence on such occasions, Frost is closer to Emerson than to Whitman. He
can be only incidentally or provisionally passive, with
none of Whitman's usually unruffled assumption (sometimes complicated by his nervously wanting to assert a
more masculine and controlling relation to what is going
on around him) that he can let himself be invaded because he is already a part of the force that flows into and
through him. Nonetheless, as already noted, Frost can
admit to something in himself responsive to the prospects of absorption or death. The desire (which he
openly reveals in certain letters to Louis Untermeyer)
for peace and lostness, the desire to throw himself away,
gets justified on occasions by his wondering if nature itself does not conspire with him by proposing that, at
last, he "come in" to the dark woods. His refusal of such
invitations is addressed both to himself and to a momentary fantasy about nature. The voice is all the stronger,
as in the poem "Come In" ("But no, I was out for
stars: / I would not come in. / I meant not even if
asked, / And I hadn't been") because it is designed to
waken him into a renewed life which, unlike the life of
nature, cannot depend on cycles or design, but only on
will and consciousness.

A poem in which this process of self-awakening is
pushed to a precarious degree is "Stopping by Woods
on a Snowy Evening":

> Whose woods these are I think I know.
> His house is in the village, though;
> He will not see me stopping here
> To watch his woods fill up with snow.

My little horse must think it queer   5
To stop without a farmhouse near
Between the woods and frozen lake
The darkest evening of the year.

He gives his harness bells a shake
To ask if there is some mistake.   10
The only other sound's the sweep
Of easy wind and downy flake.

The woods are lovely, dark, and deep,
But I have promises to keep,
And miles to go before I sleep,   15
And miles to go before I sleep.

As in "Desert Places" the seasonal phase is <u>winter,</u> the
diurnal phase is <u>night,</u> but, as in another poem of
imagined solicitation just mentioned, "Come In," the
scene, we are reminded four times over, is a wood.
<u>Woods</u>, especially when as here they are "lovely, dark
and deep," are much more seductive to Frost than is a
field, the "blank whiteness of benighted snow" in
"Desert Places" or the frozen swamp in "The Wood-
Pile." In fact, the woods are not, as the Lathem edition
would have it (with its obtuse emendation of a comma
after the second adjective in line 13), merely "lovely,
dark, and deep." Rather, as Frost in all the editions he
supervised intended, they are "lovely, [i.e.] dark and
deep"; the loveliness thereby partakes of the depth and
darkness which make the woods so ominous. The recognition of the power of nature, especially of snow, to
obliterate the limits and boundaries of things and of his
own being is, in large part, a function here of some fur-
tive impulse toward extinction, an impulse no more pre-
dominate in <u>Frost than it is in nature</u>. It is in him, nonetheless, anxious to be acknowledged, and it significantly

qualifies any tendency he might have to become a poet
whose descriptive powers, however botanically or otherwise accurate, would be used to deny the mysterious
blurrings of time and place which occur whenever he
finds himself somehow participating in the inhuman
transformations of the natural world. If Wallace Stevens
in his poem "The Creations of Sound" has Frost in mind
when he remarks that the poems of "X" "do not make
the visible a little hard / To see," that is because Stevens
failed to catch the characteristic strangeness of performances like "Stopping by Woods on a Snowy Evening."
And if he has Frost in mind when, in the same poem, he
speaks of "X" as "a man / Too exactly himself," it is because he would not see that Frost's emphasis on the dramatic and on the contestation of voices in poetry was a
clue more to a need for self-possession than to an arrogant superfluity of it.

That need is in many ways the subject of "Stopping by
Woods on a Snowy Evening." As its opening words
suggest—"Whose woods these are I think I know"—it is
a poem concerned with ownership and also with someone who cannot be or does not choose to be very emphatic even about owning himself. He does not want or
expect to be seen. And his reason, aside from being on
someone else's property, is that it would apparently be
out of character for him to be there, communing alone
with a woods fast filling up with snow. He is, after all, a
man of business who has promised his time, his future
to other people. It would appear that he is not only a
scheduled man but a fairly convivial one. He knows who
owns which parcels of land, or thinks he does, and his
language has a sort of pleasant neighborliness, as in the
phrase "stopping by." It is no wonder that his little horse
would think his actions "queer" or that he would let the
horse, instead of himself, take responsibility for the

judgment. He is in danger of losing himself; and his language by the end of the third stanza begins to carry hints of a seductive luxuriousness unlike anything preceding it—"Easy wind and downy flake . . . lovely, dark and deep." Even before the somnolent repetition of the last two lines, he is ready to drop off. His opening question about who owns the woods becomes, because of the very absence from the poem of any man "too exactly himself," a question of whether the woods are to "own" him. With the drowsy repetitiousness of rhymes in the last stanza, four in a row, it takes some optimism to be sure that (thanks mostly to his little horse, who makes the only assertive sound in the poem) he will be able to keep his promises. At issue, of course, is really whether or not he will be able to "keep" his life.

In "The Onset," only a few pages further on in *New Hampshire,* there is yet another prospect that snow and night will obliterate the human boundaries and integrities of the self. Unlike those in "Come In" and "Stopping by Woods," the natural forces of night and snow are here distinctly a threat rather than a solicitation. But more than in the other poems, there develops a confidence in the limited duration of "winter death," an assurance of the beneficent possibilities of natural cycles, which allows the speaker ultimately to retrieve himself. Before that, however, the first or threatful half of the poem seems notably melodramatic when compared even to "Desert Places," much less to "Stopping by Woods" or "A Leaf-Trader" or "The Wood-Pile," and its melodrama has an evident religious tinge to it:

> Always the same, when on a fated night
> At last the gathered snow lets down as white
> As may be in dark woods, and with a song
> It shall not make again all winter long
> Of hissing on the yet uncovered ground,

I almost stumble looking up and round,
As one who overtaken by the end
Gives up his errand, and lets death descend
Upon him where he is, with nothing done
To evil, no important triumph won,
More than if life had never been begun.

Yet all the precedent is on my side:
I know that winter death has never tried
The earth but it has failed: the snow may heap
In long storms an undrifted four feet deep
As measured against maple, birch, and oak,
It cannot check the peeper's silver croak;
And I shall see the snow all go downhill
In water of a slender April rill
That flashes tail through last year's withered brake
And dead weeds, like a disappearing snake.
Nothing will be left white but here a birch,
And there a clump of houses with a church.

While reading this poem it is worth recalling that Francis Thompson's "The Hound of Heaven" ("I fled Him, down the nights and down the days; / I fled Him, down the arches of the years; / I fled Him, down the labyrinthine ways / Of my own mind . . . .") was a poem Frost discovered in The Old Corner Bookstore in Boston not long after the trip to the Dismal Swamp when "I was trying to throw my life away." Heavily influenced by the seventeenth-century religious poetry of Crashaw, Thompson's poem of 1893 is about the pursuit by an angry God demanding self-abasements. These were in any case a part of Frost's Scotch Presbyterian heritage, which, along with Thompson's poem, makes itself felt in the first stanza of "The Onset"—"I almost stumbled looking up and round, / As one who overtaken by the end / Gives up his errand. . . ." The word "errand" (from the Latin *errare*—mission, error, and wandering all at once) has overtones of religious zeal and contrition, as does the phrase "nothing done to evil."

More than that, the syntax of the whole stanza—a long and complexly subordinated sentence—is derivatively but loudly Miltonic. The inversion manages to incorporate the "I" only eventually into a description of the storm. It appears exactly in the middle of the stanza and emphasizes the unlikelihood of anyone "counting" for very much in these poems. Still more suggestive of religious abasements, the grammatical ambiguity in the placement of "I" obliges the speaker to take some responsibility for the "hissing on the yet uncovered ground," as if he were one of the condemned of Satan's hosts. He has been cast from heaven like the "gathered snow" itself; the "night" is fated; the threat of obliteration, as in Book II of *Paradise Lost,* is "always the same," constant but never decisive. And yet the Satanic hiss is submerged, almost hieroglyphically, in the natural metaphor of the snow's sound. Again, Frost hides his allusiveness, but that he wants us to find the first stanza peculiar and that the peculiarity is meant to result from literary echoes and allusive significances is apparent as soon as we confront the markedly contrasting sounds of stanza two. "Yet all the precedent is on my side"—the metrical regularity of this (after the trochaic inversion in the first foot of the preceding line), along with its slangy idiom, belongs to someone who could have been merely posturing in stanza one. And yet the effect of the shift is not parodistic. The transition simply reminds us that a poetic tradition allows Frost the indulgence of dealing with a seasonal change, "winter death," as if it were divine intervention or retribution directed against him.

It is a bravura performance, by which, having displayed in stanza one the power and authority to use literary "precedents" in describing his situation, he can then turn round and show another kind of authority and power: he can moderate literary "precedents" by "precedents" derived from nature. This would be wholly in character both personal and poetic. His refusal to write melodramatically and apocalyptically about his occasional feelings of worthlessness or of "not counting" is in large part derived from a feeling that such writing is false. It defies what he sees as the truth about nature, namely the always limited duration allowed even its most threatening aspects. It might be equally accurate to say, of course, that Frost felt in himself a habitual brake upon extreme states of feeling, and that he transposed responsibility for emotional inadequacy to something called "nature," much as does Emerson when he complains about "reality":

> People grieve and bemoan themselves, but it is not half so bad with them as they say. There are moods in which we court suffering, in the hope that here at least we shall find reality, sharp peaks and edges of truth. But it turns out to be scene-painting and counterfeit. The only thing grief has taught me is to know how shallow it is. That, like all the rest, plays about the surface, and never introduces me into the reality, for contact with which we would even pay the costly price of sons and lovers   ("Experience").

Frost's expression of an equivalent feeling, in "To Earthward," follows immediately on "The Onset" in *New Hampshire,* with a last stanza announcing that

> The hurt is not enough:
> I long for weight and strength
> To feel the earth as rough
> To all my length.

In a letter to Bernard DeVoto on October 20, 1938, fifteen years after the poem appeared, Frost claimed that "One of the greatest changes my nature has undergone is of record in 'To Earthward' " (Thompson, *Letters*, p. 482).

It is likely that the feelings expressed in that poem represent not a change but a recognition of an aspect of himself implicit in even his earliest poetry, with its courting of excess and its fear of it. From beginning to end he was, with the Emerson of "Experience," aware that

> Human life is made up of two elements, power and form, and the proportion must be invariably kept if we would have it sweet and sound. Each of these elements in excess makes a mischief as hurtful as its defect. Everything runs to excess; every good quality is noxious if unmixed, and, to carry the danger to the edge of ruin, nature causes each man's peculiarity to superabound. Here, among the farms, we adduce the scholars as examples of this treachery. They are nature's victims of expression. You who see the artist, the orator, the poet, too near, and find their life no more excellent than that of mechanics or farmers, and themselves victims of partiality, very hollow and haggard, and pronounce them failures, not heroes, but quacks—conclude very reasonably that these arts are not for man, but are disease. Yet nature will not bear you out. Irresistible nature made men such, and makes legions more of such, every day. You love the boy reading in a book, gazing at a drawing or a cast; yet what are these millions who read and behold, but incipient writers and sculptors? Add a little more of that quality which now reads and sees, and they will seize the pen and chisel. And if one remembers how innocently he began to be an artist, he perceives that nature joined with his enemy. A man is a golden impossibility. The line he must walk is a hair's breadth. The wise through excess of wisdom is made a fool.

If Emerson seems more acutely conscious of the dangers in an excess of form than in an excess of power, Frost is warier of the excesses of power, doubtless because of his appetite for it. Each man feared the predominance of his own most repressed inclination. Like Emerson, Frost saw in nature both a provocation to excess and the retaliations for giving in to it. "To carry the danger to the edge of ruin," Emerson writes with what sounds like a good degree of appetite, "Nature causes each man's peculiarity to superabound. Here, among the farms, we adduce the scholars as examples of this treachery. They are nature's victims of expression."

Frost conspires with Emerson to the point where the very structure of a characteristic poem like "The Onset" or, as we have seen, of "Spring Pools," dramatizes the struggle in a man between contrary impulses both of which belong to nature. "Nature within her inmost self divides / To trouble men with having to take sides," and often, in a poem like "The Onset," both sides will be taken by the same man. The poem becomes a drama of his oscillation between conflicting positions. But we would misread the poem, and Frost, if we decided that he wants us to "take sides" against one of the "sides" given voice by the poem. It is easy to obscure the complications by treating him as an ironist and by reading a poem like "The Onset" as if stanza two were corrective of what thereby becomes an ironic or parodistic first stanza. But the fact that the first stanza is far more "literary" and stylistically allusive than the second does not mean that it thereby becomes less "natural." Because while Frost, to use Emerson's terms, is beautifully aware of the *form* of nature—that it is a process, a cycle, by which its destructive possibilities evolve into creative ones—he is equally aware of the *power* in nature, which at times seems to exceed the control of form and which, in doing so, lends credence, reality, and naturalness to whatever excessive feelings we might have about obliteration or apocalypse. Frost is quite willing, at his best, to let nature as power temporarily overcome his awareness of nature as form, especially when the power expresses itself through the beauties of spring or summer or the awesomeness of a winter storm.

It is in the context of such a complication of feeling that stanza two of "The Onset" should be read, especially the assertion at the beginning that "Yet all the precedent is on my side." Some precedent, yes, but not all. Stanza one is also full of precedents and the fact that they are literary, mythological, and religious does not, again, mean that they do not partake of nature as do the precedents for restitution or redemption in stanza two. This second stanza proposes to describe the release from bondage of cold and snow that will come with the spring: the snow that "hissed" in stanza one will slither away "like a disappearing snake" in the flashes of a "slender April rill." Satan begone, and the soul will be restored with the fertility of the fields!

And yet it should be noted that stanza one is in the historical present tense, describing something that is happening as it has always happened in the past "on a fated night," while the second stanza is entirely in the future tense. That is, stanza two is the vision of someone who at the time of speaking is *still* cold; he may expect more snow to fall on him before the coming of April. He can only imagine what the thaw will release from the bondage of snow, and his vision is so dominated by the whiteness of "winter death" that the elements he can envision with any particularity in the coming spring are themselves white: "Nothing will be left white but here a birch, / And there a clump of houses with a church." As Reuben Brower suggests, the description of springtime rejuvenation is not as ecstatic as anyone would expect who wants the poem to trace a progression from the threat of winter to the springtime restoration of life. Stanza two is not a decisive development from or alternative to stanza one but is still held within its gravitational field. The emphasis at the end on the winter-like whiteness of artificial as well as natural objects, once the snow melts, should be read, I think, in the light of what Emerson proposes as the special function and power of "the poet":

> For as it is dislocation and detachment from the life of God that makes things ugly, the poet who re-attaches things to nature and the Whole—re-attaching even artificial things and violation of nature, to nature, by a deeper insight—disposes very easily of the most disagreeable facts. Readers of poetry see the factory-village and the railway, and fancy that the poetry of the landscape is broken up by these; for these works of art are not yet consecrated in their reading; but the poet sees them fall within the great Order not less than the beehive or the spider's geometrical web   ("The Poet").

In a sense, therefore, "The Onset" is about the various kinds of precedents, both in poetry and in nature, for attaching oneself to "God," not to an abstraction by that name, but to what Emerson here calls "the life of God." The precedents in stanza one are more or less consistent with Frost's Presbyterian background and his devotion to religious poetry of the seventeenth century; those in stanza two are more consistent with his version of Emerson and his mother's Swedenborgianism, with its emphasis on second sight as well as a "second comings," both implicit, again, in the future tenses. Mention of the "church" as being "with" the houses affirms the expected domestication of religion within a natural redemptive cycle, though in stanza one religious sentiment had made him feel that "winter death," which is also part of the cycle, would at last have its way with him.

"The life of God" is implicit, for Frost, in the variations of the seasons. These variations posit a limited duration to suffering and also a limit to joy. It is this recognition of limits in nature—limits to form as well as to power—which releases Frost from visionary fixation with any specific manifestation in the natural world. As the titles of the *Masques* suggest, to participate in "the life of God" is to discover not only mercy but justice. This is a rather tough-minded view of human experience, and helps explain the limited liability he was willing to assume for what he considered the inescapable sufferings of others. "I suppose I am a brute," we can recall his writing to Untermeyer when his sister, Jeanie Frost, went insane, "in that my nature refuses to carry sympathy to the point of going crazy just because someone else goes crazy, or of dying because someone else dies" (Thompson, *Letters*, p. 248).

A sense of limited liability helps explain, too, his tough-mindedness in poetry—his extraordinary determination to test out the possibilities of likeness where there seem only to be differences and to look for differences where only similarities are apparent. He is thereby committed to the most subtle, insinuating, and diffident kinds of self-projection. Which brings us back to a question left unresolved at an earlier stage of discussion. How can Frost possibly be called "diffident" when voice and sound in his poems so often create an undeniably strong personal presence? The voice is often most assertive when it is denying any tendency to go with "the drift of things" or refusing to be trapped into an identification with people or with natural objects on whom sympathy would be wasted. But even while this

language of denial manages to eschew false relations, it
almost surreptitiously explores possibilities for true
ones. This is what goes on, with an illustrative clarity, in
"Good-By and Keep Cold," another poem where feelings are released and disciplined by Frost's sense of duration and the seasons:

> This saying good-by on the edge of the dark
> And the cold to an orchard so young in the bark
> Reminds me of all that can happen to harm
> An orchard away at the end of the farm
> All winter, cut off by a hill from the house.   5
> I don't want it girdled by rabbit and mouse,
> I don't want it dreamily nibbled for browse
> By deer, and I don't want it budded by grouse.
> (If certain it wouldn't be idle to call
> I'd summon grouse, rabbit, and deer to the wall   10
> And warn them away with a stick for a gun.)
> I don't want it stirred by the heat of the sun.
> (We made it secure against being, I hope,
> By setting it out on a northerly slope.)
> No orchard's the worse for the wintriest storm;   15
> But one thing about it, it mustn't get warm.
> "How often already you've had to be told,
> Keep cold, young orchard. Good-by and keep cold.
> Dread fifty above more than fifty below."
> I have to be gone for a season or so.   20
> My business awhile is with different trees,
> Less carefully nurtured, less fruitful than these,
> And such as is done to their wood with an ax—
> Maples and birches and tamaracks.
> I wish I could promise to lie in the night   25
> And think of an orchard's arboreal plight
> When slowly (and nobody comes with a light)
> Its heart sinks lower under the sod.
> But something has to be left to God.

Again, Frost, or what a purist would call the speaker,
is in a familiar stance. He is on "the edge of the
dark / And the cold." And again he is aware of "prece-

dents" in the nature of things ("saying goodby . . . Reminds me") which can be either harmful or helpful. More than half the poem is given over to what he "does not want" to happen to his orchard. There are six negative clauses; four begin with "I don't want," and the others with "It wouldn't" and "It mustn't." On the other hand, what he does want is as emphatically stated as what he doesn't—he wants the reality of winter cold unadulterated by any unseasonal warmth. His call here for the beneficent severities of nature—" dread fifty above more than fifty below"—is a piece with his blustering announcement that he is going to busy himself cutting down trees "less fruitful" than those in his orchard. The whole poem develops consistently toward his charming but chilling comparison between a freezing, dying orchard and a freezing, dying friend. Or rather it is a comparison that comes into existence, as often happens in Frost, in the act of disowning it:

> I wish I could promise to lie in the night
> And think of an orchard's arboreal plight
> When slowly (and nobody comes with a light)
> Its heart sinks lower under the sod.
> But something has to be left to God.

A lot is happening in this short passage. His denial to the orchard of a status in his emotions equal to that of a freezing and dying loved one nonetheless suggests that with the latter he would know how to act compassionately. All the more so for not being the kind of man who wastes compassion on an orchard. The rightness of the position is buttressed by the wit of the last line. It pretends to mean that what is left to God is to "think of an orchard's arboreal plight." But since God expresses Himself through the variations and durations of the seasons, and since He knows, therefore, that the orchard is

not in a "plight," He would hardly worry when its so-
called "heart sinks lower under the sod." That, after all,
is exactly what is good for it.

But the sophisticated intentions of the poem can only
be grasped along with the evidence in it of Frost's metrical genius and his total absorption of English and American verse form. These are an indispensable part of his
functioning voice, his poise of seriousness and wit. The
poem is written in anapestic tetrameter, a meter whose
history is admirably outlined by Hollander in his essay
"Romantic Verse Form and the Metrical Contract" (*Vision and Resonance,* pp. 187–211). From Palgrave, Frost
would have known the serio-comic use of the meter in
Cowper's "The Poplar-Field," and its alternate uses both
in elegiac and in satirical or comic verse by Wordsworth,
Tom Moore, Hunt, and Landor, one of the poets Frost
greatly admired. These two modalities are captured and
held brilliantly in suspense by the enjambed first line:
"This saying good-by on the edge of the dark." It seems
at this initial point like a crisis poem about death or
departure. But the next line, while continuing to exploit
the possibility ("And the cold . . .") gets us into the full
jingle of the verse from and then to the revealed object:
"good-by . . . to an orchard." Later, near the end, in
lines 25–26, the same effect is gained in "I wish I could
promise to lie in the night / And think of an orchard's
arboreal plight." The wonderful trickery of this, along
with some similarities of phrasing, is evident also in the
second stanza of the Cowper poem ("Twelve years have
elaps'd since I first took a view / Of my favorite field and
the bank where they grew"). Frost's choice of the form
with its sing-song movement and rhymes, as in "house,"
"mouse," "browse," "grouse" of lines 5–8, is an especially
vivid example of how he hedges his "seriousness" to
serious effect. He hides his poetic allegorizing—his com-

mentaries on a literary history that goes back, as Hollander shows, to the drinking songs and bawdy of earlier times—by so outrageously exploiting it as to seem almost disingenuously adroit.

Instead of ending with a cheerfully sentimental affirmation of God's mercy, the poem is a jocular and sly insider's view of God's justness, or at least the justness inherent in what Emerson calls, again, "the life of God." The poem is a joke on the whole idea of divine intercession beyond the provisions, some of them quite harsh, of already functioning arrangements. In fact, the speaker is so cognizant of the way nature works that he, and the poem, really "leave" nothing to God at all. It is the speaker who provides for the human needs in such a climate (wood and food) and who makes every provision (short of ridiculously summoning grouse, rabbit, and deer for a warning lecture) to insure an orchard cold and deserted enough for the sake of future growth.

God in Frost is never sentimental, and Frost is ever wary of depending on Him, as he suggests in "Bereft." This is a powerfully felt poem about the isolation and loneliness of someone left in a decaying house wracked by the winds:

> Out in the porch's sagging floor
> Leaves got up in a coil and hissed,
> Blindly struck at my knee and missed.
> Something sinister in the tone
> Told me my secret must be known:
> Word I was in the house alone
> Somehow must have gotten abroad,
> Word I was in my life alone,
> Word I had no one left but God.

The reiterated use of "word" suggests the pervasiveness of town gossip, of speech lending itself to old-folk clichés about a lonely man or woman having "no one left but God." Read as a kind of small-town platitude, the last three lines are not sinister or self-pitying in tone. They are a bit snickering, from a poet who never imagines that God is personally attentive to individual predicaments anyway. The "leaves" seem to be saying something but only because here, as in "The Wood-Pile," the man is lonely enough to over-read any movement as a signal of caring or antagonism. That is also why, in the beginning, he can ask the wind "What would it take my standing there for, / Holding open a restive door." As in stanza one of "The Onset," the rhetoric is one of dramatic self-posturing; about all the rhetoric asks of us is the sympathetic understanding that someone might be unhappy enough to indulge in it. Whether, by the end, the statement about God is a mockery of town gossip, of God, or of himself, does not matter. Any way of taking the last line is good enough so long as it is not taken as a subscription on the part of Frost to a belief in God's assiduous immanence in personal affairs.

In poems where Frost talks about God while also talking about seasonal change, like "The Onset," "Good-By and Keep Cold," "Bereft," and others, he does so as if "the life of God" impinged upon human consciousness—or as if it were created by that consciousness—by way of the patterns implicit in nature, in language, in some of the literary forms given to language, and in the vernacular of "sentence sounds." Language and literature are forms of human consciousness which codify patterns enacted in nature. This is not to say that the patterns *are* the codifications; language, axiomatically, is not the "thing" it tries to approximate. The cycle of death and rejuvenation is the example we have been considering. Not nature itself but the language about it and the seductiveness of that language create invitations, temptations, blandishments that can be resisted in Frost only by the power of another kind of language and within a form that contains both.

It would be convenient to identify the invitational aspect of nature-language as "literary" and the resistant aspect of nature-language as "vernacular." But any such formula would have constantly to be modified or discarded altogether as particular poems come under consideration. At a more elementary level, it could be said that Frost is continually suggesting that nature cannot "speak" at all unless we let it do so, unless we engage in the literary convention by which nature is given a tongue. Thus, we have heard him say to the tree at his window

> . . . I have seen you taken and tossed,
> And if you have seen me when I slept,
> You have seen me when I was taken and swept
> And all but lost.

But he says this only after telling the tree that "not all your tongues talking aloud / Could be profound." The awareness of the difference between self and nature is intricately tied to the fact that the self in these poems is a poet. It is his "tongue" that can be profound, his "words" that can "frame" or "make," his "verse" which protects him from believing that phoebes weep at the sight of a burned and forsaken farm.

In the voice movement of these poems, poetic processes and procedures and natural processes and procedures are shown to be intricately connected, and their possible reciprocations inquired into. Frost thereby explores the Emersonian proposal that in names of things there is a revelation of their metaphoric value. So, too, with Frostian sentence sounds, those units of expression within which words or "names" for things are only a

part. The metaphoric value of sentence sounds is that
they refer to or are "like" certain dispositions and tem-
peraments of the human mind. These sentence sounds,
to recall Frost's own claims about them, do not so much
depend upon words as actually enhance or change the
meaning of them. For Frost, a sentence sound is an example of pure form. A "system" for symbolizing, like
Yeats's, is inconceivable for Frost because for him the
power of voice in a sentence exists independently of
words and necessarily changes their significance with
each usage. Voice or sentence sound is an evidence of
human resistance to fixed meanings as well as to the im-
positional power of things or of circumstance. The shaping of sound in a sentence is the voice's way of exerting
control over particular words that can become too intimidating, words like "God," for example, or "snow."

I am describing a function of Frost's own nature, and
his personal prowess, which is in no way compromised
by our noting, once again, an equivalence in Emerson:

> Here is the difference betwixt the poet and the mystic,
> that the last nails a symbol to one sense, which was a
> true sense for a moment, but soon becomes old and
> false. For all symbols are fluxional; all language is ve-
> hicular and transitive, and is good, as ferries and
> horses are, for conveyance, not as farms and houses
> are, for homestead. Mysticism consists in a mistake of
> an accidental and individual symbol for an universal
> one   ("The Poet").

Frost did not feel as acutely as did Emerson (or Stevens)
the need to rescue life from the "old and false" sense of
things. Along with William James he preferred to play
with the barely possible virtues and the alleged necessities of "false" beliefs. Certain beliefs might seem contrary to nature, but, by a power of expression given

them in the literature of the past they have become
"true." Frost had a taste for the sheer power of linguistic
sound, and this helped make him a far more flexible
poet stylistically and an altogether more daring intellectual poet than he is generally thought to be. As in the
first stanza of "The Onset," he is willing to propose that
under certain circumstances the human mind and the
immediate compulsion of its beliefs necessitate a rhetoric which could be invalidated by any reasonable assess-
ment of what is going on: we know that inexorably the
storm will end and that spring will come.

Human consciousness is able to infer from the unself-
conscious workings of nature the likely directions of
time and its power. But in also proposing alternatives to
the inexorable movements of time, the consciousness
that shapes itself in poetry is not inviting the reply that it
is only showing its innocence or that it had better find
shelter and forgiveness in irony. Rather, it is inviting admiration, complicity, pleasure, and, not least of all, a
momentary revenge. The revenge consists of finding a
loophole in nature's own argument or, to put it another
way, of finding that since the force of nature is not
always perfectly synchronized with its forms, the force
of consciousness need not always submit to form either.
We have already seen these feelings at work in "Spring
Pools." The poem could be read to mean that the
speaker confuses the ability in nature to "reflect," to
mirror different aspects of itself, with the ability to reflect in another sense, to "think" as only human beings
can. Hence, the final caution to the trees, "Let them
think twice before they use their powers / To blot out
and drink up and sweep away / These flowery waters
and these watery flowers / From snow that melted only
yesterday." And yet the man in the language of these
closing words, so exposed to the reader's charmed con-

descensions, is not foolishly asking that time should stop
what is naturally happening. He is only reminding it
that it need not hurry. After all, those snows did melt
"only yesterday." It is a perfectly legitimate petition in
favor of a lovely confusion, the sort of thing requested
in earlier poems like "October" where the "hushed October morning mild" is asked to "begin the hours of this
day slow," or in "Rose Pogonias" where a reprieve, "a
grace of hours," is requested for a field of orchises, so
"that none should mow the grass there / While so confused with flowers."

Some of the loveliest of Frost's poems, especially in *A
Boy's Will,* are in the form of prayers, petitions, instruc-
tions to the seasons. Many of these, like the passages just
quoted, are couched in a style whose vague allusiveness
is designed to celebrate the fact that poetry—classical,
English, and American—has always taken the license of
refusing "to give all to time." Poetry can prefer *not* to
resolve the paradox—as evident in Plato as in Spenser's
Garden of Adonis—that there is death in nature but
that nature does not die. Like other prayers, the form of
"October" or "A Prayer in Spring" or "Rose Pogonias" is
obedient to the very authority being asked to restrain itself. The obedience shows forth as poetic selfconscious-
ness. By that I mean that the *un*naturalness of diction
for which Frost, the "literate farmer," is so seldom given
credit is his way of suggesting that certain aspects of nature can only be sequestered or "kept" by the human
consciousness within highly stylized fabrications of language and meter. Frost was fully aware of what it means
in "Windsor Forest" when Pope writes, expressing his
own awareness of English Renaissance poetry, that "The
Groves of Eden, vanish'd now so long, / Live in description, and look green in song." In the poems we are

about to consider, all of them early, Frost is unmistakably referring to modes of poetry, especially of the seventeenth and eighteenth centuries, and not to models
directly taken from the confines of New England.

I am concerned here with Frost's reading of nature
insofar as it was part of his life-long reading of poetry,
and with how these readings occurred *while* he was per-
forming as a writer. His attitudes about life or nature or
poetry were never innocent; they exhibit variations
rather than changes. Most important of all, however, the
variations result from the *kind* of poem he chose to write
at any given time and not the other way round. It would
be inaccurate to say that in *A Boy's Will* he exhibits a late-
Victorian anxiety, like Hopkins', about mutability; it
would be better to say that in this early period he was
experimenting with certain poetic styles which happen
also to reveal his capacity to feel beset by the obliterating
power of the seasons. He was to feel much the same
thing later in his career, as we have seen in the poems
from *New Hampshire,* like "The Onset." And when he
brought out *Collected Poems* in 1930 he felt no compunc-
tions about adding "In Hardwood Groves" to *A Boy's Will*
where its very proximity to such poems as "October"
and "Rose Pogonias" serves to emphasize its comparative jauntiness about mutability not, in this case, re-
fracted by poetic allusiveness:

> The same leaves over and over again!
> They fall from giving shade above,
> To make one texture of faded brown
> And fit the earth like a leather glove.
>
> Before the leaves can mount again
> To fill the trees with another shade,
> They must go down past things coming up,
> They must go down into the dark decayed.

They *must* be pierced by flowers and put
Beneath the feet of dancing flowers.
However it is in some other world
I know that this is the way in ours.

Necessity is acknowledged in the repeated use of the
word "must," but the third use is comically less assured,
in its italics, than the first. Is it perhaps that by the last
stanza the speaker has become so fretful of his good-boy
Lucretianism that he has to keep himself in line by un-
derscoring a requirement with which, in the first line, he
is none too happy? Whenever Frost tries to sound wise
about a situation so general, he is apt to sound unnecessary.

He is always best when most particular about *moments*
in time or *locations* in space, temporary stays. The tem-
porariness is the substance of drama: if the time be
winter night and the place deserted, the prospect is
eventual rebirth; if it be spring and in a garden or a
field accompanied by loved ones, the worry is of loss and
change. Another way of putting it is to say that Frost is
solaced in moments of particular terror or sterility by
the precedents of recurrent spring, and anguished in
particular ecstacies by the precedents in life—and in
poetry—of winter and decreativeness. In either case he
has expectations derived as much from poetry as from
climate. As an example, the speaker in "October" is only
incidentally a man begging the month to take it easy—
"Retard the sun with gentle mist. . . . For the grapes'
sake, if they were all." He is more obviously a poet who
knows that the request, having been made so frequently
in the poetry of the past, cannot wholly be a violation of
nature. He knows the peculiarity of autumn but he also
knows it, in part, because of Keats and Spenser:

O hushed October morning mild,
Thy leaves have ripened to the fall;
Tomorrow's wind, if it be wild,
Should waste them all.
The crows above the forest call;
Tomorrow they may form and go.
O hushed October morning mild,
Begin the hours of this day slow.
Make the day seem to us less brief.
Hearts not averse to being beguiled,
Beguile us in the way you know.
Release one leaf at break of day;
At noon release another leaf;
One from our trees, one far away.
Retard the sun with gentle mist;
Enchant the land with amethyst.
Slow, slow!
For the grapes' sake, if they were all,
Whose leaves already are burnt with frost,
Whose clustered fruit must else be lost—
For the grapes' sake along the wall.

The Spenserian mood here is of the "Epithalamion" with its gentle solicitations that nature relent, upon a particular occasion, in the exercise of its demonstrated powers of defoliation. It is asked to be gentle, perhaps as a lesson to the bridegroom. Nature is not asked in either poem to do anything "unnatural." Indeed, October very often does "retard the sun with gentle mist." Nature is asked to act like a poem—to be enchanting and beguiling. It is crucial to notice that it is asked to do so "in the way you know." But how does it "know"? Or, more properly, how do we "know" that it "knows"? We know because of poetry. The precedents for there being anything in nature which approximates Eden exists only on the rarest of days in a world of fact; Eden is "kept" in the traditions of poetry. And some remnant of Eden is also "kept" by the way men and women in love "keep" each other, and humanity, in perpetuation. That is why the dispensations requested here by Frost are, like those in Spenser's marriage poem, for "us," for "our hearts," "our trees." Frost's poems about seasons of mist and mellow fruitfulness, about summer and spring, are characteristically in the first person plural, while his poems about winter and barrenness are just as frequently in the first person singular. When the precedents of nature and the precedents of poetry are most nearly in conjunction, where the beguilements of nature justify and support the beguilements of poetic conventions—it is then that Frost is most likely to find himself in some kind of harmonious communion that is both poetic and sexual.

Poetry is where we *learn* to let nature "beguile" (as well as frighten) us into human love. The poetry of the past helps to teach us how to celebrate the fleeting delights of nature, how to give witness to them and to fulfill our own natures by analogous acts in sexual loving. This conjunction permeates Frost so fully and yet so instinctively that it gives his work a dimension which it almost never explicitly claims and which criticism has been reluctant to grant. "Carpe Diem," where he does choose to be explicit about these matters, is inadequate to the mixed complications it proposes to sort out, but it provides a needed vocabulary for further discussion:

> Age saw two quiet children
> Go loving by at twilight,
> He knew not whether homeward,
> Or outward from the village,
> Or (chimes were ringing) churchward.
> He waited (they were strangers)
> Till they were out of hearing
> To bid them both be happy.

"Be happy, happy, happy,
And seize the day of pleasure."
The age-long theme is Age's.
'Twas Age imposed on poems
Their gather-roses burden
To warn against the danger
That overtaken lovers
From being overflooded
With happiness should have it
And yet not know they have it.
But bid life seize the present?
It lives less in the present
Than in the future always,
And less in both together
Than in the past. The present
Is too much for the senses,
Too crowding, too confusing—
Too present to imagine.

The "past" teaches us how to "know" the delights of
nature which would otherwise elude us in the brevity of
their duration, and of course the past exists and teaches
us in the poetry we have inherited from it. This particular view of the "carpe diem" theme is far more subtly
rendered by two poems in *A Boy's Will*, "Rose Pogonias"
and "A Prayer in Spring," while the role of loving sexuality in the mythologizing of natural delight is the subject of another poem, "Putting in the Seed," written in
the same period as these two, 1906–7, but not included
in a book until *Mountain Interval*, 1916. If the two poems
in *A Boy's Will* display some of the mythological resources for adjusting to the problem of duration, the
poem in *Mountain Interval* displays those human resources by which such mythologies get created. Essentially, "Putting in the Seed," as we shall see in more detail later on, dramatizes a growth in consciousness which
is synchronized with the growth of seedlings and of the
human foetus. It is a dramatic poem in that the sense of

human participation in natural cycles is discovered at a particular point in the sonnet's development and signaled by a marked change in voice—from the familiar country-folk teasing of the first two lines ("You come to fetch me from my work tonight / When supper's on the table") to the ceremonious grandeur of line 10 ("How Love burns through the Putting in the Seed").

No such perceptible dramatic development or change of tone occurs in "Rose Pogonias" or "A Prayer in Spring," and in neither is there the slightest hint of country speech. Their having been written at the same time as "Putting in the Seed" is therefore evidence that they are "literary" by design, and not because they belong to any earlier selfconsciously poetic period. The two poems constitute a choice to write poetic exhibitions rather than dramas; he designed them to be conspicuously evocative of familiar poetic sounds and traditions, especially of English poetry from Spenser to Marvell and the early pastorals of Pope. Implicit in all three poems is the proposition that sexual love can make us aware that we participate in the larger creative processes of nature, and that poetry "keeps" or preserves that awareness in its metaphors. To read the poetry of the past, or to remember it, is to become conscious of the degree to which the idea and ideal of nature is itself a creation of poetry. Poetry "makes" nature—just as it "makes" the idea of love—available to us in moments of depression and even more in moments of delight when, as Frost would have it in "Carpe Diem," "the present / Is too much for the senses," so that we lose consciousness of the extraordinary and fleeting gift being bestowed upon us. In that sense, when Frost says that a poem is a "momentary stay against confusion" he is being more Arnold than Pater. He means that a poem is an achieved, a local act, but he could also mean that the action is a continuation of the larger life of Poetry itself. In this larger, always palpitating life of the Text we can find reassurance no matter what the terror or delight caused by some part of the Text, a single poem.

Such are the implications arrived at with a perfectly poised inexplicitness, an aristocratically casual assurance in allusiveness, at the end of the most Marvellian of his poems, "Rose Pogonias." Of course some who persist in thinking that T. S. Eliot discovered Marvell, Donne, and the seventeenth-century line for the twentieth-century will wonder that Frost was already there in 1906–7, and would not know either that Emerson put the English poets of the seventeenth century "at the head of human poetry," and that Thoreau, who figures in "Rose Pogonias," filled his Harvard undergraduate commonplace book and his early journal headings with quotations from Crashaw, Herrick, Herbert, Marvell:

> A saturated meadow,
>   Sun-shaped and jewel-small,
> A circle scarcely wider
>   Than the trees around were tall;
> Where winds were quite excluded,   5
>   And the air was stifling sweet
> With the breath of many flowers—
>   A temple of the heat.
>
> There we bowed us in the burning,
>   As the sun's right worship is,   10
> To pick where none could miss them
>   A thousand orchises;
> For though the grass was scattered,
>   Yet every second spear
> Seemed tipped with wings of color   15
>   That tinged the atmosphere.
>
> We raised a simple prayer
>   Before we left the spot,

That in the general mowing
　　That place might be forgot;   20
Or if not all so favored,
　　Obtain such grace of hours
That none should mow the grass there
　　While so confused with flowers.

The description of the meadow anticipates details in a later poem, or epigram, called "Atmosphere (*Inscription for a garden wall*)":

Winds blow the open grassy places bleak;
But where this old wall burns a sunny cheek,
They eddy over it too toppling weak
To blow the earth or anything self-clear;
Moisture and color and odor thicken here.
The hours of daylight gather atmosphere.

In both poems the wind is deprived of its power, and there is a "saturation" nearly cloying: "Moisture and color and odor thicken here," just as they become "stifling sweet" in the meadow. The effect is to create a magical poetic aura wherein earthly time seems to carry portents of timelessness. Because of the extraordinary separation of the garden from corrosive natural forces, "the hours of daylight gather atmosphere," while the meadow (where "wings of color . . . tinged the atmosphere") is given a gnomic shape and dimension ("A circle scarcely wider / Than the trees around were tall') befitting its designation as a "temple." The speaker in these poems is in the situation of Thoreau in *Walden* ("Economy"), who would "stand on the meeting of two eternities, the past and the future, which is precisely the present moment," or of Vaughan, whom Frost would have read in *The Golden Treasury*, Book Second, "When on some gilded cloud or flower / My gazing soul would dwell an hour, / And in those weaker glories spy / Some shadows of eternitie" ("The Retreat"). And we are in the vicinity, too, of Spenser's Garden of Adonis which, as Paul Alpers describes it in *The Poetry of the Faerie Queene,* "keeps changing in appearance because it is not a circumscribed world that in its innocence and perfection mocks human desire. It is really a series of pastoral images that are responsive to and complete human desires and that give them the sanction of nature" (p. 389).

Such poetic foreshadowings help us understand how the picking of "A thousand orchises" in stanza two of "Rose Pogonias" might be considered "right worship" even while in stanza three there is a call to spare the orchises from the mower. The mower in the phrase "general mowing" is also death, and the speaker immediately acknowledges a certain immoderate zeal in his request for deferment (his lack of moderation has already been indicated in the announced desire to pick "a thousand" of the flowers) by making the more possible prayer that the flowers be given only "such grace of hours" as might save them from people who would not cut them in a "right worshipful" manner. This would be anyone who failed to notice that the flowers are "confused" with grass—the Biblical equivalent of flesh and a reminder of our own destiny. The discovery of the metaphorical equivalence between the cycle of birth and death in the meadow and the cycles of human life, far from tinging the poem with melancholy, only serves to infuse the "heat" of its felt life with human sexuality. The word "burning" in line 9 compels attention and suggests how closely identified are the creative force in this "temple of the heat" and that in human life ("How Love burns through the Putting in the Seed"). Grammatically the last line can refer both to the "confusion" or mixture of grass and flowers and to our becoming "confused" and immoderate because of their beauty. The flowers ought to "stay" the hand of any indiscriminate mower. And yet to recall Frost's most renowned formulation about poetry and life is to remember that the "stay" can only be "momentary." The formula takes added significance from such a poem as this. It can mean not only the temporary amelioration of confusion but also, as here, the recognition, by withdrawing into contemplation or worship, of the *value* of confusion. Confusion is the source of metaphor and the inducement to a clarification of it, even though the clarification can be no more than locally reassuring. Metaphor helps resolve the confusion that initiated it and leads us back, if we push too far, to the point of confusion once again.

"A Prayer in Spring" shows many of the characteristics of "Rose Pogonias." There is, first, an evocation of a fortuitous moment of extraordinary natural beauty, what Gray in "Ode on Spring," which also appears in Palgrave's anthology, calls "the untaught harmony of Spring." (Gray's phrasing is of course wonderfully apt since we are discussing a kind of poetry where metrical harmonies are meant to "teach" us something about harmonies in nature.) Second, there is an allusiveness here to a poetry in which this "untaught harmony" was shown how to move by the numbers, so that we might, ever after, rediscover in meter something of Pope's "vanish'd" world. And third, there are the ubiquitous evidences in all phases of creation, natural or poetic, of human sexuality.

> Oh, give us pleasure in the flowers today;
> And give us not to think so far away
> As the uncertain harvest; keep us here
> All simply in the springing of the year.
>
> Oh, give us pleasure in the orchard white,
> Like nothing else by day, like ghosts by night;

And make us happy in the happy bees,
The swarm dilating round the perfect trees.

And make us happy in the darting bird
That suddenly above the bees is heard,
The meteor that thrusts in with needle bill,
And off a blossom in mid-air stands still.

For this is love and nothing else is love,
The which it is reserved for God above
To sanctify to what far ends He will,
But which it only needs that we fulfill.

The "prayer" is not for any unusual manifestations, but rather for the exertion by nature of its known capacity to prolong some particularly lovely phase in its development. Like "Rose Pogonias," it is a request that the people in the poem be allowed fully to participate in a moment before it passes; it is a request that nature imitate poetry by providing a "momentary stay." Both poems are essentially an appeal for a legitimate intensification of consciousness. In that sense, as in others, they resemble "October," where the month, as we have seen, is asked to "Make the day seem to us less brief," with a noticeable emphasis on "seem." In "A Prayer in Spring" the requests are similarly phrased: "Oh, give us pleasure," "make us happy," "keep us here / All simply. . . ." "All simply" might remind us that in "Rose Pogonias" "we raised a simple prayer," and the words suggest that both poems are fully aware that they are asking for the return of a lost innocence. They are also fully aware of counter-realities, like the harvest, which, while "uncertain"—as is the saving of souls—is nonetheless inexorable.

Again it should be noted that the pleasure and happiness are not for the speaker alone but are for "us"—the lovers—and that the poem is not merely about spring but about "the springing of the year," a time of leaping, an active movement of happy bees and of a bird described as a meteor who thrusts his bill into a blossom. Immediately following this image is the direct assertion that "this is love and nothing else is love." But what is "this"? It is nothing less than the human participation in "springing," in moving toward creation and recreation of body and soul. God may reserve to Himself some plan or ultimate purpose to the "springing" that can be seen in the gardens and meadows, and Frost makes due acknowledgment of this in a phrasing that sounds, in the middle lines of the last stanza, like Pope's adaptations of Milton. But the poem ends with a human claim within the larger creation. We "fulfill" His "ends."

A comparison to Hopkins is inevitable and instructive. Hopkins' celebrations of spring include sexuality but never the suggestion that he himself will celebrate it by sexual union, by the "springing" of love which brings forth the "springing" of children. The alliterative, percussive style of his poetry, of which Frost was not fond, is a way of telling us, I think, that the feelings corresponding to human "springing" existed in him by virtue of the emphatic singularity of his own poetic performance. His "doing" is in the writing only. By contrast, Frost wants to suggest that "springing" exists in "us," and in two senses: first, in the man and woman who are in love and who fulfill nature by "putting in the seed" and watching for birth; and second, in the "us" who are poets and who have internalized the poetic conventions at work in this poem and in "Rose Pogonias," conventions that help "keep" us in the "springing of the year," wherein is to be found the renewal of the body and of that innocence necessary to a renewal of the soul.

These poems have a superabundance of poetic virtuosity and read at moments like so many exercises in

Renaissance modes. Their fabricated quality should caution anyone who wants to use the poems as a declaration of religious faith. Certain religious beliefs are "there" because inseparable from the poetic traditions being explored. But they are incidental to a remarkable investigation of the possible connections among various kinds of creativity—in poetry, in the seasons, in sex. All these forms of creativity are conditioned by time and all show evidences of the human desire to "keep" things from time, to preserve or renew in human consciousness an innocence that will prevent our mistaking the starkness of reality for the whole of it. Frost is a poet who sets out to prove that nature itself wants us to "pretend" while knowing we are doing so, that it wants us to believe in something without certifying what it should be, and that, in its capacities for self-preservation, it offers a model for how we might preserve our mythologies in poetry. It is a process, to use Frost's own good way of describing it in "A Boundless Moment," of letting one's "own pretense" deceive.

> He halted in the wind, and—what was that
> Far in the maples, pale, but not a ghost?
> He stood there bringing March against his thought,
> And yet too ready to believe the most.
>
> "Oh, that's the Paradise-in-Bloom," I said;   5
> And truly it was fair enough for flowers
> Had we but in us to assume in March
> Such white luxuriance of May for ours.
>
> We stood a moment so, in a strange world,
> Myself as one his own pretense deceives;   10
> And then I said the truth (and we moved on).
> A young beech clinging to its last year's leaves.

This is a poem of highly volatile intellectual and imaginative movement. It is the drama of a mind trying *not* to make "Supreme Fictions" out of what nature might allow or discredit. It is trying to do something more difficult: to measure without disillusionment, indeed with wit and pleasure, how nature and man participate in that creation of illusion which is essential to the sequestering power of poetry. The requisite intellectual adroitness is apparent in the way ghosts are evoked in line 2 in the very act of dismissing them, or in the agitations, over the short span of the next two lines, by which a "thought," not as yet described to the reader, encounters the hesitations of a man who stands there "bringing March against his thought," only that it may then be released by his readiness "to believe the most." William James is not far away. Particularly since there is a kind of extra-sensory perception on the part of the speaker who accompanies the man: he, apparently recognizing what is going on in his friend's mind, is nonetheless also willing to play with the belief. Even knowing better, he says like a charming good fellow, "Oh, that's the Paradise-in-Bloom." If we are to take him at his word, nature itself connives in what has been recognized from the outset as an illusion—"It was fair enough for flowers." The pressure of trying to hold these contrivances together is highly stimulating, as we might guess from the punning wit of line 8: "Such white luxuriance of May for ours." The flower might have prompted the illusion that "our" month of March could vouchsafe the luxuriance of May, but we could sustain this illusion not for a month but only for "hours." (Frost uses the same pun for a similar effect in line 22 of "Rose Pogonias": "obtain some grace of hours.") This is a poem about "pretending" whenever nature gives you any sort of license, apocalyptic or redemptive, for doing so. And it is out of such moments of illusion or extremity that images emerge which belong to and are perpetuated by poetry.

Frost's sense of proper duration is in part a reading of what is natural in nature and also a reading of what are some of the visionary possibilities offered by nature and preserved in poetry. A particularly beautiful example is a poem of 1936 already alluded to, "Happiness Makes Up in Height for What It Lacks in Length":

> O stormy, stormy world,
> The days you were not swirled
> Around with mist and cloud,
> Or wrapped as in a shroud,
> And the sun's brilliant ball   5
> Was not in part or all
> Obscured from mortal view—
> Were days so very few
> I can but wonder whence
> I get the lasting sense   10
> Of so much warmth and light.
> If my mistrust is right
> It may be altogether
> From one day's perfect weather,
> When starting clear at dawn   15
> The day swept clearly on
> To finish clear at eve.
> I verily believe
> My fair impression may
> Be all from that one day   20
> No shadow crossed but ours
> As through its blazing flowers
> We went from house to wood
> For change of solitude.

The perfections and clearnesses recollected in the poem are registered in a simplicity of language and in its tri-metrical movement. Vaughan again comes to mind, as he does with Frost's "Trial by Existence." But it would be Vaughan without his devotional aspect; there is nothing here about "angel infancy." And any comparisons between Wordsworth and the Frost of this poem would also have to allow for a difference: that Frost's studious recollection is neither visionary nor entirely assured of there having been a vision to lose. "If my mistrust is right / It may be altogether / From one day's perfect weather" is not the voice of someone remembering the "fair seed time" of his soul. This poem refers us for a more revealing and distinctive comparison to Wallace Stevens of "The Latest Freed Man" who can

> suppose there is
> A doctrine to this landscape. Yet, having just
> Escaped from the truth, the morning is color and mist,
> Which is enough: the moment's rain and sea,
> The moment's sun (the strong man vaguely seen),
> Overtaking the doctrine of this landscape.

Frost's landscape is not without "doctrine," as we have been seeing, because he is more willing than the figure in Stevens to indulge in the "truth" (the literary translation of nature, or the tropes for it), from which, with Stevens, he also knows how to escape. He indulges in such "truth" because his sensuous (and sensual) experiences of things in the present encourage him to entertain certain possibilities, "kept" in the poetry of the past, which are beyond immediate verification. By the end of the poem, Frost's "mistrust" has been responsible for creating something in which he can "believe." But what he believes would not exist at all if he had not been willing in the poem to describe something in which he initially did not believe, which he mistrusted. He indulges, characteristically, in descriptions which he also negates. The mistrustful imagination of "one day's perfect weather" is transformed by line 20 into a recollection of something presumably more "actual"—"that one day"—and he then proceeds to people "that" day with "us," as he does in the other poems: "No shadow crossed but ours." The poem ends with a scene—and also with a rhyme strongly reminiscent of the Emily Dickinson of whom he had so little good to say—in which he and his beloved move from the house they share to a different solitude in the woods. Unlike the "happy bees" in "A Prayer in Spring," who encouraged a reference to the "ends" that God might have had in mind, or the "burning" in "Rose Pogonias," wherein the lovers observed what they call "right worship," the "blazing flowers" of this poem are not the prelude to any expressed belief in divinity. This is made all the more obvious by the speaker's saying that he does "verily believe"—he verily believes only in his own impressions. The perfect day and its blazing flowers are not "shadows of eternitie"; the only "shadow" is of lovers in their proximity to one another.

These poems have to be called "learned" with respect to both traditions of poetic style and religious and romantic metaphysics especially of the seventeenth and nineteenth centuries. They are not unmistakably American poems in their tone or movement, and are mostly without the kind of metrical irregularities that Frost liked to introduce into "the very regular preestablished accent and measure of blank verse" (Thompson, *Letters,* p. 128). How, to put it crudely, could he make his preoccupations with the nature of poetry more *evidently* consistent with his portrayals of rural American life? Inevitably, we are directed again to the question of the relationship between what is "gathered by the ear" from the poetic past and what is "gathered by the ear" from the vernacular, from New Hampshire and the like. More is at stake for him in this issue than the claim, large enough and also true enough by July 1913, that "To be perfectly frank with you I am one of the most notable craftsmen of my time. . . . I alone of English

writers have consciously set myself to make music out of
what I may call the sound of sense" (Letter to John T.
Bartlett, July 4, 1913, Thompson, *Selected Letters,* p. 79).
Craft was involved because, as Hollander remarks, the
"sentence sound" or the "sound of sense" for Frost
meant "the delicate but crucial modulations of phrase-
stress pattern, contrastive stress, the rhetorical supraseg-
mentals, that not only make oral communication what it
is, but which a practitioner of classical accentual-syllabic
verse must be aware of. . . . The sound of sense: the
music of speech, but of speech being watched, in its
transcribed form, within a diagramming and punctuat-
ing and annotating grid of metrical pattern" (*Vision
and Resonance,* pp. 42–43). To repeat, more is at stake
here than "craft." On his capacity to make a recognizable music of speech, poetic and vernacular, there depended his whole attempt to mythologize his role as a
poet who was also a representative natural man, notably
an American poet whose family and whose surroundings, till he was nearly forty, called his poetic vocation
into question. He wanted to be an American man of
power as well as a poet.

   To resolve the struggle or strain of voices and of natures, and to show his mastery of them in a way plainly
American to the ear—these are, in part, the concerns
of "Putting in the Seed." It is about a man who is led
through some combined use of his ordinary speech and
his ordinary natural capacities, as farmer and lover, to
the discovery of metaphor, of rhetorical eloquence, and
of myth. Frost in this poem is like Thoreau in *Walden* in
that he proposes that English poetry ("tropes and expression," as Thoreau says) can be discovered by dig-
ging in American fields. It therefore can be said that the
poem demonstrates the claim merely implicit elsewhere
in Frost and in the American and English poets he ad-

mired. The claim is that the poetry of the past exists in
nature and that nature exists in it:

> You come to fetch me from my work tonight
> When supper's on the table, and we'll see
> If I can leave off burying the white
> Soft petals fallen from the apple tree
> (Soft petals, yes, but not so barren quite,   5
> Mingled with these, smooth bean and wrinkled pea),
> And go along with you ere you lose sight
> Of what you came for and become like me,
> Slave to a springtime passion for the earth.
> How Love burns through the Putting in the Seed   10
> On through the watching for that early birth
> When, just as the soil tarnishes with weed,
> The sturdy seedling with arched body comes
> Shouldering its way and shedding the earth crumbs.

It appears that the man speaking is already at work
(he muses in line 6 on "these" soft apple petals which
are to be planted along with the beans and peas) and
that he is telling his wife, who is paying a visit to him in
the field, to come back for him when "supper's on the
table." By line 10, he is soliloquizing and in a tone noticeably lofty when compared to the affectionate teasing
in the first line. The shift is rather abrupt, however,
despite the apparent preparation for a less colloquial
tone that begins in the parentheses of lines 5 and 6, with
words like "barren" and "mingled," and in the heavily
accented elevated phrase of line 9: "Slave to a springtime passion. . . ." Read as a little drama, the change of
voice is, despite these preparatory hints, a bit startling
nonetheless, and even Donne, who liked to work toward
the same sort of transition, never tried so sharp a turn
in a sonnet.

The poem is not wholly at ease with its own ambitions,
and I suspect that this is the best clue to what those am-

bitions are. Frost wants to show how an ordinary man discovers in the round of housekeeping and planting, which he shares with his wife, the larger patterns of time that include different forms of gestation and birth. The "seed" grows in every sense: it is a seedling in the field which unlike the weeds comes arching out of the earth thanks to the human agent who planted it; it is an "arched body" emerging from the womb because of another human planting; and it is the language of poetry which begins in the opening line with "a selection of language really used by men" and develops, as Wordsworth might further describe it, toward a "personification." "Assuredly such personifications," he wrote in *Preface to Lyrical Ballads,* "do not make any natural or regular part of that language," meaning "the very language of men." But he goes on to observe that personifications are, "indeed, a figure of speech occasionally prompted by passion, and I have made use of them as such."

The poem rather intriguingly follows the sequence described in the Preface by which Wordsworth shows that the language "really used by men" necessarily evolves, in moments of high or extraordinary passion, into rhetorical enlargements and metrical movements. Indeed Wordsworth's language is replete with the idea of planting and growth which, as in Frost, unites his concern for "rustic life" with his concern for those conditions wherein "the passions of men are incorporated with the beautiful and permanent forms of nature":

> Humble and rustic life was generally chosen, because in that condition the essential passions of the heart find a better soil in which they can attain their maturity, are less under restraint, and speak a plainer and more emphatic language; because in that condition of life our elementary feelings coexist in a state of greater simplicity, and consequently may be more accurately con-

templated and more forceably communicated; because the manners of rural life germinate in those elementary feelings, and, from the necessary character of rural occupations, are more easily comprehended, and are more durable; and, lastly, because in that condition the passions of men are incorporated with the beautiful and permanent forms of nature. The language, too, of these men has been adopted (purified indeed from what appeared to be its real defects, from all lasting and rational causes of dislike and disgust) because such men hourly communicate with the best objects from which the best part of language is originally derived; and because, from their rank in society and the sameness and narrow circle of their intercourse, being less under the influence of social vanity, they convey their feelings and notions in simple and unelaborated expressions. Accordingly, such a language, arising out of repeated experience and regular feelings, is a more permanent and a far more philosophical language than that which is frequently substituted for it by poets, who think that they are conferring honor on themselves and their art, in proportion as they separate themselves from the sympathies of men, and indulge in arbitrary and capricious habits of expression, in order to furnish food for fickle tastes, and fickle appetites, of their own creation.

It might be unwise to infer any direct influence on Frost's practice as a poet of Wordsworth's theories of poetry, but the influence was nonetheless transmitted in some fashion and is obviously felt to be there. As we have seen, many of Frost's poems and much of his prose writing and talk bring sex and poetry into conjunction in the way already suggested by Wordsworth's *Preface*. In a passage in which he is trying to account for the causes "upon which the pleasure received from metrical language depends," Wordsworth observes that

Among the chief of these causes is to be reckoned a principle which must be well known to those who have

made any of the arts the object of accurate reflection:
namely, the pleasure which the mind derives from the
perception of similitude in dissimilitude. This principle
is the great spring of the activity of our minds, and
their chief feeder. From this principle the direction of
the sexual appetite, and all the passions connected with
it, take their origin: it is the life of our ordinary conversation; and upon the accuracy with which similitude in
dissimilitude, and dissimilitude in similitude are per-
ceived, depend our taste and our moral feelings.

To the extent that this and the preceding passage
about the germinations of poetry are a kind of adum-
bration of "Putting in the Seed," they confirm what I
have been trying to suggest about the degree to which
poetry and nature are fused in Frost's consciousness
without being identical, how writing about nature in poetry means for him also writing about poetry in nature
and about how all of this puts him squarely in the most
significant tradition of those poets who looked upon the
writing of poetry as a sacred vocation rather than a career. In nature or in poetry one discovers "similitude in
dissimilitude, and dissimilitude in similitude." And this
is precisely what one also discovers, as Frost continually
reiterates, in metaphor, in the play between intonation
and meter, and in marriage.

When it came, however, to the writing of certain later
poems more famous and acclaimed than those under
discussion, like "West-Running Brook," Frost increas-
ingly moved toward a kind of didactic and cleansed *description* of the pressures, conflicts, and explorations
more complexly and interestingly at work in the poems
we have been looking at. There is a pretense of conflict
in "West-Running Brook," especially in the way the husband and wife speak to each other. Apparently they
are supposed to dramatize the kind of agitations inher-

ent in the movement of the brook. But their talk is genteel to a fault; it reveals, to repeat, that slightly vulgar
side of Frost, also to be heard in the poem "New Hampshire." It is poetry written for an audience of literary
clubs. "West-Running Brook" is useful precisely because
its weakness derives from Frost's giving himself away for
very little, going explicit, as American writers tend to do
once their careers are more or less set and they become
cerebrally conscious of what they have been up to. The
poem opens with a young couple who explicate one another with a wholly tiresome premeditation:

"Fred, where is north?"

"North? North is there, my love.
The brook runs west."

"West-Running Brook then call it."
(West-Running Brook men call it to this day.)
"What does it think it's doing running west
When all the other country brooks flow east   5
To reach the ocean? It must be the brook
Can trust itself to go by contraries
The way I can with you—and you with me—
Because we're—we're—I don't know what we are.   9
What are we?"

"Young or new?"

"We must be something."

They then see a familiar wave, and Frost, breaking the
dramatic frame, describes it in a parenthesis:

(The black stream, catching on a sunken rock,
Flung backward on itself in one white wave,   20
And the white water rode the black forever,
Not gaining but not losing, like a bird

White feathers from the struggle of whose breast
Flecked the dark stream and flecked the darker pool
Below the point, and were at last driven wrinkled   25
In a white scarf against the far-shore alders.)

When the young woman persists in thinking of the
wave as a signal to them or as "an annunciation," her
husband corrects her with the charge that she is taking
them "off to lady-land." The poem itself has already
done that, but it is worth noting nevertheless that Frost
once more proposes here the necessity for a masculine
power of form, a masculine willingness to recognize conflicts and limitations, as a correction to the extravagant
and romantic feminine tendencies which he also wants to
see indulged. The husband in response to the wife—and
it is clear that he would not produce his arguments were
it not for her prodding—offers us a large-minded,
mythy "reading" of the wave, about which more will be
said in the next chapter:

"Speaking of contraries, see how the brook
In that white wave runs counter to itself.
It is from that in water we were from   40
Long, long before we were from any creature.
Here we, in our impatience of the steps,
Get back to the beginning of beginnings,
The stream of everything that runs away.
Some say existence like a Pirouot   45
And Pirouette, forever in one place,
Stands still and dances, but it runs away;
It seriously, sadly, runs away
To fill the abyss's void with emptiness.
It flows beside us in this water brook,   50
But it flows over us. It flows between us
To separate us for a panic moment,
It flows between us, over us, and *with* us.
And it is time, strength, tone, light, life, and love—
And even substance lapsing unsubstantial;   55

> The universal cataract of death
> That spends to nothingness—and unresisted,
> Save by some strange resistance in itself,
> Not just a swerving, but a throwing back,
> As if regret were in it and were sacred.   60
> It has this throwing backward on itself
> So that the fall of most of it is always
> Raising a little, sending up a little.
> Our life runs down in sending up the clock.
> The brook runs down in sending up our life.   65
> The sun runs down in sending up the brook.
> And there is something sending up the sun.
> It is this backward motion toward the source,   70
> Against the stream, that most we see ourselves in,
> The tribute of the current to the source.
> It is from this in nature we are from.
> It is most us."
>
>   "Today will be the day
> You said so."
>
>   "No, today will be the day
> You said the brook was called West-Running Brook."
>
> "Today will be the day of what we both said."

The reference is not to the day "when" but to "the day of *what* we both said." The poem thus suggests that speaking or saying is a true measure of time, that human exchange, like poetry, is a manifestation of life resisting any unimpeded movement toward death. The poem tries, most tepidly (except for the powerful description of what it then rejects, "The universal cataract of death" in lines 51–57), to register in their marriage the contraries within coherence which the two lovers also celebrate and mythologize in the brook at which they are looking, and it thus becomes, familiarly, a celebration of metaphor and of its tensions. But it is an over-clarified and relatively complacent poem.

V

"The exception
I like to think I am
in everything"

From the late twenties until his death in 1963, Frost
regarded himself as the necessary enemy of two forces
in American cultural life which had formed an unex-
pected and perplexing alliance: the political left and the
modernist literary élite. No matter the many honors he
received from universities, no matter four Pultizer
Prizes—for *New Hampshire* in 1923, *Collected Poems* in
1930, *A Further Range* in 1936, and *A Witness Tree* in
1942—or the appreciation of distinguished fellow poets
like Edward Thomas, Edwin Muir, Auden, Graves, Robert Penn Warren, and, later, Randall Jarrell, Robert
Lowell, and Richard Wilbur, Frost in his lifetime was
somehow denied the status accorded Eliot by the con-
sensus of the most respected kind of criticism. Like
many other American writers who have been popularly
successful, Frost never quite made his mark where it
eventually came to matter most to him. What such
writers finally want is the kind of sustained critical attention that will establish them securely within the academic
curricula and at a central intersection on the literary-his-
torical map. Even now, Frost has not escaped the gravi-

tional pull of general popularity which keeps him from
orbiting in a constellation of the "great" poets.

A writer's reputation dictates the reader's behavior.
Any reader of Eliot has been led to expect (and respect)
more difficulty with the poems than has any reader of
Frost, and if some passage is hard to negotiate in Pound
or in Yeats, then the fault is assumed to be in the be-
holder rather than in the author. Frost's own self-
projection in his many public appearances and interviews helped in the process by which a poet was created
from whom no great difficulties were to be anticipated
and before whom, most assuredly, no reader was to be
made to feel inadequate. Some highly complex poems,
like "A Star in a Stoneboat," rest in limbo because
readers simply cannot see or hear intricacies which are
not supposed to be there, and the situation is even more
deadening when it comes to the old familiar pieces like
"After Apple-Picking." Frost chose to make a reputation
for himself in America with a mixed constituency: a literate general public and a college-university audience
who tended to reject the presuppositions of modernism
and to resent the Europeanized intellectualism of New
York. He became known as a bard and sage who was
versed in literary as well as in country things, someone
who could talk about anything with a casual self-assurance and a remarkable memory. That is how he
wanted to be taken. In 1913, in a letter to John Bartlett,
he remarks that

> There is a kind of success called "of esteem" and it but-
> ters no parsnips. It means success with a critical few
> who are supposed to know. But really to arrive where I
> can stand on my legs as a poet and nothing else I must
> get outside that circle to the general reader who buys
> books in their thousands. I may not be able to do that. I
> believe in doing it—don't you doubt me there. I want

to be a poet for all sorts and kinds   (Thompson, *Letters*, p. 98).

And so he was—to the point where he was systematically neglected by that "critical few" who began to look to Eliot as the "great" American modern poet. Feeling inadequately understood, Frost began, as early as some of the poems in *New Hampshire* in 1923, to explicate himself. It was like an open declaration of intentions from somebody who wondered if perhaps he had been too coy. If he had hidden himself too much "behind light words that tease and flout," so that nobody had been able properly to "find [him] out," maybe it was time for him to "speak and tell us where" he had been ("Revelation"). By the thirties and with the advent of the New Deal and of Roosevelt, a man whose promises to America in the Depression era prompted Frost to call him "His Rosiness," it seemed as if he might lose America altogether. The bitterness gets expressed with representative force at about the time of *A Further Range,* whose publication coincides with Frost's visits to Harvard in 1936 as the Charles Eliot Norton Lecturer. Writing to Louis Untermeyer on May 9, 1936, he places himself in an antagonistic relationship to certain poets and critics whose assumed alliance is given, though without his defining it, a distinct political and cultural significance.

I don't feel I made too big a hit with the dignitaries and authorities. There was a moment in March when I thought perhaps they were giving me back my father's Harvard. But probably I was fooling myself. I'm imperfectly academic and no amount of association with the academic will make me perfect. It's too bad, for I like the academic in my way, and up to a certain point the academic likes me. Its patronage proves as much. I may be wrong in my suspicion that I haven't pleased Harvard as much as I have the encompassing barbarians. My whole impression may have come from the Pound-Eliot-Richards gang in Eliot House here. I had a really dreadful letter of abuse from Pound in which he complains of my cheap witticisms at his expense. I may have to take him across my page like this: It is good to be back in communication with you on the old terms. My contribution was the witticisms: yours the shitticisms. Remember how you always used to carry toilet paper in your pocket instead of handkerchief or napkin to wipe your mouth with when you got through? Etcetera.—I suspect the same dirty sycophant of having reported me to him as reported me to Wallace Stevens. I think its Matteson. Never mind. Peace hath her victories no less renowned than war   (*The Letters of Robert Frost to Louis Untermeyer,* p. 277).

The nastiness about Pound is juvenile, but more important is the reference to "the Pound-Eliot-Richards gang in Eliot House here," and the contemptuous reference to Matthiessen. Eliot House was a center of literary and cultural Anglophilia at Harvard. And by virtue of his position at the university, which in those days was one of the most influential centers for the training of academic literary critics and scholars in America, Matthiessen was a powerful contributor to the critical revaluation and reshaping of American literature. In addition to *American Renaissance,* he wrote what is generally regarded as the first important book on T. S. Eliot in 1935, a fact which by itself would have generated animosity in Frost. Matthiessen was later to figure prominently in the Waldorf Peace Conference of 1949 which was designed to moderate the Cold War, or at least to point to its dangers, and he was to commit suicide the next year. That year, 1950, also marks the publication of his *Oxford Book of American Verse.* Along with Stevens and

Robinson, Frost was given more space than either Eliot
or Pound, and the selection of his poems remains one of
the best anyone has ever made. But Matthiessen was
nonetheless a natural enemy. Combining a taste for difficult, culturally saturated literature on the one hand
and, on the other, an announced sympathy for the political left and for the Soviet Union, he epitomized a new
force in American cultural and academic life which
brought Frost's literary position and the politics implicit
in it into serious question.

It is perhaps difficult now to realize how high were
the stakes on all sides. At issue was not simply the appreciation of talent. So far as that went, Matthiessen's selection in the Oxford anthology indicates his generous understanding of what is best in Frost. It was not even a
matter of the relative standing of Frost, Eliot, Pound, or
Stevens. It goes beyond that and into an area which
Frost demarcates himself when he says of Marx, in another letter to Untermeyer on November 25, 1936:
"Marx had the strength not to be overawed by the metaphor in vogue . . . great is he who imposes the metaphor" (*The Letters of Robert Frost to Louis Untermeyer,* p.
285). This is an important statement not for what it says
about Marx but for what it suggests about cultural
power. I am proposing that in the thirties Frost began to
suspect that the metaphors, including that of *laissez-faire,*
which governed his thinking and his poetry were being
substantially displaced within the national consciousness
by two others. On the one hand, there were metaphors
of "wasteland," or apocalyptic disillusion, against which
individual resistance was presumably useless; and on the
other, the metaphor of "planning," of the New Deal, of
provision, which, as Frost saw it, was designed to relieve
the individual of responsibility for his own fate.

That was the essential problem, and measured against

it Frost's lapses of taste, his occasional paranoiac inaccuracies, and his petty complaints should be treated as inessential. We should concern ourselves with deeper reverberations in his expressions of discontent. There was, for example, no "Eliot House gang" that included Pound (who was in Italy), or I. A. Richards (who was at Cambridge University), or T. S. Eliot, who was in London, though he had already been at Harvard as Norton Lecturer, a fact which did not deter Frost from claiming in a letter, again to Untermeyer, that he was himself the first American to be asked to deliver the series. There could be said, however, to have been a "gang" led by Matthiessen which was trans-Atlantic in its interests and which thought of culture and of civilization as involving the burdens of an inheritance principally European. Correspondingly, they exhibited a predilection for direct rather than for minimal or covert allusiveness and for a poetry in which allusion was meant to highlight those difficulties in contemporary civilization which Frost chose not to acknowledge or was unable to see.

Frost's most disabling intellectual weakness, as I have intimated, was that he could look into nature but was blind to social systems. He was especially insensitive to the way social systems can, as Hawthorne said long ago, take on the appearance and force of nature. It is this that sets him off also from a group of literary critics who were themselves quite distinct from one another in practice and taste, like Matthiessen and Hicks, or Newton Arvin and Rolfe Humphries, or Malcolm Cowley as compared to any of these. Frost had signaled his differences from them long before the publication of the poems in *A Further Range*. That volume was simply the most obvious occasion for his being attacked, though the battle lines had been drawn somewhat earlier, especially, as we shall see, by Hicks. Frost had previously revealed his political antagonism toward the liberalism that was to be institutionalized by the New Deal in his 1935 introduction to Robinson's *King Jasper,* in his letter to *The Amherst Student* of March 9, 1935, and in his preface to Sarah N. Cleghorn's *Autobiography* in 1936: "Security, security! We run in all directions," he complains in the preface, "for security in the game of Pussy-wants-a-corner" (Thompson, II, 414).

As far back as 1923, in the poem "New Hampshire," based in part, it seems likely, on the second and third epodes of Horace—allusive in that easy and unbothering way of his—Frost could include the question "How are we to write / The Russian novel in America / As long as life goes so unterribly?" Asked in the year following *The Waste Land,* three years before *The Great Gatsby,* and seventy-odd years after *Moby-Dick,* the question is facetious, but only to the extent that we choose to remember Frost as the author of "The Hill Wife" and the other terrible "novels," as he liked to call them, that appeared in the same volume. Frost knew that life could go "terribly" anywhere. What he insisted upon was that there was no reason to think that America or modern civilization had anything out of the ordinary to do with it. What he chose to talk about in conversation, what he makes clear in the Introduction to *King Jasper* and in his correspondence, is that life everywhere and at all times has its griefs and terrors. "You will often hear it said," he writes in a letter to *The Amherst Student,* "that the age of the world we live in is particularly bad," and he continues:

> I am impatient of such talk. We have no way of knowing that this age is one of the worst in the world's history. Arnold claimed the honor for the age before this. Wordsworth claimed it for the last but one. And so on back through literature. I say they claimed the

honor for their ages. They claimed it rather for themselves. It is immodest of a man to think of himself as
going down before the worst forces ever mobilized by
God   (Thompson, *Letters,* pp. 417–18).

Frost is in effect saying here that the recurrence of a
complaint only proves that the cause of the complaint is
inevitable. He talks as if history not only partakes of nature but is identical with it. He never asks himself if
perhaps Eliot and before him Arnold and before Arnold Wordsworth and before all of them Shakespeare of
Troilus and Cressida, to think only of writers in English,
were not *all* justified in their suggestions about the
badness of the age because they were all talking essentially about the same age, the same historical phenomena, the shapings and systems peculiar to western civilization, and the beginnings of capitalism. Frost did not
have the historical vision which would have allowed him
to see that perhaps even what he calls "grief" rather
than "grievance" is not necessarily an inevitable result of
the nature of life. It can be, instead, ultimately the result
of systems which are an unnatural imposition upon life,
systems that could include Christianity itself. Frost was
disinclined to see modern life as in any significant degree different from what life had ever been because he
did not recognize that he lived in a period in which the
structurings implicit for at least five hundred years had,
by the slow processes of economic, political, and social
acculturation, at last become unmistakably grotesque.
   If Frost in 1936 saw a new "gang" arrayed against
him, they saw him, too. They were not the old gang—
the editors of magazines, possible reviewers, judges of
literary competitions whom Frost, all through his life,
had out-maneuvered or bullied. Theirs was a power
more subtle than the power to print a poem or not print

it; their reviews were meant to articulate cultural positions and not merely to announce whether a book of poems was good or bad; and they could not very easily be dismissed as could Edgar Lee Masters or Vachel Lindsay or Amy Lowell as practitioners of a rival and demonstrably inferior poetic style. Along with great authority in the academy, the new "gang" exercised a wider general influence through magazines on the left, like *The New Republic, The Nation,* and *Partisan Review,* all of which were trying to assess literary works as evidences of the larger directions of contemporary culture. In doing this, they brought into sharp relief what had up to that time gone mostly unnoticed—the political implications of Frost's poetry and of his theories, implicit and explicit, about the functions of literature.

The differences I am trying to describe are political in an ideological sense, and this is not the way Americans habitually think of politics. It is of no consequence to our considerations, for example, that Frost was given Lee as a middle name by a father of such strong Copperhead sympathies that he had wanted to enlist in the army of General Robert E. Lee. Nor is it important that Frost could sometimes express himself rather charmingly about the possible political implications of his poetry insofar as the American two-party system was concerned:

> They think I'm no New Dealer but really and truly I'm not, you know, all that clear about it. In "The Death of the Hired Man" that I wrote long, long ago, long before the New Deal, I put it two ways about home. One would be the manly way: "Home is the place where, when you go there, they have to take you in." That's the man's feeling about it. And then the wife says, "I should have called it / Something you somehow haven't to deserve." That's the New Deal, the feminine way of it, the mother way. You don't have to deserve your

mother's love. You have to deserve your father's. He's more particular. One's a Republican, one's a Democrat. The father is always a Republican toward his son, and his mother's always a Democrat. Very few have noticed that second thing; they've always noticed the sarcasm, the hardness of the male one   (*Writers at Work: The Paris Review* Interviews, Second Series, p. 25).

This is pleasant, but innocuous, like the politics in "Build Soil" or in "To a Thinker," both written before Roosevelt's ascendancy, in 1932 and 1933 respectively, though when the latter was printed in 1936 it was taken by some to be crudely allusive to Roosevelt's paralysis: "The last step taken found your heft / Decidedly upon the left. / One more would throw you on the right. / Another still—you see your plight." There is a tendency in Frost's more directly political utterances to chuckle, as he does in the *Paris Review* interview, over opinions he thinks outrageous. But even to an admirer—perhaps especially to an admirer—such opinions are the more platitudinous for being simplifications of, say, the poignant and mysterious threats to individualism implicit in "Stopping by Woods on a Snowy Evening." Frost begins in the thirties, as I have said, unnecessarily to explicate himself with what are to me mostly embarrassing results, as in the series called "Ten Mills":

> I never dared be radical when young
> For fear it would make me conservative when old.
> > (Precaution)

or

> Let chaos storm!
> Let cloud shapes swarm!
> I wait for form.
> > (Pertinax)

Such poetry—(and there are samples sprinkled throughout *A Witness Tree* (1942) and *Steeple Bush* (1947), the next two volumes—is the result of having not the courage but the discouragement of one's convictions. And the evidence of insecurity goes beyond politics into a kind of assertiveness about poetry itself and his characteristic poetic practices. He becomes self-conscious about his tone, not in any critical way, but as if the reader should now appreciate it as among the predictable eccentricities of someone in the family:

> Some things are never clear.
> But the weather is clear tonight,
> Thanks to a clearing rain.
> The mountains are brought up near,
> The stars are brought out bright.
> Your old sweet-cynical strain
> Would come in like you here:
> "So we won't say nothing is clear."

Even if the "you" is supposed to be someone else, it is obvious from the title alone—"Voice Ways"—that the reader is to think of Frost's preoccupation with voice and of *his* presumably "old sweet-cynical strain." Or there is the kind of thing found in "A Missive Missile"— "Why will I not analogize? / (I do too much in some men's eyes)"—or in "The Lesson for Today" ("I would have written of me on my stone: / I had a lover's quarrel with the world"), or the couplet ending "A Considerable Speck" ("No one can know how glad I am to find / On any sheet the least display of mind"), or the last two lines of "The Fear of Man" ("May I in my brief bolt across the scene / Not be misunderstood in what I mean").

Frost's self-consciousness about politics was also, then, a self-consciousness about poetic habits, and the public awareness of them. As is evident in some of his best poetry, his politics and his poetics are inseparable, but when he becomes defensively explicit about this, he reveals the cost of his having spent a lifetime with mostly second-rate literary minds, or with academics, some of them brilliant men and women, who were bound to be deferential to the great man on campus, or with people ignorant of social theory. It is not necessary to say that it is possible to be a great poet despite such a pattern of associations. Of course it is—and Frost is the example. I am talking rather about his decisions, in specific poems, to propose himself to us as a poet whose thinking should matter, who chose to display a cogitating mind in verse, and was unembarrassed by the sometimes trivial results.

And yet, even as he nearly succumbed to his worst possibilities, he somehow managed to save himself. He confounded his critics by writing (and resurrecting) some poetry whose complications are both fresh and wonderful, and he did so at exactly the time when the better critics who attacked him, like Arvin and Blackmur, revealed that they could not read him at his already published best. They were locked into simplistic expectations and their readings yielded correspondingly simplistic results. Frost, they would have us believe, was hurt by his confinements to New England and by his conservative politics. Would he have been a better poet, or Faulkner a better novelist, if either had chosen to live in New York? or had a different politics? More likely, Frost would have been no poet at all. Politics is only one aspect of a larger commitment of feeling, even of sexuality. That Frost, as if imitating his adverse critics, sometimes abstracted his politics and made the worst of them is no reason why his critics should do the same thing.

There are a number of questions before us. First, in what sense is some of his poetry a response to the threat articulated in a criticism written from the left and often from the point of view of the Waste Land ethos? Second, to what extent does this criticism derive from a reading of Frost that is superficial and that expects from him far less than he offers? And third, are not his politics incidental to the deepest impulses of his genius and to such larger dispositions about the nature of life as to make his flashes of vulgarity and even his limitations of historical vision—something no writer is without—the necessary conditions of an ennobling achievement?

A Further Range, the volume that occasioned the sharpest attacks, happens to include some of Frost's strongest poems: among them, "The White-Tailed Hornet," "Neither Out Far Nor In Deep," "Desert Places," "Design," "The Strong Are Saying Nothing," "Provide, Provide." It also includes obnoxiously preachy pieces addressed to an audience of the already convinced, like "At Woodward's Gardens" (an attack on Darwinian evolution) and a garden club evocation called "Iris by Night," wherein a rainbow encircles a group, including Frost, "in a relation of elected friends." It is one of the best of Frost's books, better than the earlier *West-Running Brook* and easily as good as *New Hampshire.* The attacks on it from critics associated with the left thus allow us to ask some questions about a more general balkiness in modern criticism when it comes to Frost. Politics offered a conveniently loud and just as conveniently crude form for an attack already implicit in critical negligence. Politics was at last the way, and 1936 was at last the right time, to go after him. And it should be remembered that this was also a time when these same critics were for the most part reverential about two "great" poets, Pound and Yeats, who were flirting with Fascism, and with another, Eliot, who was still being anti-Semitic on grounds of a question-begging definition of culture and of a specious anti-cosmopolitanism that went with it.

Some of the adverse reviews of *A Further Range* came from critics of considerable sophistication, notably Newton Arvin in *Partisan Review* and R. P. Blackmur in *The Nation*. Both came round to the complaint, as did Horace Gregory in *The New Republic,* and Rolfe Humphries in *The New Masses,* that Frost was simply not "major": Arvin's piece is entitled "A Minor Strain," and Blackmur dismisses Frost as a "mere easy-going versifier"—this, when before him was a book full of dazzling metrical accomplishments. The very title was taken to mean that Frost was illegitimately laying claim to new poetic territories. People who had not sufficiently explored the territory already made available in earlier books were now provoked to say that Frost was not one of the important poets of the time, because like "A Drumlin Woodchuck," he wanted only to be "more secure and snug." The ending of that poem, especially where its phrasing resembles the letter to *The Amherst Student* of 1935, could be taken as a nearly smirking declaration of territorial confinement: ". . . though small / As measured against the All, / I have been so instinctively thorough / About my crevice and burrow."

Despite Frost's direct excursion into politics and other "further ranges," including the quasi-philosophical effort of "West-Running Brook," the charge made against him was that his ambitiousness only directed attention to his being, in Blackmur's term, "an escapist" from the modern world. He was said to be so anxious for "mastery" that he chose only those subjects, large or small, which he could most easily control. Granville Hicks had already put the matter more succinctly in an unsigned review eight years before, at the time of *West-Running Brook:* "He has created the ordered world in which he lives by the exclusion of many, many chaotic elements in the real world. Perhaps it is this fact that explains why Frost is, even at his best, a very perfect minor poet, not the major poet America is looking for" (in the Springfield *Union Republican,* 30 December 1928, p. 7). Hicks was a leading communist critic in this period, an editor of *The New Masses,* and author in 1933 of a Marxist interpretation of American literature since the Civil War, *The Great Tradition.* His objections to Frost provide what little grounding there might be for the later trifling criticisms of Arvin, Blackmur, Humphries, and Cowley, though not for Yvor Winters, the flat-minded irrelevance of whose criticism of Frost must look for its excuse not to political ideology but to Winters' loyalist admirers and to his own tone-deaf rationalism. Thanks to Marxist training, Hicks's objections are more incisive than are the pretentious stretch-outs of Arvin in *Partisan Review* ("It is the New England of . . . skepticism and resignation and retreat") or the smirky sarcasms of Cowley in *The New Republic* ("He is rather a poet who celebrates the diminished but prosperous and self-respecting New England of the tourist home and the antique shop in the abandoned gristmill.") The ignorance displayed by attacks of this kind is the more astonishing for its self-assurance. Such exercises in confident ineptitude, the first by Hicks in 1928, the second by Arvin in 1936, the next by Cowley in 1944, followed by the Winters essay in 1948, in *Sewanee Review,* can pass for criticism only in a literary climate that fosters the twinned reductions of modernism and socialist realism.

Frost was fair game for critics writing for the more urbane and urban journals like *The New Republic* and *Partisan Review.* He did not cope with issues and subjects considered, though not by him, unique to the twentieth century and recognized as central by both left- and right-wing adherents to ideas of social decline and dete-

rioration, ideas implicit in literary modernism and in
arguments for the necessity of centralized social planning. At its most reductive, the operative assumptions of
this criticism are that we go to a poet the way we go to a
grocer's—with a shopping list calling for Freudianism,
science, industrialism, chaos, the city, or whatever. I
would expect that the discussion up to now has sufficiently answered the charge that Frost is merely a so-
called New England poet (an allegation resurrected with
some vitality in A. Alvarez' *Stewards of Excellence*); and
in any case no one should go to any writer with a shopping list. When the "items" are graspably in stock they
are invariably shoddy. With Frost, the items can be
found only if, in order to give prominence to a few sal-
able commodities, you move out of the way everything
that he chiefly offers. Why propose, as Brower does, for
example, that "If as Randall Jarrell says ["Acquainted
with the Night"] connects Frost with Dante, it shows as
surely his kinship with Baudelaire and all seers of the
modern city"? (*The Poetry of Robert Frost,* p. 126). Such a
statement is a concession to topicality that ought not to
be made, particularly since it provokes the reply that
"Acquainted with the Night" is the only poem by Frost
that remotely could suggest Baudelaire. Once is not
enough.

Genius, it is said, exists in limitation. Frost is or is not
a great poet within the limits, and thanks to them, imposed by his idea of form in poetry and in nature.
There is no point in trying to prove that he exceeded
these when in fact he did not. Anyone is free to conceive
of these limits as a handicap, but in so doing might
wonder at the same time if the opinion does not derive
from a system of belief hierarchically structured by what
Frost sardonically calls "the larger excruciations." How
Frost chose to live with his limitations, be they a defect

or a virtue, how, indeed, to live *in* them, to explore them with a passion for excess, as Henry James recommended—this is what matters. And all the more because any admirer like myself must honestly face evidence that beginning with his fourth volume, *New Hampshire,* through some of *A Further Range* and *West-Running Brook,* on through nearly the whole of the second half of *A Witness Tree,* Frost had dogmatized himself with his own hierarchical schemes to a point where he sometimes showed a satisfaction so smug, an irony so steeped in the vanity of popular acclaim, as to invite repudiation. He can repudiate his best self, most disreputably, by his ironies. Not those local ones which follow necessarily from his trying to keep in conjunction a visionary and a real world, but the larger kind that exert a control, often retrospectively, over a whole poem, invalidating rather than modifying the compact initially established with the reader. Under such circumstances—I think of "Once by the Pacific"—"irony is the wound," as Octavio Paz somewhere remarks, "through which analogy bleeds to death."

In a curious way Frost was saved from his debilitating tendencies by the very political-literary opposition which prompted so crass a reaction from him. As we will see, he began to develop a view more pronouncedly mystic and visionary than before; of the poet as the truly exceptional man in any scheme, Darwinian, Christian, political, or in the country life around him. The poet is someone who will not "come in" even if asked, who "has promises to keep" which prevent him from doing more than "stopping by." The same talent for making an exception of himself that is evident in his poetry of natural enticement helps Frost in the more political poems of *A Further Range,* as when the two tramps come "out of the mud"—an image of undifferentiated mass flow—and want him to surrender what he has to them. With this volume, Frost shows more than ever an affinity to Lawrence and to the Emerson of the later, less idealistic strain. In *Conduct of Life,* published in 1860, Emerson declares, as against the liberalism and social unrest of his own day, that "masses are rude, lame, unmade, pernicious in their demands and influence. . . . I wish not to concede anything to them, but to . . . divide and break them up, and draw individuals from them. . . ." Emerson shows in such a passage how Frost himself could appeal, in defense of his own formalism, against the "mass," against "tides" of opinion, and against the programs of political liberalism.

Interestingly enough, there begins to appear in Frost's poetry of the 1930's a more concerted critique of "design," of formal regularity, of form itself. This is especially noticeable in the metrical angularities of a verse essay like "The White-Tailed Hornet." *A Further Range* includes, then, an earlier Frost already familiar, a more recent one who too much enjoys what is familiar—a Frost who has given himself over to his own formulae— and another Frost of which he has given only fleeting glimpses and who is writing against any relaxations into what, in one poem, he calls "the stated plan." If he becomes tiresomely explicit about his pieties, he becomes explicit also, and with a new surge of poetic energy, about aspects of himself that are most profitably conflicted.

More than ever, he seems to withhold total assent from what is simultaneously being affirmed in a poem. This has always been true of the realities of a natural scene, which can get undermined by the repeated use of negatives or of phrases like "as if." But now Frost hints at a much greater willingness to test and question some of the operative principles, the sincerities behind his

own writing. Form, as we know, is for him characteristically a protection against chaos while being at the
same time a provocation to elude security systems; it is
now, more than ever, treated as a possible threat of fix-
ity. The "wisdom" of ordinary folk, teased enough in
earlier poems, can now be freakish, a conformity of dull
staring, as in "Neither Out Far Nor In Deep." And the
prescription of 1929 in "Preface to *A Way Out*" that "everything written is as good as it is dramatic," is violated
by some of the best poems, like "The Strong Are Saying
Nothing," which are not dramatic in any sense; their
power resides precisely in an induced feeling of near
stasis. The same is true, by Frost's admission, in "Design." "It's one of those that is very undramatic in the
speech entirely. It's a kind of poker-face piece," he remarked in 1958 during a public appearance where he
read the poem three times over (Cook, p. 126). In a
subsequent talk, when he read "Design" twice, he remarked that "this is a harder one . . . see, that hasn't
any tune at all. That's a new way to write. That's getting
all the resonance out of it that you can get out of it"
(Cook, p. 135).

Given the often hidden distance between the time
when some of Frost's central poems were written and
the time of their publication, the precariousness of any
discussion of "development" might be more positively
viewed as a forced lesson in the caution of thinking of
any writer in terms of "development." What more often
happens is that a writer remains pretty much the same
but finds new terminologies, new challenges, and new
opportunities for testing the self and refreshing it.
Structurally, as I argued in the second chapter, the
Joyce of the little story "The Sisters" is the Joyce of the
massive novel *Ulysses;* the Eliot of "The Preludes" is the

Eliot of *The Waste Land;* the development in each case is the translation into terms of greater historical-cultural currency of the feeling of potential paralysis and fragmentation which obsessed each author from the beginning.

This same repetition with a difference is observable in the characteristics that come into sharper focus with *A Further Range.* "Design" is one of the best poems in it, giving evidence, as we have heard Frost say of himself in 1959, of a "new way to write." And yet the poem was actually first printed in *American Poetry 1922, A Miscellany.* What changed between 1922 and 1936 was not the poem but Frost's feelings about it, his decision, at last, to lay full claim to it. But even in 1950 he can say, with remarkable casualness, that he had forgotten it until "someone turned it up and began to get it said about and I put it in the book" (Cook, p. 126).

But what exactly does he mean by "it"? There are in fact two remarkably different versions of "it," the earlier of which goes back even before 1922—a poem called "In White," which he sent to Susan Ward with a letter dated January 15, 1912. At the time of composition Frost was teaching William James's *Psychology* ("Briefer Course") and *Talks to Teachers on Psychology* to his students at Plymouth Normal School in New Hampshire. He was also reading *Pragmatism.* Along with the works of Emerson and Thoreau, *Pragmatism* was a source of metaphors for him and for certain exercises of mind in his poetry. In Lecture Three, "Some Metaphysical Problems Metaphysically Considered," Frost came upon a passage that is the likely source for the poem we know as "Design" and for the earlier version called "In White." I will quote first the extensive passage from James and then both versions of the poem:

Let me pass to a very cognate philosophic problem, the *question of design in nature.* God's existence has from time immemorial been held to be proved by certain natural facts. Many facts appear as if expressly designed in view of one another. Thus the woodpecker's bill, tongue, feet, tail, etc., fit him wondrously for a world of trees, with grubs hid in their bark to feed upon. The parts of our eye fit the laws of light to perfection, leading its rays to a sharp picture on our retina. Such mutual fitting of things diverse in origin argued design, it was held; and the designer was always treated as a man-loving deity.

The first step in these arguments was to prove that the design *existed.* Nature was ransacked for results obtained through separate things being co-adapted. Our eyes, for instance, originate in intra-uterine darkness, and the light originates in the sun, yet see how they fit each other. They are evidently made *for* each other. Vision is the end designed, light and eyes the separate means devised for its attainment.

It is strange, considering how unanimously our ancestors felt the force of this argument, to see how little it counts for since the triumph of the darwinian theory. Darwin opened our minds to the power of chance-happenings to bring forth 'fit' results if only they have time to add themselves together. He showed the enormous waste of nature in producing results that get destroyed because of their unfitness. He also emphasized the number of adaptations which, if designed, would argue an evil rather than a good designer. *Here,* all depends upon the point of view. To the grub under the bark the exquisite fitness of the woodpecker's organism to extract him would certainly argue a diabolical designer.

Theologians have by this time stretched their minds so as to embrace the darwinian facts, and yet to interpret them as still showing divine purpose. It used to be a question of purpose against mechansim, of one *or* the other. It was as if one should say "My shoes are evidently designed to fit my feet, hence it is impossible that they should have been produced by machinery." We know that they are both: they are made by a machinery itself designed to fit the feet with shoes. Theology need only stretch similarly the designs of God. As the aim of a football-team is not merely to get the ball to a certain goal (if that were so, they would simply get up on some dark night and place it there), but to get it there by a fixed *machinery of conditions*—the game's rules and the opposing players; so the aim of God is not merely, let us say, to make men and to save them, but rather to get this done through the sole agency of nature's vast machinery. Without nature's stupendous laws and counterforces, man's creation and perfection, we might suppose, would be too insipid achievements for God to have proposed them.

This saves the form of the design-argument at the expense of its old easy human content. The designer is no longer the old man-like deity. His designs have grown so vast as to be incomprehensible to us humans. The *what* of them so overwhelms us that to establish the mere *that* of a designer for them becomes of very little consequence in comparison. We can with difficulty comprehend the *character* of a cosmic mind whose purposes are fully revealed by the strange mixture of goods and evils that we find in this actual world's particulars. Or rather we cannot by any possibility comprehend it. The mere word 'design' by itself has no consequences and explains nothing. It is the barrenest of principles. The old question of *whether* there is design is idle. The real question is what is the world, whether or not it have a designer—and that can be revealed only by the study of all nature's particulars.

Remember that *no matter what* nature may have produced or may be producing, the means must necessarily have been adequate, must have been *fitted to that production*. The argument from fitness to design would consequently always apply, whatever were the product's character. The recent Mont-Pelée eruption, for example, required all previous history to produce that exact combination of ruined houses, human and animal corpses, sunken ships, volcanic ashes, etc., in just that one hideous configuration of positions. France had to be a nation and colonize Martinique. Our country had to exist and send our ships there. *If* God aimed at just that result, the means by which the centuries bent their influences towards it, showed exquisite intelligence. And so of any state of things whatever, either in nature or in history, which we find actually realized. For the parts of things must always make *some* definite resultant, be it chaotic or harmonious. When we look at what has actually come, the conditions must always appear perfectly designed to ensure it. We can always say, therefore, in any conceivable world, of any conceivable character, that the whole cosmic machinery *may* have been designed to produce it.

Pragmatically, then, the abstract word 'design' is a blank cartridge. It carries no consequences, it does no execution. *What* design? and *what* designer? are the only serious questions, and the study of facts is the only way of getting even approximate answers. Meanwhile, pending the slow answer from facts, any one who insists that there *is* a designer and who is sure he is a divine one, gets a certain pragmatic benefit from the term—the same, in fact, which we saw that the terms God, Spirit, or the Absolute, yield us. 'Design,' worthless tho it be as a mere rationalistic principle set above or behind things for our admiration, becomes, if our faith concretes it into something theistic, a term of *promise*. Returning with it into experience, we gain a more confiding outlook on the future. If not a blind force but a seeing force runs things, we may reasonably expect better issues. This vague confidence in the future is the sole pragmatic meaning at present discernible in the terms design and designer. But if cosmic confidence is right not wrong, better not worse, that is a most important meaning. That much at least of possible 'truth' the terms will then have in them.

In White

A dented spider like a snowdrop white
On a white Heal-all, holding up a moth
Like a white piece of lifeless satin cloth—
Saw ever curious eye so strange a sight?

Portent in little, assorted death and blight   5
Like the ingredients of a witches' broth?
The beady spider, the flower like a froth,
And the moth carried like a paper kite.

What had that flower to do with being white,
The blue Brunella every child's delight?   10
What brought the kindred spider to that height?
(Make we no thesis of the miller's plight.*)
What but design of darkness and of night?
Design, design! Do I use the word aright?

Design

I found a dimpled spider, fat and white,
On a white heal-all, holding up a moth
Like a white piece of rigid satin cloth—
Assorted characters of death and blight
Mixed ready to begin the morning right,   5
Like the ingredients of a witches' broth—
A snow-drop spider, a flower like a froth,
And dead wings carried like a paper kite.

What had that flower to do with being white,
The wayside blue and innocent heal-all?   10
What brought the kindred spider to that height,
Then steered the white moth thither in the night?
What but design of darkness to appall?—
If design govern in a thing so small.

James's extensive influence can be located both in particular images—the statement about eyes, for instance, might have something to do with the last stanza of "All Revelation" ("Eyes seeking the response of eyes")—and in Frost's general disposition. The idea that creation might prove insipid if it did not work against opposition and counterforce (as in getting a ball over a goal line) is similar to Frost's notion of the process of a poem in

* miller-moth

"The Figure a Poem Makes" or his contention that "Every single poem written regular is a symbol small or great of the way the will has to pitch into commitments deeper and deeper" ("The Constant Symbol"). With respect to "In White" and "Design," the very clumsiness of the first indicates Frost's studious dependency on the passage from James. The line "Saw ever curious eye," for instance (whose? when? where? why?), can escape ridicule only by appeal to some antecedent authority. Such authority lies not, I think, in emblem poems, though "In White" does seem rhetorically to court that form; it lies instead in James's description of the inveterate thrust of investigation and "curiosity." "Nature was ransacked for results," he tells us, adding that "the real question is what *is* the world, whether or not it have a designer—and that can be revealed only by the study of all nature's particulars." So, too, with the unfortunate word "thesis" in line 12. It carries a nervous reassurance as if to someone checking up on his coverage of the subject, and so does the school-boy display of verbal-philosophical scrupulousness in the last line: "Design, design! Do I use the word aright?"

The later poem is freed of such sophomoric concern about correct usage or responsible modes of perception. By contrast to "In White," "Design" is a rather playful poem, much closer to the charmingly confident willingness in James to allow for alternate or conflicting possibilities. There is less worry about whether the word "design" is used "aright" because the speaker is his own man. If the word is not used "aright," then the responsibility lies in some collusion between reality and the perception of it. As in "The Most of It," reality here appears to form itself in shapes that one "finds"; it sends signals that offer, according to how you read them, more than you can cope with and less than you need.

The same is true, of course, for the "design" of a "thing so small" as a poem, particularly a sonnet like this one. Understandably, the poem ends with two questions. The first, while grammatically in the form of a question ("What but design of darkness to appall?"), is more assertive than the second, which is grammatically a conditional clause ("If design govern in a thing so small"). The first question is pronounced by two heavily accented syllables on either end ("What but . . . appall"). And yet the very emphasis on "appall" brings with it a demand for attention which, as alternative meanings begin to emerge, dissolves the fright initially induced by the word. It is related to the word "pale" and suggests therefore that in our fright we might become as white as the horrid little cluster of things we are looking at. "Appall" also suggests "pale" in yet other ways, however. A "pale" can be a spike (is that an image of how the spider is "holding up a moth"?) and, most importantly, a "pale" can be a slat in a fence, as every farmer knows. "Darkness" has fenced in or enclosed these "assorted characters." It has given them a "design." Thus, an extended and potentially self-canceling reading of the line would be "What but design of darkness to" . . . design. This would be an extraordinarily witty way to gather up and transform the meanings being groped for in the clumsy ending of the original: "Design, design! Do I use the word aright?" As a tautology the line would also give a still more problematic and sardonic turn to the last line of the poem. A design whose purpose is only to "design" cannot be said to "govern" much of anything, large or small.

A reading of this kind is assisted by James's observation about the woodpecker and the grub, an observation full of that ingratiating, warm-hearted sarcasm of his (so like Emerson of the later and shorter essay "Nature"),

when he is exposing the affrontery of human schema-
tizations: "to the grub under the bark the exquisite
fitness of the woodpecker's organism to extract him
would certainly argue a diabolic designer." The word
"appall" is therefore marvelously apt not only because it
can end up meaning "design" but because in doing so it
maintains its connotations of terror. The implications of
design are "appalling" in every sense if we try to infer
from any assortment of things the presence of something or someone, a Creator who "governs." Melville
and the "whiteness" of his whale are a glimmering presence here, much as in "For Once, Then, Something," a
poem written in 1917, between "In White" and "Design": "What was that whiteness? / Truth? a pebble of
quartz? For once, then, something." In this poem, written in hendecasyllabics—Frost's affectionate nod to Catullus—there is, as in "Design," the enticement of significances simultaneously denied by the tone and the terms
in which they are offered, as note the comic alliteration
of "w" and how an assertive beginning ("For once,
then,") gives way to the hesitancy of the word "something."

Christianity for Frost is only one of the ways in which
he can feel baffled to some probably good effect; it is a
form of belief, and so is poetry, which excites as many
questions as it answers. Even when he is most expressly
Christian in his poetry, as in the *Masques,* little is affirmed that is not implicit in "Design," as we can see
from Job's speech in "A Masque of Reason" when God
begins to fudge on an answer to a direct question: "Why
did you hurt me so?"

JOB.   All right, don't tell me, then, 270
If you don't want to. I don't want to know.
But what is all this secrecy about?
I fail to see what fun, what satisfaction

A God can find in laughing at how badly
Men fumble at the possibilities   275
When left to guess forever for themselves.
The chances are when there's so much pretense
Of metaphysical profundity
The obscurity's a fraud to cover nothing.
I've come to think no so-called hidden value's   280
Worth going after. Get down into things,
It will be found there's no more given there
Than on the surface. If there ever was,
The crypt was long since rifled by the Greeks.
We don't know where we are, or who we are.   285
We don't know one another; don't know You;
Don't know what time it is. We don't know, don't we?
Who says we don't? Who got up these misgivings?
Oh, we know well enough to go ahead with.
I mean we seem to know enough to act on.   290
It comes down to a doubt about the wisdom
Of having children—after having had them,
So there is nothing we can do about it
But warn the children they perhaps should have none.
You could end this by simply coming out   295
And saying plainly and unequivocally
Whether there's any part of man immortal.
Yet You don't speak. Let fools bemuse themselves
By being baffled for the sake of being.
I'm sick of the whole artificial puzzle.   300

Job is noticeably overwrought here, but through him
Frost manages nonetheless to say a number of things
that can now be recognized as important to him. Among
these is the remark, that "obscurity's a fraud to cover
nothing" (line 279). The little passage where this occurs
is a jab, I would guess, against the cult of obscurity in
the kind of modern poetry Frost was not writing. In the
subsequent argument it is suggested that obscurity can
successfully defraud only those who assume that there
really *is* ("for once, then,") something important hidden
under the surface of things. Life, as Job would have it,

consists of going ahead not because some underlying meaningfulness is assured, some "so-called hidden value," but because one is in doubt that life is meaningful at all and has "misgivings" about committing anyone or anything to the future even while the commitment is being made. Far from being stalled or stopped by not being able to predict what is going to happen, by not being able to pin God down to a "plan" or "design," Job instead gets incensed, in a lovably feisty and tongue-tied way, about any suggestions (even those cast off by his own language) that one needs to be provided for in order to go on living: "We don't know, don't we? / Who says we don't? Who got up these misgivings? / Oh, we know well enough to go ahead with" (lines 287–89). In his momentary fretfulness Job says something about fools that is wiser than he knows and that represents what Frost thinks best about human beings generally: "being baffled for the sake of being" (line 299). "Being" here is both a gerund and a noun. Humans attain their "being" by a willingness to be baffled, or, as noted earlier, "confused"; the "puzzle" is "artificial" or unnecessary or in need of solution only to those who want a "design" which will take care of everything. Job's confusion here is Frost's own clarification. Job wants an answer but he would just as soon get along without one; he calls on God for a clue, but is at the same time aware that this presupposes a "puzzle." The puzzle may be no more than the fact that "life" exists at all. We are again in an area where Frost's positive attitude toward elusiveness of meaning applies at once to the difficulties of life and of poetry. Like Job's experience, some of the poems, as William Pritchard acutely, and admiringly, remarks, are "ultimately not quite understandable" ("The Grip of Frost," *Hudson Review,* Summer, 1976, p. 200).

"Designs" are themselves a part of mystery, the subject as well as the object of imagination. The dizzying denials in Job's speech of what is also his expressed appetite for certainties would, if put to work on the subject of political planning, have predictably contemptuous consequences, as we will eventually see. The highly mobile, even unstable, movement of attitudes in Job is what Frost would think most commendable about him, and it offers a clue to how we ourselves should proceed—and what we can expect to find—when we think about the career of certain of Frost's poems, including "Design." We cannot be sure why Frost left the poem behind for ten years, from 1912 to 1922, and then allowed a version to be printed, or why he then ignored it another fourteen, during which he published two volumes of poetry, before at last including it in *A Further Range.* It is possible to know, however, that the poem belongs to the "design" of this volume more than it would have to any other, and that it fits into a smaller design created by the five poems immediately following it, each of which is a variation on the theme already observed in Frost of walking or of "extra-vagance," the desire to get out of a rut, out of a form, the desire to break, at least for a brief spell, the apparent rules of duration. Some of these five poems—"On a Bird Singing in Its Sleep," "Afterflakes," "Clear and Colder," "Unharvested," and "There Are Roughly Zones"—will be discussed later on.

For the moment, let us look once again at "Design" itself. The meaning it acquires when placed in the context available to it in 1936 makes it in part a political poem, a poem of social commentary. Of course, it does read, and was initially intended to be read, as a poem about the philosophical and, inferentially, religious issue of design. But as already noted, the poem in its final form emphasizes, as "In White" does not, a distinct personal

presence. The voice at the end is of someone highly
skeptical about any kind of "design," and this is the
same person who pushes himself forward in the very
first phrase of the poem: "I found," etc. Someone who
announces that he has "found" something has probably
been looking for it, and, as James makes rather caus-
tically clear, someone looking for any kind of "design" is
doubtless going to find it: "When we look at what has actually come, the conditions must always appear perfectly
designed to assure it." The speaker of "In White," by
contrast, takes no responsibility for anything. Below the
level of the apparent, he cannot even be sure that he is
using the word "design" properly, whereas the speaker
in "Design" actively participates in the creation of what
he finds. We feel this most subtly in the way the metaphors and similes of the earlier poem are now given
some reverberation and point. What the speaker finds in
"Design" is not a "dented spider," whatever that could
be or imply, but a "dimpled" one who is also "fat" and
"white." It has the characteristics of a healthy baby,
though its color may be a bit off, a suggestion consistent
with "paper kite" in line 8, the words "blue and innocent" in line 10, and even with the phrase "mixed
ready to begin the morning right." Breakfast cereal?
The connotations are macabre. But they are also ridiculously cheery, and the combination is nicely evident in
the way "satin cloth" could evoke either a wedding gown
or, in the attribution of "rigid," a pall.

In the submerged reference to advertisements for
breakfast cereal and to the fat and dimpled babies who
might be seen in such an advertisement, "Design" manages, as it appears in *A Further Range,* to become socially
topical. That is, much of what the speaker finds is on the
verge of being "designed" in the sense of being "pack-
aged." One might say that the images seem sporadically

to mimic a possible "design for living." That is not what the poem is "about," but it is a consequence of the words in the poem, a kind of surplus meaning. Advertising slogans or political jingoism is even more directly at work in the other poems near by in the same volume. Note only the title of "On Taking from the Top to Broaden the Base" or the lines in "The Strong Are Saying Nothing" which evoke *Good Housekeeping* ("The final flat of the hoe's approval stamp / Is reserved for the bed of a few selected seed."). Or one of the poems with which "Design" is grouped, "Clear and Colder": it begins with a recipe for the weather ("Wind, the season-climate mixer, / In my Witches' Weather Primer / Says, to make this Fall Elixir / First you let the summer simmer, / Using neither spoon nor skimmer, / Till about the right consistence")—and it ends with a selling puff ("Wait and watch the liquor settle. / I could stand whole dayfuls of it. / Wind she brews a heady kettle. / Human beings love it—love it. / Gods above are not above it.").

If "Gods above" are not "above" recipes and formulas even for the weather, then the human "designs" on life have come a fair way toward accounting for Everything. Except, as the gusty-contemptuous mimicry of the poet suggests, they really have not come as far as they intend. They have contrived no more than have earlier witch-crafts, and the references to "witches' broth" in "Design" and to "Witches' Weather Primer" in "Clear and Colder" get echoed in a famous poem a little further on about the folly of trying to "design" your life by putting things aside for a rainy day. In "Provide, Provide" the central illustration of the hazards of fortune is another kind of witch:

> The witch that came (the withered hag)
> To wash the steps with pail and rag
> Was once the beauty Abishag,

The picture pride of Hollywood.
Too many fall from great and good
For you to doubt the likelihood.

If witchcraft has no power over the accidents of life,
then supposedly "planning" has. Frost once took delight
in reading the poem to an audience which included his
left-liberal friend Henry Wallace. He did so not because
he wanted the poem read as a mockery of efforts to
"provide" for oneself. I think he rather toughly suggests
that the effort is worth making despite the odds. What
he was doing on that occasion was setting the stage for
his *ad hoc* political aside to Wallace when he had finished
the poem—"Provide, provide! . . . Or somebody else 'll
provide for ya."

It might seem as if Frost's attitude toward "design" is
at odds with his earlier confidence in the virtues of
form, but no contradiction emerges if it is kept in mind
that from the beginning he demonstrated a habitual suspicion of any form or "design" or "provision" that does
not find itself by almost lucky accident. Form, like the
act of love, induces a sense of pleasure and security
which fortunately cannot be permanent. If it were, then
the form would be without the efficacy and pleasure
that comes from the act of discovering and shaping it,
time after time. "Momentary stays against confusion"
are the best of all, as Frost wants always to show, and the
only significant difference, at this later stage of his career, is in the terms for expressing this preference. Earlier, the terms derived from his concern with durations
and with entrapments—in a place, a circumstance, a
metaphor. Now, his terminology tends also to refer to
those political nostrums or popular styles that insist on
conformity, on our settling into a mold. His feelings on
this score are apparent in his imitations and parodies of

the political and advertising vocabularies meant for contemporary mass audiences. And there are other poems
in which his delight in the flexibility of form in nature
and in poetry is set against the deadening inflexibilities
of political or social formulae. He can discover within
the conflict a freedom that once again depends on the
rich and sustaining resources of the past, especially in
the poetry of the seventeenth century which has "kept"
certain myths and images alive. A lovely example is a
short poem called "Unharvested," one of the group that
immediately follows "Design":

> A scent of ripeness from over a wall.
> And come to leave the routine road
> And look for what had made me stall,
> There sure enough was an apple tree
> That had eased itself of its summer load,   5
> And of all but its trivial foliage free,
> Now breathed as light as a lady's fan.
> For there there had been an apple fall
> As complete as the apple had given man.
> The ground was one circle of solid red.   10
>
> May something go always unharvested!
> May much stay out of our stated plan,
> Apples or something forgotten and left,
> So smelling their sweetness would be no theft.

To some extent, this, too, is a poem about "walls" and
"extra-vagance." Walls have a power of confinement
which creates a counter-movement of "mischief" if we
are reading "Mending Wall," or irresponsible invention
if we are reading "A Star in a Stoneboat," or "profanation" if we are reading "Good Hours," or, as here,
"theft." But what is stolen is not an object, not even an
apple. Instead it is a "scent," the "theft" of an emana-
tion, of something no one can possibly own. Frost toys

with the idea of ownership the way Thoreau does, who likes, as he says, to walk over other men's "premises," or as Emerson does when he remarks that while particular people may own a farm, "none of them owns the landscape. There is a property in the horizon which no man has but he whose eye can integrate all the parts, that is, the poet. This is the best part of these men's farms, yet to this their warranty-deeds give no title" (*Nature*). In his beautiful dedication of *A Further Range* to his wife, Frost himself allows the attractions of visionary possession: "To E. F. for what it may mean to her that beyond the White Mountains were the Green; beyond both were the Rockies, the Sierras, and, in thought, the Andes and the Himalayas—range beyond range even to the realm of governments and religion."

In "Unharvested," the "scent of ripeness from over a wall" reveals the "best" of someone's apple orchards, precisely because it is the most ephemeral part, the "sweetness" of unharvested apples, all that has been "forgotten and left." In other words, what appeals to him most cannot fit any "design" or "stated plan," economic or legal. In 1934, when the poem was first printed, the phrase "stated plan" was full of political connotations of state planning in the United States as well as in Italy and the National Socialism, so called, of Nazi Germany. The term can refer to any kind of presumptuous planning. Significantly, it is an accident rather than premeditation, the accident of an odor coming over a wall, which takes the speaker out of what is already a somewhat "designed" experience. It makes him "stall." "Stall" is a peculiar, an odd-sounding word here, and it reminds us of the casualness implicit in common phrases like "stalling for time," or "stalling around" in violation of a set schedule. These connotations are consistent with the fact that the speaker leaves a "routine road"—the road both as it cuts through wilderness toward a predetermined goal and as it forces movement into a "routine." As the old farmer in the poem "From Plane to Plane" says to the young college boy with whom he is working in a field, " 'A man has got to keep his extrication. / The important thing is not to get bogged down / In what he has to do to earn a living.' " And in a poem published still later in *In the Clearing*, there is a kind of scanning of what the apples mean in "Unharvested" in the beautiful image of a pod of milkweed that keeps its grip upon a plant because it is inquisitive about "some dim secret of the good of waste" ("Pod of the Milkweed").

The speaker of "Unharvested" in his "extrication" from routine and in his confrontation with "waste" is able to offer us more than a scene of randomly fallen apples: they form "one circle of solid red." Like the "saturated meadow" in "Rose Pogonias," which was "Sunshaped and jewel-small, / A circle scarcely wider / Than the trees around were tall," the arrangement of the apples creates an aura associated with ceremonious or ritualistic re-enactment. The anapestic tendency of the poem is pronounced and at times dominant, as in the four anapestic beats of line 6: "And of all but its trivial foliage free." The poem begins to pick up a gravity and slowness of movement when the vocabulary, while giving full credit to the seasonal fall, implicates itself with the great mythic Fall. Hence, the relaxed but witty implications of saying that an apple tree of "all but its trivial foliage free, / Now breathed as light as a lady's fan. / For there had been an apple fall / As complete as the apple had given man." The word "free" is infused with Miltonic and Biblical possibilities and makes the otherwise merely picturesque reference to the "lady's fan" something that might, in this context, remind us of the seductiveness of an Eve.

If the fall of the apples in "Unharvested" is to be as-

sociated with the fall of man, then it is with the *felix
culpa* or fortunate fall of *Paradise Lost*. It was this that
made it possible for humans to take control of their own
destiny and to have those "passionate preferences," a
phrase of which Frost was particularly fond, by which
they might freely choose either to save or lose themselves. In one of the many remarkably energetic poems
from *In the Clearing*—he was eighty-six at the time of its
publication—Frost explicitly connects the violation of
"design" with the attainment of an earned salvation, either in earthly love or in the love of God:

> Whose purpose was it? His or Hers or Its?
> Let's leave that to the scientific wits.
> Grant me intention, purpose, and design—
> That's near enough for me to the Divine.
>
> And yet for all this help of head and brain
> How happily instinctive we remain,
> Our best guide upward further to the light,
> Passionate preference such as love at sight.
> ("Accidentally on Purpose")

The language here, echoing a much earlier poem,
"The Master Speed," again reflects Frost's indebtedness
to the notion of *élan vital* which he found in Bergson
and which he used frequently to counteract evolutionary
theories by which human passions or preferences are
left out of the "stated plan" of deterministic biology.
This conjunction of poems allows us to see significances
about which "Unharvested" is by itself appealingly cir-
cumspect. We can say, that is, that if the best part of the
unharvested apples is the "scent" then the best part of
man, as the poets George Herbert and Henry King
suggest, is the odor of sanctity. It is the soul which is
"unharvested," an idea beautifully developed in "After
Apple-Picking." In that poem the glory and possibility

of life exists, the open chance (to quote the last line of Herbert's "Our Life is Hid with Christ in God") "To gain at harvest an eternal *Treasure.*" The same idea is evident in one of the most mysterious and wonderful of Frost's earlier poems, first printed in 1906, "The Trial by Existence," and in "A Masque of Reason" in 1945:

> For instance, is there such a thing as Progress?
> Job says there's no such thing as Earth's becoming
> An easier place for man to save his soul in.
> Except as a hard place to save his soul in,
> A trial ground where he can try himself
> And find out whether he is any good,
> It would be meaningless. It might as well
> Be Heaven at once and have it over with.

Anything outside a "stated plan," anything "unharvested" is an encouragement to that "extra-vagance" which, throughout Frost, is necessary to those who want to create "homes" or "forms" that are more conducive to freedom and the rejuvenation of the self than are the homes one starts from. The knowledge that no one can at last depend on being taken care of by governments—or even by God—is the necessary inducement to further creation in life, in poetry, in the imagination of the self.

The "things" that one wants most, and that nature makes us want, are in Frost, as in Thoreau and Emerson, elusive of already existing or "provided" forms. "There is in woods and waters a certain enticement and flattery," Emerson observes, "together with a failure to yield a present satisfaction . . . always a referred existence" ("Nature," *Essays, Second Series*). There is a "scent of ripeness," an odor of "sweetness" more important than apples to be gathered. What is most desired is

always in the future and unnamed. In one of his interviews Frost gives a clarification of these matters which,
again, is much indebted both to Emerson and to William
James:

> The Founding Fathers didn't believe in the future. . . .
> they believed it *in*. You're always believing ahead of
> your evidence. . . . the most creative thing in us is to
> believe a thing in, in love, in all else. You believe your-
> self into existence. You believe your marriage into exis-
> tence, you believe in each other, you believe that it's
> worth while going on, or you'd commit suicide
> wouldn't you?   (Lathem, *Interviews with Robert Frost*, p.
> 271).

Frost takes his place in an American tradition which
proposes that since you are most inconsequential when
you are most "included" in any system or "stated plan,"
you are, paradoxically, most likely to find yourself, and
to be saved, when you risk being excluded or periph-
eral. This is a tradition full of political implications. The
placement of the self in relation to the apparent organi-
zations of things is one of the major concerns of Frost's
later poetry, but it is a political concern only while it also
reveals his more general contempt for a tendency in
modern liberalism to discredit the capacity of ordinary,
struggling people to survive in freedom and hope without the assistance of state or any other kind of planning
and despite the arrogant solicitude of those who think
that such people would be better off if "provided" for.
"On a Bird Singing in Its Sleep" is a nice example, coming immediately after "Design," in the group of associated poems already mentioned:

> A bird half wakened in the lunar noon
> Sang halfway through its little inborn tune.

Partly because it sang but once all night
And that from no especial bush's height,
Partly because it sang ventriloquist   5
And had the inspiration to desist
Almost before the prick of hostile ears,
It ventured less in peril than appears.
It could not have come down to us so far,
Through the interstices of things ajar   10
On the long bead chain of repeated birth,
To be a bird while we are men on earth,
If singing out of sleep and dream that way
Had made it much more easily a prey.

If the song is "inborn," then so is the caution with
which it gets stopped; it is not a fearful or timid caution,
but an "inspiration to desist," like something breathed
in. The bird "sang ventriloquist": its lyricism is inherited
yet somehow learned. So is its decorum. Otherwise, it
"could not have come down to us so far, / Through the
interstices of things ajar." The poem is about a native
shrewdness which has allowed this little creature to per-
petuate itself while taking risks that are nearly taunt-
ing—it stops singing just a moment too late, "almost
before the prick of hostile ears." Survival in the passage
through nature or through life is not managed and it
cannot be planned; it is the result, inborn and instinctive, of finding your way not through a structure but
through the gaps in it, through things "ajar," things in
conflict, and of doing so with a daring playfulness.

Frost seldom misses a chance to bring Darwinism into
question, more in a teasing than a dogmatically orga-
nized way. Darwinian evolution for him implied too
much linear predictability, and while it proposed the
necessity of waste it was indifferent to its virtues. He was
resolutely committed, as he shows in his commentary on
Amy Lowell and in the structure of his poems, to the
contrary notion mentioned earlier: that "the most excit-

ing movement in nature is not progress, advance, but
expansion and contraction," instinctive assertion and inspired caution.

The terms at work in these poems—"interstices,"
"ajar," "extrications," "waste," "unharvested"—describe
conditions of existence available to human beings only
when they act to free themselves from "routine" and
"planning." We create this opportunity by acts of extrication, by "waste" or "extravagance," by preferences,
passions, and above all, by the determination to resist
rather than participate in what is deemed progress. In
"West-Running Brook" this gets expressed in the image
of the brook that "can trust itself to go by contraries," to
resist, with a backward motion, a forward thrust that is
part of the "universal cataract of death": "It is this backward motion toward the source, / Against the stream,
that most we see ourselves in." The same image occurs
in another poem from *A Further Range,* a kind of Pro-
thalamion which Frost wrote to his daughter Leslie on
her marriage, called "The Master Speed." He endows
the young married couple in the poem with a speed
greater than that "of wind or water rushing by," but it is
a speed curiously enough conducive not of movement
forward but rather of "the power of standing still— /
Off any still or moving thing you say."

The central image for both poems owes something to
Emerson, who makes the "backward motion" synonymous with the conservatism of art: "The direction is forever onward, but the artist still goes back for materials
and begins again with the first elements on the most advanced stage: otherwise all goes to ruin" ("Nature," *Essays, Second Series*). But more directly Frost is indebted to
Henri Bergson's *Creative Evolution,* another book he
read, along with a great deal of James, in 1912. He
found there the Lucretian image of life as a stream or

river and the statement that "our consciousness is . . .
continually drawn the opposite way. . . . This retro-
spective vision . . . must detach itself from the *already
made* and attach itself to the *being-made*," Emerson's "advanced stage" of "first elements." In choosing images of
resistance and contrariness to "drift," "design," or
"stated plan" Frost was at the same time enacting them;
he was expressing his own stubborn contrariness to
dominant intellectual movements that were full of of-
fensive political implications. That is why in arguing
with scientists at the University of Michigan during his
visit there in 1917 he cared as much for the *posture* as
for the substance of what he said. Even philosophical
thinking was for Frost very much a matter of stance and
of tone, and he writes to Untermeyer on January 1,
1917, about being "so fond of seeing our theories
knocked into cocked hats." He continues, in a passage
quoted at the beginning of this book, that

> What I like about Bergson and Fabre is that they have
> bothered our evolutionism so much with the cases of
> instinct they have brought up. You get more credit for
> thinking if you restate formulae or cite cases that fall in
> easily under formulae, but all the fun is outside saying
> things that suggest formulae that won't formulate—
> that almost but don't quite formulate. I should like to
> be so subtle at this game as to seem to a casual person
> altogether obvious. The casual person would assume
> that I meant nothing or else I came near enough mean-
> ing something he was familiar with to mean it for all
> practical purposes. Well well well   (*The Letters of Robert
> Frost to Louis Untermeyer*, p. 47).

Saying things that almost but do not quite formulate is
a central achievement of Frost's poetry from the first
volume onward. It is to be seen as a conscious effort to
extricate himself from poetic and intellectually fashion-

able concoctions. For that reason, poems in which people decline invitations from nature to "come in" or give
up can be re-read or re-experienced as parables of intellectual as well as physical and moral courage. By 1934,
when "Desert Places" was first printed, the tropes it
shares with "Stopping by Woods on a Snowy Evening"
(1923)—of a snow and a landscape that can threaten to
"include me unawares"—had political implications. The
threats in landscape are also threats and oppositions of a
literary and cultural kind. Not only does the danger at
the end of the penultimate stanza sound curiously like a
threat to the act of writing itself ("A blanker whiteness
of benighted snow / With no expression, nothing to express"), but it is immediately followed by what could be
an allusion to "the Pound-Eliot-Richards gang" with
whom Frost associated Matthiessen. "They cannot scare
me with their empty spaces" takes us, as I mentioned
earlier, to the Eliot whose poetry had already implicit in
it the lines which were to appear in "East Coker" as an
echo of Pascal's "The eternal silence of those infinite
spaces": "O dark dark dark. They all go into the
dark, / The vacant interstellar spaces. . . ."

As against formulae of any kind and against views of
existence which he thought to be fashionable in the thirties, Frost's recalcitrance might amount to no more than
standing still or even saying nothing instead of something. The poems in the volume are filled with an anapestic movement meant (though the frequent anapests
in the dramatic narratives were used with no such intention) to suggest two quite opposite kinds of foot-drag-
ging. On the one hand are his objections to panaceas
and promises, as evoked by the first and third foot of a
line like "But the stróng | are sáy | ing noth | ing untíl |
they sée," and on the other a near total lassitude, the
passive resistance implicit in the anapestic feet in

> The péop | lé álong | thé sand
> All túrn | and look | one wáy.
> They túrn | their báck | on the land.
> They look | át the séa | all dáy.
>
> As long | as it takes | to pass
> A ship | keeps rais | ing its hull.
>
> ("Neither Out Far Nor In Deep")

The landscape of these poems is in every sense impoverished. It gives no sustenance to life; it promises little in the future, and none at all to the imagination. It is impoverished both in Wallace Stevens' sense and in Henry Wallace's, so that the only hint of metaphoric activity in "Neither Out Far Nor In Deep," aside from the mockery in the title, is the observation that "The wetter ground like glass / Reflects a standing gull." These lines, and others in the poem, emphasize the total *un*reflectiveness of "the people" who merely sit all day and look at the sea. And what is further emphasized is the fact that no detail of the poem mirrors or reflects anything except inertia and conformity. By contrast, the men who work alone in "The Strong Are Saying Nothing" have a sort of Beckett-like heroism in the stoic separateness of their probably useless labor. That is why the word "harrowed" in the second stanza has a peculiarly right double meaning, suggesting both the clods that have been broken up and the feelings that have been lacerated or tormented:

> There is seldom more than a man to a harrowed piece.
> Men work alone, their lots plowed far apart,
> One stringing a chain of seed in an open crease,
> And another stumbling after a halting cart.

If the land is niggardly in what it promises to yield to
the people who till it, the landscape is no more yielding
to the poet.

These are poems of almost blank observation and, for
Frost, a near tonelessness. When it comes to "metaphors
we live by," of which he speaks in "Education by Poetry," he would rather have "trivial ones of my own
. . . than the big ones of other people"; he would rather
have even his own "desert places," and in the poems we
have just looked at there is a studied avoidance of the
kind of metaphors that would even sustain, much less
exalt, life. "The White-Tailed Hornet," near the beginning of the volume, is an amused meditation on the fate
of metaphor under Darwinian and "liberal" auspices. In
the table of contents for the 1939 *Collected Poems* and in
most reprintings thereafter, it bore the subtitle "The
Revision of Theories." It is a witty essay whose iambic
pentameter is thrown into prose-like movements nearly
every other line by a lurch into hendecasyllabics. A hornet who lives in a "balloon"—actually a Japanese crepe
paper globe that floats in the woodshed—darts out to
sting the poet because of the mistaken assumption that
he wants to steal the globe and hang it over his bookcase. The hornet acts out of "instinct" and with an aim
that is "unerring." "Verse could be written on the certainty / With which he penetrates my best defense," the
speaker tells us in his prosy line. And yet the hornet's instinct is not sufficient to let him make proper comparisons. He cannot, the speaker complains, "recognize in
me the exception / I like to think I am in everything,"
someone, that is, who would never want to hang such a
balloon over his bookcase. Nor does "instinct" work
more efficiently where it might be expected to—in locat-
ing flies, the hornet's natural prey. Here is a case where
"instinct" does not appear to be governed at all by the

kind of laws which evolution would lay down for it. Instead, the hornet strikes with great accuracy on nail-
heads and on huckleberries, and when he at last finds a
fly

> He shot and missed;
> And the fly circled round him in derision.
> But for the fly he might have made me think
> He had been at his poetry, comparing
> Nailhead with fly and fly with huckleberry:
> How like a fly, how very like a fly.

The derision in the speaker is more than charming Horatian humor or playful philosophizing. The
speaker's reference to the hornet's "poetry," coupled
with his saying earlier that "verse could be written on
the certainty / With which he penetrates my best defense"—these should alert us to the fact that the poem is
concerned with the difficulties of making or sustaining
comparisons of a kind that constitute an education
about human potentiality. The Horatian mode, that is,
has played itself out in a post-humanistic world where
Darwinism and related theories from Pavlov and Freud
have "instituted / Downward comparisons." The ending
shows an elegant unruffled skepticism. This is someone
who, with a kind of deviltry, is exploding the very
theories that, so he pretends, initially encouraged him in
his observations:

> Won't this whole instinct matter bear revision?
> Won't almost any theory bear revision?
> To err is human, not to, animal.
> Or so we pay the compliment to instinct,
> Only too liberal of our compliment
> That really takes away instead of gives.
> Our worship, humor, conscientiousness
> Went long since to the dogs under the table.

And served us right for having instituted
Downward comparisons. As long on earth
As our comparisons were stoutly upward
With gods and angels, we were men at least,
But little lower than the gods and angels.
But once comparisons were yielded downward,
Once we began to see our images
Reflected in the mud and even dust,
'Twas disillusion upon disillusion.
We were lost piecemeal to the animals,
Like people thrown out to delay the wolves.
Nothing but fallibility was left us,
And this day's work made even that seem doubtful.

The middle of the passage is Great Books paraphrase: Oh, what a piece of work is a man. It is saved, I think, by a sometimes homey, sometimes paradoxical wit: as in the comic image from a Russian novel of pursuing wolves; the near-oxymoron of "nothing but fallibility"; and the comic clumsiness in the monosyllabic sprawl of the last line, meant perhaps as an example of how fallibility can get into the writing itself.

A reciprocal pressure can be felt between this poem and the one which immediately precedes it in the volume, "Two Tramps in Mud Time." The latter is an exceptionally strong example of Frost's political and poetical resistance to "liberal compliment" and "downward comparisons." Ostensibly the poem is about a choice facing the speaker on a day when there are stirrings of early spring in the air and in himself. Should he continue to do something that gives him pleasure, like chopping wood, so as to release his body and his muscles to the seasonal possibilities of relaxation, or, alternatively, should he turn the task over to two tramps who "wanted to take my job for pay"? There is no dialogue; the poem is essentially an interior monologue by a man who considers these alternatives while he chops wood under the watchful and intimidating scrutiny of the two strangers. They are "downward" indeed: he says at the outset that they "came . . . out of the mud," a sluggish mass. However, he also says that they "caught me splitting wood," so that while his view of their anonymous inferiority is prejudicial, there is a chance that his phraseology about them is charged with a paranoiac guilt implied by the word "caught." It is a word whose implications are never brought wholly under the control of the poem.

This failure is the first clue to larger deficiencies. The poem is all the time retreating from its powerful Laurentian inclinations. It aspires and sometimes nearly manages to be about the desire of this man to do what he wants to do only because he wants to do it; his being demands it. But it is an inexplicably embarrassed and apologetic effort, and the rhetoric at the end attempts to make the man's desire socially, morally, and politically acceptable. The best parts avoid evocations of general standards, like those that mar the closing of stanza two:

> The blows that a life of self-control
> Spares to strike for the common good,
> That day, giving a loose to my soul,
> I spent on the unimportant wood.

and also avoid efforts to implicate the reader ("You know how it is with an April day"). Instead, they are strongly self-exonerated and self-delighting:

> The time when most I loved my task
> These two must make me love it more
> By coming with what they came to ask.
> You'd think I never had felt before
> The weight of an ax-head poised aloft,
> The grip on earth of outspread feet,
> The life of muscles rocking soft
> And smooth and moist in vernal heat.

There are no "downward comparisons" or even any "comparisons . . . stoutly upward" here. There is an assertion of self and of being, and that is enough. But the moment is short-lived. The ending of the poem shows how, characteristically, Frost's need of "comparisons" can be at times poetically and intellectually compromising:

> But yield who will to their separation,
> My object in living is to unite
> My avocation and my vocation
> As my two eyes make one in sight.
> Only where love and need are one,
> And the work is play for mortal stakes,
> Is the deed ever really done
> For Heaven and the future's sakes.

The ending involves "comparisons . . . stoutly upward," but to what? "Need" is not being compared to "play," which would take the kind of courage demanded by the poem itself; it is instead being compared to what can only be called Renaissance humanism, and the poem is the loser thereby. It may be that the word "vocation" is meant to reveal its original sense of "voice" and, therefore, of poetry. But otherwise there is no evidence of what the speaker's "vocation" might be or why "love" has anything to do with his desire to chop wood. Nor is there suggested any of the connections, which support some of Frost's best poems, between human love and the creative promises of seasonal change and poetic inspiration. As a result, the last line, "For Heaven and the future's sakes," lacks the force and resonance of similar conjunctions in "A Prayer in Spring," an otherwise less interesting poem. It is therefore scarcely a sign of the strength of this poem that the observation "And the work is play for mortal stakes" is so detachably memorable.

Lurking in this performance is a mistrust of poetry. Mistrust can be the begetter of great poetry rather than a bar to it, as Eliot repeatedly shows, beginning with "The Preludes" and through the "Four Quartets," and it is in Stevens often an excuse for luxuriance. Frost is a poet by vocation; but his avocation is something like chopping wood. That is, his visionary life is linked ineluctably to physical sensations and realities generally considered "natural." So subtle are his driftings from one kind of experience to another that is possible in reading "Birches," for instance, to forget that the trees are bent because of ice storms and not because boys have been swinging in them. The latter is only the poet's preference: "I should prefer to have some boy bend them." Such "preference," as it functions to determine the evolution and shape of a poem, is the same as the "passionate preference" which, in Frost's thinking about evolution, helps determine the shape and form of life itself. Preference can be the determination only to "stand still" within the fluctional movements of nature and of history, to "stand still" not for the confirmation of vision but only to attest the possibilities, momentarily, of entertaining one, even the vision of obliteration. Unlike Yeats or Stevens or Lawrence, Frost never let his visions abstract him from a sense of persistent and demanding daily reality. He can be as great as they because in the management of certain poems—like "After Apple-Picking," "Never Again Would Birds' Song Be the Same," "All Revelation," or "A Star in a Stoneboat"—he invents occasions when conflicting kinds of reality are resolved, as Emerson wished they would be, in the mythic properties of language itself. This is what happens in poems where he thinks least about any audience or any reader, where he is reading himself, in all arrogance and daring, but in humility before the "thing" done by poetry as well as by himself. Often, as it turns out, these are poems about work which, unlike "Two Tramps in Mud Time," are filled with the best kind of vanity about the writing of poems; writing becomes a kind of work superior to any other, the poet becomes the best of workers by virtue of being the most inclusive, and also the most free of self-accusing moralisms.

VI
The Work
of Knowing

But if, instead of identifying ourselves with the work, we feel that the soul of the Workman streams through us, we shall find the peace of the morning dwelling first in our hearts, and the fathomless powers of gravity and chemistry, and, over them, of life, pre-existing within us in their highest form.

Emerson, "Nature" (*Essays, Second Series*)

In "Two Tramps in Mud Time," the woodchopper is also, as obviously, a poet, and it is suggested that ideally the work of hands and of mind are one. Implicit in this claim is a special pride in the superiority of Frost's kind of poet. Other poets, it is suggested, and certain other day laborers, are able in work to make use of only a limited amount of their potential powers; they therefore never come into full possession of the "thing" produced, of the "fact," which in "Mowing" is "the sweetest dream that labor knows." Thoreau is the precedent here in the great chapter of *Walden* called "The Bean Field." He allows that there may be others besides himself who want to grow beans. But his point is that only a Poet,

one who, in Emerson's words, "stands among partial
men for the complete man" ("The Poet") can really
"know" them. "I was determined to know beans," he asserts, demonstrating in the very phrasing his authority
to transfigure the most common and popular jargons.

How does anyone "know beans"? More perplexing
still, how does anyone know that he knows them? This is
a question set and answered by Thoreau and, with more
subtlety and less show-off wit, by Frost in his poems of
work and in the work of his poems. The answer is that
you "know" a thing and know that you know it only
when "work" begins to yield a language that puts you
and something else, like a field, at a point of vibrant intersection. Thoreau by this process, "dabbling like a
plastic artist in the dewy and crumbling sand," arrives at
a moment when he can say that "It was no longer beans
that I hoed, nor I that hoed beans"; he "works" as "some
must work in fields if only for the sake of tropes and
expression." What you finally can know that you know is
mysterious and dream-like. And yet, in its mythic pro-
pensities, the knowledge is less ephemeral than are the
apparently more practical results of labor, like food or
money—or poems if no different from those already
harvested by the poets of the past.

Frost's poetry of work is quite directly about the cor-
relative work of writing a poem and of reading it. Any
intense labor enacted in his poetry, like mowing or
apple-picking, can penetrate to the visions, dreams,
myths that are at the heart of reality, constituting its articulate form for those who can read it with a requisite
lack of certainty and an indifference to merely practical
possessiveness. "Throughout nature," Emerson writes in
a phraseology that may remind us of Frost's early poem
"The Demiurge's Laugh," there is

something mocking, something that leads us on and
on, but arrives nowhere; keeps no faith with us. All
promise outruns the performance. We live in a system
of approximations. Every end is prospective of some
other end, which is also temporary; a round and final
success nowhere. We are encamped in nature, not domesticated. Hunger and thirst lead us on to eat and to
drink; but bread and wine, mix and cook them how
you will, leave us hungry and thirsty, after the stomach
is full. It is the same with all our arts and performances. Our music, our poetry, our language itself are
not satisfactions, but suggestions ("Nature," *Essays,*
Second Series).

The work of hands alone is not sufficient—and reality,
in the form of a buzzsaw, can even leap out to cut off
the hand and the life of a young man as in "Out,
Out—." But manual labor in Frost is often an image of
the effort to penetrate matter. Such penetration is the
precondition for the discovery of an intermediate realm
where something in the self and something in "things"
can meet in "a system of approximations."

Frost is a rigorous formalist to the extent that he is
also a witty one. He knows the elusiveness of the forms
that attend on any labor of perception, and in the poems
we will mainly consider—"The Ax-Helve," "Mowing,"
"After Apple-Picking," "Kitty Hawk," and "A Star in a
Stoneboat"—it is the difficulty of knowing *that* you know
anything, even when you may, which charms and ob-
sesses him. The first of these, "The Ax-Helve," was
doubtless on Frost's mind in 1916 (the poem first appeared in 1917) when he gave an interview to a reporter
from the *Philadelphia Public Ledger:*

Never larrup an emotion. Set yourself against the
moon. Resist the moon. If the moon's going to do anything to you, it's up to the moon. . . . Love, the moon,

and murder have poetry in them by common consent.
But it's in other places. It's in the axe-handle of a
French Canadian woodchopper. . . . You know the
Canadian woodchoppers . . . [make their own] axe-
handles, following the curve of the grain, and they're
strong and beautiful. Art should follow lines in nature,
like the grain of an axe-handle. False art puts curves on
things that haven't any curves   (quoted in Thompson,
II, 77).

In the poem, the speaker, who at the outset is cutting
wood in his yard, is interrupted when his French Canadian neighbor, Baptiste, catches his lifted ax from behind and proceeds to criticize the ax because its helve
was " 'made on machine.' " Baptiste invites him to his
house with the promise that " 'I put you one in / What's
las' awhile—good hick'ry what's grow crooked, / De second growt' I cut myself—tough, tough!' " Clearly we are
to take note of the accent here, and notice also how
markedly different it is from the speaker's at the
beginning of the poem:

> I've known ere now an interfering branch
> Of alder catch my lifted ax behind me.
> But that was in the woods, to hold my hand
> From striking at another alder's roots,
> And that was, as I say, an alder branch.

This is not the sound or figure of "art following the
lines of nature": there is instead the poeticism of "ere,"
the poetical fanciness of ascribing to a branch the intention not only of "interfering" but of doing so in order to
protect a fellow branch from being hit. Additionally,
there is the speaker's desire to call attention to his own
inventiveness in the self-congratulatory phrase "as I
say." Later in the poem, when this evidently educated
and literary type does visit the neighbor's house for the

first time, and sees a display of ax-helves, we get a passage which on the face of it simply illustrates to him and to us the principle by which work or art can "follow the lines of nature" rather than of bookishness.

> He showed me that the lines of a good helve
> . Were native to the grain before the knife
> Expressed them, and its curves were no false curves
> Put on it from without. And there its strength lay
> For the hard work.

It is tempting to read this passage as if it were a statement of poetic theory. But that would be a mistake. The passage belongs at this point to the developing relationship between two quite different men who happen to be neighbors, one of them an immigrant laborer, the other someone akin to Frost himself. The relationship is not unlike those in other work poems, such as "Mending Wall" or even "Two Tramps in Mud Time." In both of these, as here, the reader is asked more or less to trust the figure who stands for the poet, though, as we have seen, the trust is not to be either complete or uncritical. In "Mending Wall" the poet-figure who voices his opposition to wall-building is also the man who each year informs his taciturn neighbor that it is time to build them; in "Two Tramps in Mud Time" there is at least some possibility that the hortatory tone of the speaker is meant to characterize him as someone on the defensive, someone trying to justify to himself as well as to us his claim—that in his chopping of wood, even as two hungry tramps in need watch him do the job, he is exercising a prior right because somehow in the exercise of manual labor he has discovered that his vocation and avocation have become one, a job done for "Heaven and the future's sake."

In all these poems there is a social snobbishness in the

assignment of styles of speech—the two tramps are
given no voice at all, except for the idiot phrase of one
of them, "Hit them hard"—while there is at the same
time a hint that the poet-speaker is guilty now and again
of "false art," of "putting curves on things that haven't
any curves," of being too "knowing" in a merely received way. If a false knowingness is evident in the
opening lines of "The Ax-Helve," it becomes by the end
something more than a matter of social significance.
When Baptiste is finished talking he "stood the ax there
on its horse's hoof, / Erect, but not without its waves,
as when / The snake stood up for evil in the Garden." A
bit of gratuitous and "educated" fanciness? An effort to
give a mythic and Miltonic curve to what is by nature
curved anyway? To some extent, but it is important that
Baptiste himself seems to have an intimation of mythic
potentialities in the loving pride of the last line where
he, too, sees the ax-helve as a snake: "See how she cock
her head?" The image becomes an appropriate one for
the occasion, for the Frost we have been getting to
know, and for a poem about the labor of hands—
something that came into the world with the Fall. Just
before this passage, the speaker reveals his suspicion
that Baptiste has in fact lured him to the house to talk
less about ax-helves than the education of children. He
wants reassurances, from a man who has been to college, that it is permissible to keep children out of school;
and he is apparently aware, besides, that the speaker
(like Frost himself) has also tried to educate his own
children at home. Reference is made not to "his" but to
"our doubts / Of laid-on education."

Disingenuously, the speaker wonders what such education "had to do / With the curves of his ax-helves,"
when the connection between machine-turned handles
and school-bred children is almost too obvious. But the

disingenuousness is to good effect; it makes us look beyond the obvious and ask where this, like any metaphor in Frost, breaks down. What we begin to see by the end is that the educated speaker is no more exonerated from the Fall and its consequences than is the uneducated Baptiste. They have, he tells us, talked about education, but the word he uses initially is "knowledge": "what we talked about was knowledge." The poem ends, then, with a reminder, in the image of the snake in the garden, that we cannot in a fallen world know anything except by approximations. Nature, including our own, is fallen; it takes hard work and a willingness to respect the particular form of individual things—a respect which a machine cannot show and a schoolroom tends to neglect—if we are to recover any approximations of what nature ideally intended. But hard work means, in turn, that children cannot simply be left to nature, any more than can a piece of wood be left as it is if it is to serve as an ax-helve, machine made or hand made. That is why the doubts about education expressed both by Baptiste and the speaker have to remain doubts. They cannot be just what they are, whatever that is. At the end the two men also have doubts about each other, even though the one needs help with ax-helves and the other needs help with education. What joins them is a shared perception: that work is necessary if we are to get down to the grain of things, the lines in nature which we cannot otherwise know or see. The work, the labor, and the subsequent discovery of the "lines in nature"—all these bring to consciousness both the Fall which made labor necessary, and the good fortune of our having henceforth to discover the world anew for ourselves. That is in part what Frost means when he says at the end of his great poem about penetration that "All revelation has been ours."

In the same interview with the *Public Ledger,* Frost observed that Puritanism "hasn't had its day, and it might
be fun to set it up as an artistic doctrine." This, it seems
to me, is what he does, though never in any systematic
way, in his poems about penetration of matter by
various kinds of work, including the reading and the
writing of poetry. To work is to cope with "facts" in
much the way the poet, ideally, confronts his medium—
as something that, in response to his exertions of personal power, will lay bare an essential form which will at
last absorb and transform such power into expression
that is more than personal. Again, he observes in the interview that "The curse of our poetry"—this was
1917—"is that we lay it on things. . . .

> But people say to me: "The facts themselves aren't
> enough. You've got to do something to them, haven't
> you? They can't be poetical unless the poet handles
> them." To that I have a very simple answer. It's this:
> "Anything you do to the facts falsifies them, but any-
> thing the facts do to you—yes, even against your will;
> yes, resist them with all your strength—transforms
> them into poetry" (quoted in Thompson, II, 77–78).

There is no use pretending that statements such as
this make any immediate sense. And there are no terms
other than those Frost is using here which can make
clearer what he means by the insistence that one should
"resist" facts and by the promise that this will "transform
them into poetry." It is simplistic to say, as Thompson
does, that there is operative in Frost the Puritan doctrine, winnowed from Emerson and Thoreau, that "any
fact may and should be viewed as a type or emblem or
symbol of some element in the divine plan" (Thompson,
I, 550). Where there is the inclination to do so in Frost,
there is, as strongly, the struggle not to. Frost's sense of

fact does not elucidate an idea so much as a state of mind about the proper *way* to think and to perceive, the proper way to "educate" yourself by the reading and the writing of poetry, and by the dramatic trying out of metaphor. You may save your soul in the process, because it is the process that will save it, not any theological faith prior to it. In his feeling for "facts" and for the special kind of work required by those who would discover the poetry that is in them, Frost varied but did not change between his very early poems, written on the Derry farm between 1900 and 1906, and the very late poems like "Kitty Hawk," published in his final volume. "Mowing," written in that early period and published in *A Boy's Will,* is both an example of his extraordinary self-possession as a young poet and of tendencies that pass on into later poems like "Mending Wall," "Two Tramps in Mud Time," and "The Ax-Helve," along with others I have not yet discussed at length, "After Apple-Picking," "Putting in the Seed," "A Star in a Stoneboat":

There was never a sound beside the wood but one,
And that was my long scythe whispering to the ground.
What was it it whispered? I knew not well myself;
Perhaps it was something about the heat of the sun,
Something, perhaps, about the lack of sound—   5
And that was why it whispered and did not speak.
It was no dream of the gift of idle hours,
Or easy gold at the hand of fay or elf:
Anything more than the truth would have seemed too weak
To the earnest love that laid the swale in rows,   10
Not without feeble-pointed spikes of flowers
(Pale orchises), and scared a bright green snake.
The fact is the sweetest dream that labor knows.
My long scythe whispered and left the hay to make.

The poem begins by decisively dispelling the notion that nature manifests its significance, if any, without the intervention of human labor: "There was never a sound beside the wood but one." This is not a likely "fact." Indisputably, there have been sounds other than mowing "beside" the wood: of the wind, the rustle of grass, or leaves, so that the disavowal, a very strong one in the word "never," must refer to sounds other than natural ones. Nature is silent for him except for sounds that result from human labor or that have been dignified and made worth listening to by the labor of poetry, by folklore or myth, such as the myth of the mower. In his conception of sound, that is, this speaker wants us to recognize that he is not the passive, sometimes fearfully receptive listener of Wordsworth or the ravished seer of Emerson, with his faith in the power of imagination to see "every dull fact," as Perry Miller puts it in *Errand into the Wilderness,* "as an emblem of spirit." For him, any sound of consequence apparently has to involve a human agency, and the whispering scythe, even at this early point, is potentially analogous to poetic "making."

Once past this discrimination, however, the speaker almost at once begins at least to allow for other possibilities and conjectures. It is as if, after all, he would be willing to entertain Wordsworthian or Emersonian impulses. The Frostian negatives of uncertainity come into play almost at once, as if to erode the initial negative of denial: "I knew not well," it "did not speak" but only "whispered," along with those tentative phrasings characteristic of his inquiries about the potential significance of sights and sounds in nature. "What was it it whispered?" "Perhaps it was something . . . Something, perhaps." The sound made by his scythe creates as much expectation as would any heard directly off a field or wood by a Swedenborgian or mystical pantheist. The metrical movement of the first eight lines of the sonnet registers an effort of mind to cope with mysteries that by tradition belong to the world of transcendental imagination or the world of romance and faerie, but which in this case issue, unexpectedly, from the world of practical effort, what Emerson would call the world of the "understanding," or Thoreau the world of "actual fact."

Frost wants none of the "easy gold" that other writers have already mined for him. The poem asserts itself both against and within the traditions it evokes. "Anything more than the truth" is whatever would be "laid-on" the experience from the outside merely, whether from Virgil or Marvell, or from the more distinctly American traditions to which Frost frequently acknowledged an indebtedness. All the same, something of that "more" gets into the poem in the very gesture by which he pretends to exclude it. The third line, for instance, "What was it it whispered? I knew not well myself," might for some readers be a reminder of the bucolic diaresis of Greek and Latin pastoral. And it is to the Latin and Greek derivation of the word "earnest" that we are invited to turn when reading of the "earnest love that laid the swale in rows." This is love that is more than zealous or serious; it is "earnest" also in the sense of being a promise or token of something to come, the harvest of his labor, the "sweetest dream" and the "harvest" of the poem itself. The last phrase of the poem, "and left the hay to make," seems to insist on such connections. By his laboring in the field, where he meets with feeble flowers and bright snakes, he has shown what it means to "make hay while the sun shines"; he has shown, also, how the very process of knowing what he is up to constitutes the "making" of a poem; and he can leave the "hay" to "make" what it will of whatever it can. As Thoreau said of his beans, the hay can have "results which are not harvested by me."

When the sonnet arrives at the conviction that "Anything more than the truth would have seemed too weak," it also arrives at an oxymoron. And this is one evidence that the "truth" or facticity which is promised for the sestet, far from being denuded of poetic and intellectual tradition to which the whole poem responds, will instead transcend these. The special strength of this "truth" is that it is without modification, without limiting substance—the hay is merely left to its own makings. The speaker has the satisfaction not in the results of his labor but in the labor itself, and his earnestness, in every sense of the word just mentioned, is communicated both in the grammatical simplicity of his declaration and in its open-endedness. "The fact is the sweetest dream that labor knows."

This discovery results from what the poem has done and what the worker has done to dispose of false dreams and expectations; the poem moves ahead by speculative probing, by wonderments that leave intact the essential mystery of the relationship thus developed between men and scythes, landscape and poet. Not everyone is vouchsafed such knowledge of "the fact" as the lines promises. Only some of Frost's laborers—like the apple-picker or the man in "Putting in the Seed"—are so privileged, and the poet as laborer, or the reader for that matter, can only hope to approximate the "dream" in the making of verse. In its odd syntactical bareness the line sounds itself like a "fact," and its lovely directness shames any challenge to what it says about the factual status of dreams.

The line defies rephrasing. We are not invited even to metaphoric speculations; the fact is not said to be "like" a dream; it *is* a dream. And it is "known" not by a person but by "labor." In the analogous labor of writing the line or of reading it we pass from "fact" to "dream" to "knows" but the sequence is not as conventional as the words in isolation might suggest. The line is not saying that we first labor hard with facts and then dream of our accomplishment and then become aware, in the dream, of how the facts we have physically encountered yielded a mysterious benefit. Again, it is "labor," not any meditation afterwards, that "knows." It is the activity, something that may be felt later on, in "After Apple-Picking," as a physical pain in the instep—it is this that "knows." And what "labor" knows is not *a* fact but *the* fact. It knows a type or composite which includes every aspect of the thing done: the hay, the scythe, the sound of the scythe, the silence of the wood, the margin between wood and field, the orchises, the snake, and so forth. Isn't "the fact" in that sense, isn't any "fact," always a dream since it cannot in any other state of consciousness hold in suspension all the varieties of truth and reality that impinge upon it? This is something athletes know as well as laborers of a certain kind. To do any job well requires the capacity to concentrate on the labor with a full and simultaneous awareness of the different orders of experience that get brought into play. This is what Frost tries to argue—without having made the argument inevitable—in his coda to "Two Tramps in Mud Time," with its proposal that "Only where love and need are one, / And the work is play for mortal stakes, / Is the deed ever really done / For Heaven and the future's sakes." In his work poems, as in a garden poem like "A Prayer in Spring," Frost uses the word "love" in a way that points again to his receptivity to seventeenth-century lyric poetry where the term can refer to the love of God and also to those human acts, including sex, by which we participate in the creation. The "earnest love" of "Mowing" is an example, and it il-

lustrates what Frost means in "Education by Poetry"
when he remarks that "Belief in God is a relationship
you enter into with Him to bring about the future."

A relationship between humans and God in Frost can,
as in the *Masques,* be consciously and explicitly founded
in complaints and in wonderings about mercy and justice. But the relationship very often comes about without calculated effort, even without a full consciousness
of its having been achieved, as in poems of work, of sexual love, or a combination of both, like "Putting in the
Seed." Any intense exercise of human creative powers in
Frost is apt to touch some larger creative force in the
universe. "How Love burns through the Putting in the
Seed"—the way that line, with its sudden appropriateness, glorifies the workaday activities of a farmer in
the field, the way it magnifies the workaday language of
a farmer in his marital playfulness, constitutes, as we
saw, the eloquence with which the sonnet comes to
terms with itself. The terms are appropriately those less
of an asserted fact (e.g., "Love burns through . . .")
than of an exclamation that has the elements of an awed
question ("How Love burns through . . ."). Like "Mowing," "Putting in the Seed" moves into a language that
redeems labor from drudgery and discovers in it a creative fulfillment of life: in the first, an inclusive
dream, and in the second, a sort of vision. But in the
same sure rhythm with which this expansively liberated
movement is registered, it is made to circle back on itself, back to earth. The last line of each poem returns to
work and to the soil: in the one case, to the ground over
which the scythe sweeps, and in the other, to the earth
crumbs which are shed by the "arched seedling," which
is also a new-born child. In one of his earliest poems,
"Bond and Free," from the period 1896 to 1900, Frost
describes this circuit in a way that has stylistic and tem-

peramental affinities to Marvell's "On a Drop of Dew." I
quote the first and last stanzas:

> Love has earth to which she clings
> With hills and circling arms about—
> Wall within wall to shut fear out.
> But Thought has need of no such things,
> For Thought has a pair of dauntless wings.
>
>   .   .   .
>
> His gains in heaven are what they are.
> Yet some say Love by being thrall
> And simply staying possesses all
> In several beauty that Thought fares far
> To find fused in another star.

The equivalent of "Thought" for Frost's laborers is
not ratiocination, or the kind of talk that goes with it.
"Thought" for them is the knowing that comes only in
labor, what is called "the sweetest dream" of labor. The
extraordinary tact, delicacy, and refinement of feeling
by which Frost shows how possession of this "dream"
constitutes "a relationship to God" is nowhere drama-
tized with more intimacy, or with a finer eloquence that
strains ever so gently within that intimacy, than in
"After Apple-Picking":

> My long two-pointed ladder's sticking through a tree
> Toward heaven still,
> And there's a barrel that I didn't fill
> Beside it, and there may be two or three
> Apples I didn't pick upon some bough.
> But I am done with apple-picking now.
> Essence of winter sleep is on the night,
> The scent of apples: I am drowsing off.
> I cannot rub the strangeness from my sight
> I got from looking through a pane of glass
> I skimmed this morning from the drinking trough
> And held against the world of hoary grass.
> It melted, and I let it fall and break.

But I was well
Upon my way to sleep before it fell,
And I could tell
What form my dreaming was about to take.
Magnified apples appear and disappear,
Stem end and blossom end,
And every fleck of russet showing clear.
My instep arch not only keeps the ache,
It keeps the pressure of a ladder-round.
I feel the ladder sway as the boughs bend.
And I keep hearing from the cellar bin
The rumbling sound
Of load on load of apples coming in.
For I have had too much
Of apple-picking: I am overtired
Of the great harvest I myself desired.
There were ten thousand thousand fruit to touch,
Cherish in hand, lift down, and not let fall.
For all
That struck the earth,
No matter if not bruised or spiked with stubble,
Went surely to the cider-apple heap
As of no worth.
One can see what will trouble
This sleep of mine, whatever sleep it is.
Were he not gone,
The woodchuck could say whether it's like his
Long sleep, as I describe its coming on,
Or just some human sleep.

The poem has become so familiar and revered that it
is difficult to recognize its strangeness. But it would
probably seem familiar in any case; it is a prime example
of how even the very great poems of Frost can induce a
kind of ease about their deeper intensities. It is a proud
poem, as if its very life depends upon a refusal to justify
itself by any open evidence of what it is up to. The apparent "truth" about the poem is that it is really concerned with the actualities of its announced subject. But

is that "truth" even residually enough if, not thinking so, one takes the risk of burdening the poem with "more than the truth"? Brower has written meticulously about its rhythmic form, but he has not let himself feel the deeper pulsations in its metaphors. There are energies in the poem as well as a dream of potential experience that include but are passionately larger than that recorded in his otherwise useful observation that "From the opening lines, apparently matter-of-fact talk falls into curious chain-like sentences, rich in end-rhymes and echoes of many sorts" until "memories of waking fact and their sleepy distortions become impossible to tell apart" (*The Poetry of Robert Frost,* pp. 24, 25).

Once again, "The fact is the sweetest dream that labor knows." It is a muscular and active knowing, and should not be confused with Santayana's rather too fastidious proposition that "The artist is a person consenting to dream of reality." Consent is not at issue—as if reality were propositioning us. What is required is toil and labor, the exertion of body and mind necessary to bring anything to birth. Labor, again, is both one of the unfortunate consequences of the Fall and a way of overcoming them, of transforming them into fortunate ones. The "dream" that "labor knows" in Frost's poems of work is often "sweet" because it frequently involves images of the birth or rebirth of the self, of redemption offered those who try to harvest reality.

"After Apple-Picking" is a dream vision, and from the outset it proposes that only labor can penetrate to the essential facts of natural life. These include, in this case, the discovery of the precarious balances whenever one season shifts to another, the exhaustions of the body, and the possible consequences of "falling," which are blemish and decay. When the penetration of "facts" or of matter occurs through labor, the laborer, who may also be the poet, becomes vaguely aware that what had before seemed solid and unmalleable is also part of a collective "dream" and partakes of myth. This is in part what is signified by Emerson's paradigm at the beginning of "Language" in *Nature:* "1. Words are signs of natural facts. 2. Particular natural facts are symbols of particular spiritual facts. 3. Nature is the symbol of spirit." The penetrating power of labor can be evinced in "apple-picking" or in writing or reading about it, and any one of these activities brings us close to seeing how apples and all that surround them can be symbolic of spirit. The easiness of voice movement and vocabulary in the poem will seem at odds with deeper possibilities only to those who do not share Frost's perception, following Emerson and Thoreau, that the possibilities are simply *there* to be encountered. When at the very outset the apple-picker remembers "My long two-pointed ladder's sticking through a tree," he is, without any self-consciousness, committed by "natural facts" to a mythological or symbolic statement, as he is immediately thereafter in the further "fact" that the ladder is pointing "toward heaven still." "Heaven" is not the destination awaiting anyone who climbs ladders, but it can become part of his consciousness of destinations.

A version of this image will appear later in "Directive," where "The height of the adventure is the height / Of country where two village cultures faded / Into each other. Both of them are lost. / And if you're lost enough to find yourself / By now, pull in your ladder road behind you. . . ." But this "ladder" is essentially lateral. The journey is back into time, into geological and cultural debris. Though I would not, with Helen Bacon, think that the two towns refer to the twin cults of Apollo and Dionysus, the poem lets itself be read as an attempted journey to poetic and personal sources where a self can be discovered this side of heaven. By comparison, the ladder in "After Apple-Picking" is quite graphically vertical, and it points to a destination beyond itself. It is, also, a ladder that is not "pulled in"; it is "still"—"still" there, "still" to be climbed again, and "still" pointing as if, despite its being "long," it merely directs us to a place toward which it provides the initial steps. It sticks "through" a tree and not against it.

And yet for all these suggestions, the ladder is very much a real one. The phrase "two-pointed ladder" is itself less directly metaphorical than is "ladder road" of "Directive." In a context where every word seems so much by nature to be metaphorical, "two-pointed" trembles with possibilities of meaning that adhere to its very essence. The phrase could signify metaphor itself and reminds us that for Frost metaphor was the true source and method of all thinking. Not only do we think in metaphors that are contrived for the purpose, like "ladder road"; more than that, we cannot so much as use a word or a phrase without committing ourselves, often unknowingly, to metaphor and therefore to some form of unconscious "thought." Thinking in Frost *is* metaphoric or "two-pointed," and it directs us at last to what is beyond the metaphor, to things we cannot "know" and whereof, as Wittgenstein suggested, we should not speak.

A "two-pointed ladder" is very much like a metaphor as Frost describes it. Its two terms head in a parallel and mutually supporting direction; ultimately, however, the relationship comes to an end or leaves off; the metaphor necessarily breaks down. The progress or movement of analogy brings us to something beyond it, like faith or a belief. Metaphor, that is, both controls us and propels us into exaggerations, into the idea of God, for instance, with whom we enter into a relationship, as Frost says at the end of "Education by Poetry," in order "to believe the future in—to believe the hereafter in." As in much of Frost's prose the syntax here is aggressively vernacular and irregular, and the effect is to make the word "in" a part of the verb. By a relationship to God, about which we cannot say very much and have little to show, we can, however, try, as in "Carpe Diem," to bring the future and the hereafter "in" close, to bring it "in," as by climbing ladders for the picking of apples, from remoteness or abstraction. In this same talk—it was stereographically recorded and printed first in 1931—Frost seems to have borrowed the image of the ladder and the sky from "After Apple-Picking" in order to talk about metaphor, about thinking, and about the hereafter or the future, the sky which waits at the end of the ladder. "We still ask boys in college to think, as in the nineties, but we seldom tell them what thinking means; we seldom tell them that it is just putting this and that together; it is just saying one thing in terms of another. To tell them is to set their feet on the first rung of a ladder the top of which sticks through the sky."

In his rambling somnolence, his driftings among the terms of his own obsessive experience, the apple-picker is "thinking" only less consciously than is the poet in his more directly exploratory use of language. From the outset the materials of the poem belong to the apple-picker: it is "my" and not "a" ladder that is sticking through the trees, and in Frost's formula the apple-picker's "saying" of one thing in terms of another *is* "thinking" even though he might not credit himself with doing so. Indeed, the conceptual frame of the poem, if so heavy a phrase is appropriate to it, is held together by the way "dream" gets stated in terms of waking experience, waking experience in terms of "dream." This is an

occasion when the precondition of metaphor itself
seems to be that the normal distinction between dreaming and waking be suspended. Even the verb tenses of
the poem contribute to this suspension: before he begins
his last day of apple-picking he "could tell" while awake
"What form my dreaming was about to take." It is as if
he woke before work into a kind of reality that had all
the strangeness of dream, and he looks to sleep after
work almost in the hope of dispelling the dream:

> I am drowsing off.
> I cannot rub the strangeness from my sight
> I got from looking through a pane of glass
> I skimmed this morning from the drinking trough
> And held against the world of hoary grass.
> It melted, and I let it fall and break.

There is both daring and genius in the lines that follow: "But I was well / Upon my way to sleep before it
fell." So confused are states of consciousness here that
perhaps we are to think that he slept all through the day
of work, perhaps he dreamed the day itself, with its
"hoary grass." This grass could be real, "hoary" in the
sense that it is coated white with morning frost; or it
could be other-worldly grass, "hoary" in the sense of
"ancient," part of a mythic world derived from the Bible
and Milton. We are not to decide which is which; we are
instead meant to equivocate. The larger possibilities are
made inextricable in our, and in his, experience from
smaller, more detailed ones. Thus, "essence" can mean
something abstract, like an attribute or even a spirit that
is fundamental to winter nights, and it is also something
very specific to apple-picking, the perfume of a harvest.
So wonderfully does the language of the poem subvert
any easy regulation that some readers might want to
think of the "perfume" in Herbert's "Life" or in King's

"Contemplation upon Flowers" or in Frost's own "Unharvested" which emanates from a soul that has sanc-
tified itself. So, too, with "harvest." It is called a "great
harvest," and while "great" can refer to numbers—
"There were ten thousand thousand fruit to touch"—it
soon begins to accumulate other than quantitative implications in its linkage to the word "cherish," the phrase
"not let fall," and the reminder, in the suddenly exalted
phrasing of "struck the earth" (when the word "ground"
might have been used), that the ladder was pointed not
at the "sky" but "toward heaven." The phrasing has a
Marvellian reticence, only a bit less pronounced than in
"The Silken Tent" where the "central cedar pole" is "its
pinnacle to heavenward."

   The apple-picker (and Frost) seems almost reluctantly
involved in these implications. Perhaps that is one reason why he is "overtired" of a harvest "I myself desired."
The intensity of labor has brought him in touch with a
vocabulary of "apples," "trees," "scent," "ladders," "har-
vests," of ascents and descents that make it impossible
for him not to say one thing in terms of another. To
speak of apples *is* to speak of the Fall and the discovery
of the benefits from it that both require and repay
human toil. The only explicitly metaphorical statement
in the entire, highly metaphoric poem—the only time
the apple-picker tries directly to generalize his experience ("One can see . . ."), and the only spot
where he admits to a sense of audience ("As I describe . . .)—occurs at the end:

> One can see what will trouble
> This sleep of mine, whatever sleep it is.
> Were he not gone,
> The woodchuck could say whether it's like his
> Long sleep, as I describe its coming on,
> Or just some human sleep.

It is appropriate to the whole intention of the poem that where the apple-picker sets out *wakefully* to accomplish what he has all along been doing in a daze, unconsciously—to make metaphors and to generalize on his experience—the result is a tangle of confusions. He is a successful "poet" only when he does not try to be. Obviously, the "woodchuck" could not "say" anything, and its capacity to make a metaphoric discrimination between its own and human sleep is rendered comic by the speaker's ascription to himself of the power only to "describe" the coming on of sleep. "Just some human sleep" sounds at first like an unfortunate infusion of the coy Frost—one of those calls for a trivially self-deprecating irony that reveal at times his peculiar embarrassment with the power of his own sincerities. But the line is saved from disingenuousness, just barely, by the "fact" that in his overtired state the apple-picker might indeed want a sleep equivalent to the hibernation of a woodchuck rather than a "human sleep." His sleep will be human precisely because it will be a disturbed, dream- and myth-ridden sleep. Human sleep is more than animal sleep for the very reason that it is bothered by memories of what it means to pick apples. After that famous picking in the Garden, human life, awake or sleeping, has been a dream, and words are compacted of the myths we have dreamt of the fall and redemption of souls.

"After Apple-Picking" is hardly an instance of how while Eliot was playing Eucharist, Frost, as he liked to say, was playing Euchre. And yet he cannot be called a religious poet in Eliot's sense. "Belief" in God and a hereafter, belief also in the "Fall," are rather the inescapable consequences of his feelings about life and especially about language. The language he wants to use, the acts, poetic and human, for which he has a "passionate preference," partake of mythologies whose forms happen to be Christian. Like Emerson, he finds his miracles not in dogma or antiquities but in human actions, especially those which, through labor, reveal and help create nature. The Fall is a human invention; it is one of the metaphors that helped him to "think," to make sense of human life and language.* And the things he wanted to say, as we saw in the last chapter, almost invariably involved reactions against general fallings or drifts, against any movement or current, in thought or nature, which tended to standardization, conformity, and the repression of the individual spirit.

Mythically and historically the most notorious and graphic example of standardization, calling forth a redeeming individual resistance, was the Fall itself. Frost plays with the image, as he does with any other, for all that it is worth; his poems are full of fallings: the fall of leaves, of snow, of apples, and "Brown's Descent." And besides the Fall of man there is another fall which redeems him, the descent of spirit into matter, ". . . risking spirit / In substantiation," is the way he puts it in "Kitty Hawk." It is this particular kind of "fall" which, in turn, allows us to ascend into or penetrate the "matter" which is the sky, using ladders, telescopes, the eye, poetic flight, or the airplane, all of which figure prominently in his numerous poems, probably as much as one-tenth of all of them, which are in whole or part concerned with stars. We can recall that in "On Extravagance," apropos of "Take Something Like a Star," he admits that "By star I mean the *Arabian Nights* or Catullus or something." That word "something" is not simply an

---

* Emerson can be recalled here, too: "It is very unhappy, but too late to be helped, the discovery we have made that we exist. That discovery is called the Fall of Man" ("Experience").

affectation of country talk to cover an uncustomary bookishness. It also means what it says, namely anything, any kind of work done by anyone that can extend the capability of human dreaming.

"Kitty Hawk," the long poem (471 lines) which appears in his last volume, *In the Clearing*, celebrates "something"—the first flight into air achieved by the Wright brothers—which, like any great effort of metaphor or poetry, was a successful penetration into the unknown. This feeling about scientific achievement is typical of Frost's refusal to join the poetic pack in their attacks on science and technology. For him, these are only the best kind of competition, which poetry ought to meet and profit from, and he chooses to recall the occasion of his suicidal trip at eighteen to the Dismal Swamp near the site of the Wright brothers' flight in order to suggest that, in his own way, he might have anticipated their accomplishment:

> It was on my tongue   40
> To have up and sung
> The initial flight
> I can see now might—
> Should have been—my own
> Into the unknown,   45
> Into the sublime
> Off these sands of Time
> Time had seen amass
> From his hourglass.
> Once I told the Master,   50
> Later when we met,
> I'd been here one night
> As a young Alastor
> When the scene was set
> For some kind of flight   55
> Long before he flew it.

Just supposing I—
I had beat him to it.

The poet as Shelleyan adventurer into the heavens,
and into the literary realm of "the sublime," can com-
pare himself to the Wright brothers, but the metaphor
can work only to a point. The poet's is "some kind of
flight," similar to but also different from that of air-
planes. Both are examples of the "mighty charge / On
our human part / Of the soul's ethereal / Into the material" (lines 254–57), and the metaphorical similarity between apparently physical and apparently only imaginative or spiritual flights extends to the Incarnation, which
unites both aspects. It was this "descent" which re-es-
tablished the capability of humankind for ascent into the
heavens:

> Pulpiteers will censure
> Our instinctive venture
> Into what they call   215
> The material
> When we took that fall
> From the apple tree.
> But God's own descent
> Into flesh was meant   220
> As a demonstration
> That the supreme merit
> Lay in risking spirit
> In substantiation.

As Frost phrases it, the Incarnation of God was an
achievement similar to the writing of a poem, to the
"figure a poem makes." For both, "the figure is the same
as for love" and both are creatively beyond the rhetoric
subsequent to them of "sects and pulpiteers." The difference is in the way of knowing. For the "figure" of
Christ or of poets, "knowing" is through the act of reve-

lation, of working with and into "facts" so that they take on the properties of dream and mythology. While "a schoolboy may be defined as one who can tell you what he knows in the order in which he learned it, the artist must value himself" (and here the Incarnation is rather clearly implied) "as he snatches a thing from some previous order in time and space into a new order with not so much as a ligature clinging to it of the old place where it was organic" ("The Figure a Poem Makes"). Art, like the Incarnation, is an attempt at the concentration of sky and earth.

The wonderful and neglected master poem, "A Star in a Stoneboat," is really about these phenomena, but it speaks with a comedy and wit which insist less on mythologies than on the labor involved in discovering and experiencing them. As do the other great poems of Frost, it enacts rather than extols a process by which sky and earth are brought into a reciprocal conjunction in man-made forms. It is a poem that insists on being read as in itself an act of labor, some of it rather foolhardy, and it calls on the reader for an effort of belief which should be necessarily playful and roughhouse as we move through the turns and twists of the poem. It should be read with the exhilarated tension with which the writing seems to come at us off the page; and it provides an occasion to take heed of Frost's own account of the reading-writing experience in "The Constant Symbol," a critical utterance which, along with "Education by Poetry," "The Figure a Poem Makes," and "On Extravagance," is as essential as any by Eliot, Stevens, or Pound:

> The freshness of a poem belongs absolutely to its not having been thought out and then set to verse as the verse in turn might be set to music. A poem is the emotion of having a thought while the reader waits a little anxiously for the success of dawn. The only discipline

to begin with is the inner mood that at worst may give
the poet a false start or two like the almost microscopic
filament of cotton that goes before the blunt thread-
end and must be picked up first by the eye of the needle. He must be entranced to the exact premonition.
No mystery is meant. When familiar friends approach
each other in the street both are apt to have this experience in feeling before knowing the pleasantry they will
inflict on each other in passing.

Probably there is something between the mood and
the vocal imagination (images of the voice speaking)
that determines a man's first commitment to metre and
length of line.

Suppose him to have written down "When in dis-
grace with Fortune and men's eyes." He has uttered
about as much as he has to live up to in the theme as in
the form. Odd how the two advance into the open pari
passu. He has given out that he will descend into
Hades, but he has confided in no one how far before
he will turn back, or whether he will turn back at all,
and by what jutting points of rock he will pick his way.
He may proceed as in blank verse. Two lines more,
however, and he has let himself in for rhyme, three
more and he has set himself a stanza. Up to this point
his discipline has been the self-discipline whereof it is
written in so great praise. The harsher discipline from
without is now well begun. He who knows not both
knows neither. His wordly commitments are now three
or four deep. Between us, he was no doubt bent on the
sonnet in the first place from habit, and what's the use
in pretending he was a freer agent than he had any
ambition to be? He had made most of his commitments
all in one plunge. The only suspense he asks us to
share with him is in the theme. He goes down, for instance, to a depth that must surprise him as much as it
does us. But he doesn't even have the say of how long
his piece will be. Any worry is as to whether he will
outlast or last out the fourteen lines—have to cramp or
stretch to come out even—have enough bread for the
butter or butter for the bread. As a matter of fact, he
gets through in twelve lines and doesn't know quite
what to do with the last two.

The "inner mood," to look back at the beginning of the passage, or "self-discipline" which initiates "A Star in a Stoneboat," the moment of "entrance" into it for the speaker, is also, Frost nicely intimates, "en-tranced," a commitment to a vision the implications of which have not as yet been thought out:

> Never tell me that not one star of all
> That slip from heaven at night and softly fall
> Has been picked up with stones to build a wall.

This has very much the quality of one "familiar friend" approaching (and reproaching) another. In the essay Frost allows for a certain pointedness in the "pleasantry" of exchange—it is "inflicted"—but at the very end of his *Paris Review* interview he is more revealing in calling it "animus": "You see somebody coming down the street that you're accustomed to abuse, and you feel it rising in you, something to say as you pass each other. Coming over him the same way. And where do these thoughts come from? Where does a thought? Something does it to you. It's him coming toward you that gives you the animus, you know. When they want to know about inspiration, I tell them it's mostly animus." Jocular teasing of this sort is a form of "inspiration" even physiologically—in the drawing in of the breath as one friend approaches the other. Just as soon as the voice is heard and hears itself, it becomes committed to one kind of "discipline from without," in this case an image of a recognizable temperament ("Never tell me . . ."), and it then becomes further committed, this time to forms poetic rather than social, to meter and length of line, iambic pentameter triple rhymes. The meter and line length represent a commitment more than ordinarily formal, especially since the voice is so blustering and torrential in its movement over the lines, undeflected by so much

as a comma. The "wordly commitments are now three
or four deep" and then some. The voice, that is, com-
mits itself to a proposition about stars in a form that is
distinctly of this world; in his mood and in his articula-
tion of it, he is a man who wants worldliness and other-
worldliness to coincide; he wants a concentration, even
if in "walls," of earth and sky. And as we have noticed
earlier, "walls" are for Frost an elementary or vulgar
expression of the human need for form, of which poetry is the masterly example.

We catch the speaker in mid-passage. Presumably he
is in an argument, more animated than any in "Mending
Wall," and at issue is whether or not walls in the neighborhood have been built in part with stars, or meteor-
ites, fallen from the heavens. Obviously this blunt
speaker, with enough country knowledge to back up his
opinion, believes that at least one star has met such a
fate, though whether this is good or bad from his point
of view is something he has not yet confided to anyone
listening. He seems to care mostly that some such intersection has occurred. But the form of his reply or of his
"mood," especially in the rush of his movement, is likely
to induce the very uncertainty in the reader which it is
meant to correct in the skeptic to whom the lines are
addressed. Anyone who would later write "There was
never naught / There was always thought" would be
aware of the power of the sequence of negatives and
quantifiers in the opening line: "Never . . . not . . .
one . . . of all." Despite his air of confidence, this man
cannot say that even one star has, to his knowledge,
been picked up "to make a wall." He can only say that
he will "never" let anyone say that this has not happened.

The alternative here to "Never . . . not" can only be,
once again, "thought" or belief. But it is a rather conten-

tiously stated thought or belief, and in that the suspense resides. What does it mean to believe, so energetically and with such investment of feeling, in the claim that stars or maybe only one star was accessible to the labor of mind and body for the making of a wall? This is where we find ourselves as we proceed into the next several of the poem's nineteen stanzas:

> Some laborer found one faded and stone-cold,
> And saving that its weight suggested gold
> And tugged it from his first too certain hold,
>
> He noticed nothing in it to remark.
> He was not used to handling stars thrown dark
> And lifeless from an interrupted arc.
>
> He did not recognize in that smooth coal
> The one thing palpable besides the soul
> To penetrate the air in which we roll.
>
> He did not see how like a flying thing
> It brooded ant eggs, and had one large wing,
> One not so large for flying in a ring,
>
> And a long Bird of Paradise's tail
> (Though these when not in use to fly and trail
> It drew back in its body like a snail);
>
> Nor know that he might move it from the spot—
> The harm was done: from having been star-shot
> The very nature of the soil was hot
>
> And burning to yield flowers instead of grain,
> Flowers fanned and not put out by all the rain
> Poured on them by his prayers prayed in vain.

At first the condescensions directed against "some laborer," hardly an admiring introduction, seem decisive enough. Nearly every stanza begins by putting us on no-

tice that the laborer is remarkable chiefly for his deficiencies of perception: "He noticed nothing . . . He did
not recognize . . . He did not see . . . Nor know."
However, the reader will want to "interrupt" the swift
"arc" of the speaker's own movement when he gets to
the stanza about the soul. There is a delightfully arrogant subordination in its second line, nearly smirking in
the suggestion that one reason this laborer perceives so
little is that he does not "know" that the soul is "pal-
pable" and can "penetrate the air in which we roll" as effectively as can a star. Frost would say as much. We are
alerted here, if we have not been from the outset, that
everything in the poem so far—the argument, the star,
the wall, the laborer, and of course all the properties of
stars which the laborer cannot appreciate—that all this is
mere "thought" or belief, all of it the result of the
speaker's imagination. It is an obtusely, comically demanding imagination, zany in its particularities and
dizzy expertness about the aeronautical characteristics of
this star, which has by now become variously a "smooth
coal," and "like a flying thing" or "a snail." We might
guess that the speaker here is a flightier version of the
speaker in "Mending Wall," impatiently insisting on the
predominance of his powers when it comes to providing
for extraterrestrial possibilities—possibilities of the sublime—in the human scheme of things.

   The poem has made itself ready for the direct admission—in the last eleven stanzas—that it is about Frost
himself, or more precisely about his somewhat feverish
imagination of himself, caricatured only that he may
come to the more astringent view at the very end of the
poem.

> He moved it roughly with an iron bar,
> He loaded an old stoneboat with the star
> And not, as you might think, a flying car,

Such as even poets would admit perforce
More practical than Pegasus the horse
If it could put a star back in its course.

He dragged it through the plowed ground at a pace
But faintly reminiscent of the race
Of jostling rock in interstellar space.

It went for building stone, and I, as though
Commanded in a dream, forever go
To right the wrong that this should have been so.

Yet ask where else it could have gone as well,
I do not know—I cannot stop to tell:
He might have left it lying where it fell.

From following walls I never lift my eye,
Except at night to places in the sky
Where showers of charted meteors let fly.

Some may know what they seek in school and church,
And why they seek it there; for what I search
I must go measuring stone walls, perch on perch;

Sure that though not a star of death and birth,
So not to be compared, perhaps, in worth
To such resorts of life as Mars and Earth—

Though not, I say, a star of death and sin,
It yet has poles, and only needs a spin
To show its wordly nature and begin

To chafe and shuffle in my calloused palm
And run off in strange tangents with my arm,
As fish do with the line in first alarm.

Such as it is, it promises the prize
Of the one world complete in any size
That I am like to compass, fool or wise.

This is a comically frenzied performance. The
speaker claims that "to right the wrong" he goes about

"as though / Commanded in a dream forever," that
"from following walls I never lift my eye," and that he is
too harassed to answer even important questions: "I do
not know—I cannot stop to tell." It is a poem about possibilities of motion, on the ground, in the sky, in the
mind, in the voice. Put another way, it is about different
kinds of "transport," poetic and vehicular, or both at
once. It is assumed that anyone who would be caught
reading the poem would also care about poetic carriers,
even to the point of knowing so little about laborers and
walls as to "think" the stone had been loaded not on a
stoneboat—a sled-like wagon once used by upland New
England farmers to clear their rocky fields—but on a
"flying car." After all, "even poets would admit" (and
the laborer is hardly one of these; neither, quite, is the
reader) that such a "car" would be "More practical than
Pegasus the horse" (the winged horse of Greek mythology and also the constellation associated with poetic inspiration) "If it could put a star back in its course." But
in fact this is not an ambition credited to anyone, except
perhaps "you," the naive reader. "Practical" transport is
not the issue; neither, for that matter, is ultimate destination. When the reader, perhaps after reading Frost's
own "Birches" ("I don't know where it's likely to go
better") is again presumably slow-witted enough to ask
"where else" except into building material the star
"could have gone as well," the speaker hurriedly brushes
the query aside by saying that the star might simply have
been left where it landed.

The obsession, in the voice and in the form, with its
accelerating rhymes, is with motion rather than placement, and with efforts to sustain motion. There are reiterated images of flying, fanning, spinning, running off
in tangents, showering, and the pun on the "worldly nature" of the star. This is also a poem of "measuring," of

the inertial pull of the unimaginative laborers who can only drag stars across the ground, of "stone walls, perch on perch," of "interrupted arcs," and "charted meteors." In the imagination of the speaker, these "measurings" constitute the limit against which we can appreciate movement and "extra-vagance." The dragging of the star through "the plowed ground" is a poor substitute for its heavenly motion, but is reminiscent, however faintly, of the movement of rocks "in interstellar space." Even there, he imagines they are "jostling," as if stars crowd in on one another in the urgency of getting someplace. This star is not, like the earth and Mars, a "resort," with connotations of relative inactivity; it "stands" for none of the larger abstractions like "death" and "birth" or, since the Fall, "sin." Rather, it partakes of a "worldly nature" partly by being "whirldly"—it has poles and can therefore be provoked from rest into restlessness. Even in his hands, it can be made to "chafe" and "shuffle" just as it "jostles" in space. It resists stasis or manipulation, as does everything Frost believes in, or believes in-to being.

As applied to a star, however, there is a sort of diminishment in words like "chafe" and "shuffle" and in the comparison of the star to a fish on a line. The poem as it nears its end begins to de-accelerate, to tone down, and the star becomes little more than a toy. "Such as it is"—it is what Frost has made it or made up about it. The star is his own imagination, an inspiration to venturesomeness but also to domestication. The harsher disciplines "from without" which, in Frost's account, gradually impinge on Shakespeare's sonnet are at work here, too. The poem's "worldly commitments" emerge very early, as we have seen—in Frost's election of meter, stanza, and rhyme and in his characterization of the speaker as a man of a particular temperament in a definably circumscribed ambiance. These "commitments" are increased by his decision to populate the poem with imaginations unlike or antithetical to his own—the person who apparently sets him off on his initial near-tirade in stanza one, the "laborer" in stanza three, and the "you," the supposititious reader who is directly addressed in stanza nine. While each of these exhibits a different kind of inadequacy as compared to the poet, they nonetheless require that he somehow moderate his speed and freedom of movement in order to take them into account. His imagination must "jostle" its way among competitors if it is to attain a requisite authenticity, a "worldly nature." The measure proper to it is discovered at the end, in the "compass," a word that implies all at once something that can plot the direction of the thing in motion, an en-compassment of divergent possibilities, and an act of apprehension. The poet "compasses" the world by "thought," which moves, for Frost, like a falling star as early as "Bond and Free" and as late as "One More Brevity," his Christmas poem for 1953. In both, the star Sirius, the brightest in the heavens, allows the dispatch to earth of figures—a Dalmatian hound in the later poem—who find it a temporarily habitable place:

> Thought cleaves the interstellar gloom
> And sits in Sirius' disc all night,
> Till day makes him retrace his flight,
> With smell of burning on every plume,
> Back past the sun to an earthly room.
> ("Bond and Free")

"A Star in a Stoneboat" is an altogether remarkable poem, and the more so for being close at times to self-ridicule. The speaker is "fool or wise" in his eager imaginings. And perhaps we are also to wonder, in those sections of unmeasured hyperbolic indulgence where he berates the laborer for his lack of vision and condescends to the reader who is slower moving than himself, if Frost is not sharing with us a critical awareness that extravagances so quirky constitute their own repression, a correction, in course, of flights toward the sublime. If so, then the poem is, again, one of those with, as he said, "a lot of literary criticism in them—*in* them," a criticism of the life of writing itself, its living motions out of form and back again so that the poet might at last be, as he once remarked to Robert Penn Warren, "the happy discoverer of your ends."

Works Cited

Following is a list of works frequently referred to in the text by short title only:

The Poetry of Robert Frost, edited by Edward Connery Lathem. New York: Holt, Rinehart and Winston, 1969.

Selected Prose of Robert Frost, edited by Hyde Cox and Edward Connery Lathem. New York: Collier, 1966.

Robert Frost: Poetry and Prose, edited by Edward Connery Lathem and Lawrance Thompson. New York: Holt, Rinehart and Winston, 1972.

Selected Letters of Robert Frost, edited by Lawrance Thompson. New York: Holt, Rinehart and Winston, 1964.

The Letters of Robert Frost to Louis Untermeyer, edited by Louis Untermeyer. New York: Holt, Rinehart and Winston, 1963.

Interviews with Robert Frost, edited by Edward Connery Lathem. New York: Holt, Rinehart and Winston, 1966.

Writers at Work: The Paris Review Interviews, Second Series, edited by George Plimpton. New York: Viking, 1963.

Cook, Reginald L. *Robert Frost: A Living Voice.* Amherst: University of Massachusetts Press, 1974. (Includes transcripts of twelve talks given by Frost in the last decade of his life.)

Thompson, Lawrance. *Robert Frost: The Early Years, 1874–1915.* New York: Holt, Rinehart and Winston, 1966.

———. *Robert Frost: The Years of Triumph, 1915–1938.* New York: Holt, Rinehart and Winston, 1970.

Thompson, Lawrance, and Winnick, R. H. *Robert Frost: The Later Years, 1938–1963.* New York: Holt, Rinehart and Winston, 1976.

Index